JAPANESE SCIENCE

Japan's performance in the field of scientific research has been less than might be expected. There is a curious dichotomy between what has gone on in the laboratory and the country's outstanding technical sophistication and economic success. However, this may be about to change.

This new ethnograpic study of Japan's scientists looks firsthand at the career structures and organizational issues that have hampered their advancement. It provides an analysis of the problem of career mobility in science, the status quo in university and government laboratories, relations between scientists and lay administrators and the problems encountered by women scientists.

Japanese Science: From the Inside contests the view that Japan's relatively poor scientific record has been the product of unique thought patterns and instead demonstrates the crucial importance of moribund policy decisions in holding back dynamic and ambitious scientists.

Samuel Coleman is an independent researcher who has written extensively on Japanese science and society. In his former position as Associate Director for Research and Program Development at the North Carolina Japan Center, he led the effort to establish the Harry C. Kelly Fund for United States–Japan Scientific Co-operation.

ROUTLEDGE STUDIES IN THE GROWTH ECONOMIES OF ASIA

JAPANESE SCIENCE

From the Inside

Samuel Coleman

Routledge
Taylor & Francis Group

LONDON AND NEW YORK

First published 1999
by Routledge
2 Park Square, Milton Park, Abingdon, Oxon OX14 4RN

Simultaneously published in the USA and Canada
by Routledge
270 Madison Ave, New York, NY 10016

Transferred to Digital Printing 2008

Routledge is an imprint of the Taylor & Francis Group, an informa business

© 1999 Samuel Coleman

Typeset in Garamond by
MHL Typesetting, Coventry
Printed and bound in Great Britain by
TJI Digital, Padstow, Cornwall

British Library Cataloguing in Publication Data
A catalogue record for this book is available
from the British Library

Library of Congress Cataloging in Publication Data

Coleman, Samuel J., 1946–
Japanese science: from the inside/Samuel Coleman.
p. cm. – (Routledge studies in the growth economies of Asia; 25)
Includes bibliographical references and index.
1. Science–Research–Japan. 2. Scientists–Japan. I. Title.
II. Series.
Q180. J3C66 1999
509.52–dc21   99-27363
                                                                                              CIP

ISBN 10: 0-415-20169-1
ISBN 13: 978-0-415-20169-8

IN MEMORY OF MY FATHER,
DAVID M. COLEMAN

CONTENTS

FOREWORD
BY ARTHUR KORNBERG

Progress in science depends on discoveries by trained, able, and motivated scientists; virtually all industrialized societies have or can have an abundance of such scientists. What is lacking in most societies is the cultural environment and the sustained financial support that scientists need to contribute their creative talents. In the coming decades, when science and technology will be increasingly vital for the welfare of a society, an adequate volume of research support and its proper organization are crucial.

In this needed book by Dr. Sam Coleman, the management of bioscience in Japan, the world's second largest economy, is examined critically to provide a case study which is instructive for other societies, as well as an internal audit for Japan itself. Considering the essentiality of bioscience research and the huge investment being made in the enterprise, such an analysis is timely and of the greatest importance.

As a mentor since 1950 for some twenty Japanese bioscientists and a close colleague of as many more, I have been attentive to how their careers were affected by their research support. Also, on frequent visits to Japan, I have observed the organization of funding of academic and governmental science and on occasion have been asked to advise on future planning. For these reasons, I especially welcomed this in-depth analysis of Japanese support of bioscience by someone with the qualifications of the author.

Sam Coleman, trained in anthropology and possessing a professional command of the Japanese language, has conducted extensive studies on Japanese health and science policies and related issues. In this most recent research, he has focussed on how bioscience research is performed and how it is funded by several governmental agencies in a variety of settings. His findings and conclusions are presented clearly in chapters that dwell on government institutes, university groups, and quasi-independent research institutes along with chapters containing reflections on social issues: insularity, hierarchy, mobility, gender, bureaucracy, and status quo.

His data and interviews with a wide spectrum of scientists and administrators presented in this book corroborate and extend the impressions I have gained over the years from Japanese colleagues and former students. In the post-World War II period, governmental spending on basic bioscience training and research, has until very recently, been abysmally poor. Virtually all postdoctoral training was funded and directed by American laboratories: the National Institutes of Health (NIH) in Bethesda and academic groups supported by the NIH at universities and institutes. The young scientist upon returning to Japan, and fortunate enough to obtain an academic appointment, was indentured to a professor who controlled the meager funds and dictated the research program. Those who climbed the slippery pyramid to a professional appointment then reenacted the hierarchical pattern. University appointments virtually excluded graduates from other institutions; mobility between university departments was uncommon. Both the university administrations and the granting agencies have been and still remain under centralized governmental control, enmeshed in layers of bureaucracy, and dominated by an "old-boy" network. Opportunities for women in academic life remain severely limited.

On the positive side, Coleman did encounter some hopeful signs – effective management of the autonomous Osaka Bioscience Institute, voices of concern and dissatisfaction from many young scientists and a few elders, stirrings in the government that indigenous basic science is needed for long-term technological development, and large increases in the bioscience budgets even in the face of the current downturn in the general economy.

With regard to severe criticism of the magnitude and organization of Japanese bioscience support, it needs to be said that similar patterns have, with few exceptions, also prevailed in the European countries and were extensions of the practices in the pre-World War II period. By sharp contrast and a departure from the accustomed patterns was the magnitude and the organization of bioscience funding by the NIH in the post-World War II period. Although this subject is not treated in this book, I believe that such a comparison between the Japanese and American styles needs to be made.

With the conclusion of World War II, the NIH started something in biomedical science research support that was utterly unique. Competitive applicants are judged by committees of peer scientists from outside the government; grants are now given to some 40,000 individual scientists, young and old, for four to ten years. With the award of a grant, the scientist becomes his own boss. Success or failure depends on what the scientist accomplishes. Research is directed from the *bottom up*. By contrast, in Japan and most other countries, much of research direction is vested in a relatively few senior scientists or administrators. Research is directed from the *top down*.

Were the NIH record to be described for publication as an experiment in research administration, an impartial reviewer, even in this social area of science, might well question whether other factors might have been responsible for the good result. Such an experimental control does in fact exist in the support program of agricultural science in the United States during the same postwar period. The considerable, federally supported research activity remained in the tight grip of the Department of Agriculture, which retained all authority within its own bureaucracy. Research programs were limited to the established regional laboratories around the country; there were no grants to universities or private institutes. With this old-fashioned system of management, the knowledge base for agriculture remained stagnant. Little was learned about the basic biochemistry and genetics of plants and farm animals. Only recently, with the introduction of recombinant DNA technology, funded largely by the NIH, has there finally been an awakening of interest and activity in basic agricultural science.

The independence of an American scientist to initiate and pursue his own research program in the biomedical sciences has sometimes been attributed to the policies of American universities and institutes. Not really. This independence has been achieved because the individual scientist is not indebted to a senior professor, to a department head, to a dean or is prey to university politics. The university has no choice but to give scientists their independence in order to compete for their teaching contributions, the prestige of their discoveries, and for the very considerable income from the indirect costs attached to their grants. Yet it should be recognized that the very competition for grantees is an essential ingredient of the success of the NIH granting system because both the private and public universities are free from centralized government controls, something also virtually unique in the United States. With all its success, this system is constantly under strong pressures to centralize and collectivize research support; constant vigilance is needed to restrain these pressures.

Science is a global enterprise; instant communications have made it more so. Curiosity, ability, and pursuit of knowledge have no national boundaries. Japan like other nations can have an unlimited reservoir of scientific talent. Proper nourishment of talent is the crucial element. Coleman's book makes a major contribution in identifying many of the ways in which Japan can nourish this talent for the welfare of Japan and all mankind.

Arthur Kornberg
Stanford, California

ACKNOWLEDGMENTS

In the course of this project I became indebted to a very large number of people and organizations. The United States' National Science Foundation (NSF) gave me indispensable funding through a joint grant from its Studies in Science, Technology and Society Program and Japan U.S. Fellowship Program (DIR 8911539), and a continuation grant from the NSF Studies in Science, Technology and Society Program (SBR-9511897). The findings and conclusions presented in this book do not, of course, necessarily reflect the views of the National Science Foundation or any of its individual staff members. I also received support from the Joint Committee for Japanese Studies of the Social Science Research Council and the American Council of Learned Societies. William Purcell and colleagues at the University of New South Wales' School of Asian Business and Language Studies graciously provided me a professional berth during data analysis and initial manuscript drafting.

Introductions from Genya Chiba and Osamu Hayaishi gave me invaluable access to research institutes in Japan. Shoichi Kobayashi, Morio Ikehara, the late Tatsuo Miyazawa, Peter von Hippel (for his laboratory in the United States), Keiji Umeda and Hideo Matsumoto also deserve my warmest thanks for their roles in allowing me access to research sites and related assistance. My "subjects" and "informants" in Japan – the individual research scientists, technicians and administrators who shared their professional lives with me – also made this study possible through their generosity in time and candor. Some of the subjects' real names appear in the text, but limitations of space and some interviewees' preference for anonymity prevent me from thanking all of them in print individually. I thank as well American researchers in the life sciences. Jack Heinemann and Mark Young responded especially patiently when I came to them with questions, even though I sorely tested Peter von Hippel's axiom that "there are no stupid questions, only stupid answers."

A community of colleagues guided me with their insights, encouragement, and constructive critiques. Eleanor Westney, long-time friend and mentor, gave me professional inspiration via conceptual insights and her wisdom throughout this project. Ellis Krauss encouraged me as only a long-time friend and respected colleague could. Shigeru Nakayama has been a wellspring of knowledge in both historical fact and the intellectual landscape of Japanese science studies. He and Morris Low have helped me often and unstintingly. Justin Bloom also very generously shared his extensive knowledge of Japanese science and technology. My thanks go also to Catherine Lewis, Susan Orpett Long, and an anonymous manuscript reviewer for Routledge who, along with Jack, Eleanor and Justin, made suggestions for portions of early drafts that improved the manuscript greatly. I can only hope that the final product approaches the quality of their input. The faults and mistakes that remain are of course mine alone.

I have also made more requests for help than I would care to count to other colleagues, chief among them Shigeaki Yamazaki, Keiichi Yamada, Shinichi Yamamoto, Kozo Iwata, and Yasuo Kagawa. Jun-ichi Aoyagi made available to me the resources of the journalist community, and Masanobu Miyahara provided guidance for governmental information sources; Ken-ichi Arai, Shin'ichi Kobayashi, Haruki Nakamura, Mitsuhiro Yanagida, and Kazumasa Iinuma generously shared their time and knowledge also. The thoughtful assistance of colleagues and staff at the National Institute for Science and Technology Policy (NISTEP) in Tokyo made my 1996 stay productive and rewarding. I thank especially Akiya Nagata and Manami Shimoda. After I returned to the United States, NISTEP's Kumiko Morishita responded to my multiple requests for documents and information with wonderful alacrity and kindness. When gaps in information appeared as the manuscript neared completion, I called on Izumi Koide at the International House Library for help many times, and always received timely responses far beyond my expectations in accuracy and thoroughness. My dear friend Makoto Ikeda provided me important statistical information without hesitation. Mihoko Miki at UCLA's East Asian Library helped fill in some important blanks. I thank also George Argyrous and Hervey Allen for computer-related assistance, without which my data analysis would have stopped dead in its tracks.

My introduction to the Science, Technology and Society community came from Ronald Overmann, now retired National Science Foundation program officer. In 1983 the eminent historian of technology Ruth Schwartz Cohen wrote that all historians and philosophers of science owed Ronald Overmann much; twelve years later he was still helping immensely. For decades Marvin Harris' writings have raised for me a guiding beacon of intellectual rigor and insight into the human condition. I thank him for the bright light.

Illustrations convey what words alone cannot. This book is the richer for the kind consent of Ken-ichi Arai, who originally composed the figures in Chapter 2, and Noriko Sasaki for a sketch from her delightful *The Animal's Doctor* that graces Chapter 9. Equally, thanks to Norio Yamanoi and *AERA* for the cartoon appearing in Chapter 6, and to Take-emon Sato, Isao Ando, and their publisher, Takarajimasha, for cartoons appearing in Chapters 5 and 8; they helped me convey the wit and irony of editorial commentary on Japanese science. The radar graph in Chapter 1 appears courtesy of the British Council and Brendan Barker. I also thank the Society for Applied Anthropology and the Association of Japanese Business Studies for their permissions to reproduce portions of my papers on the Protein Engineering Research Institute that originally appeared in *Human Organization* and *Best Papers* of the AJBS, respectively, in 1995.

Sam Coleman
Fountain Valley, California

CONVENTIONS

The yen value for figures given in US dollars is 125/$US. All Japanese names appear in the Western fashion, i.e., personal name first and then surname, as in international scientific journals. Romanization of Japanese language follows the Hepburn system, but where individual Japanese have transliterated their names differently I have followed their preference. English translations of Japanese publication titles and organizational names appear as written by their Japanese authors or organizations.

Abbreviations used in the text

ARS	Agricultural Research Service (United States Department of Agriculture)
BERI	Biomolecular Engineering Research Institute
GRE	Graduate Record Examinations
IMSUT	Institute for Medical Science, University of Tokyo
JBS	Japanese Biochemical Society
JRDC	Japan Research and Development Corporation
JSC	Japan Science Council
MAF	Ministry of Agriculture, Forestry and Fisheries
MHW	Ministry of Health and Welfare
MITI	Ministry of International Trade and Industry
MOE	Ministry of Education, Science, Sports, and Culture
MRC	Medical Research Council (Great Britain)
NIH	National Institutes of Health (United States)
NISTEP	National Institute of Science and Technology Policy
NSF	National Science Foundation (United States)
OBI	Osaka Bioscience Institute
PERI	Protein Engineering Research Institute
RIKEN	(Rikagaku Kenkyūjo) Institute of Physical and Chemical Research
SRF	Science Research Fund
STA	Science & Technology Agency

1

INTRODUCTION

This is a book about the careers and aspirations of Japan's scientists, with special attention to its bioscientists (the laboratory scientists who study the workings of the cell through biology, chemistry, and physics). At first glance, Japan would not be a particularly interesting country in which to study any of the sciences. As the twentieth century closes, Japan has yet to capture more than 1 per cent of the Nobel Prizes ever awarded in the sciences. And many commentators, Western and Japanese, have stated that good science, after all, requires original and innovative expression, which Japanese society seems to suppress in the name of consensus and group discipline. But what if there were Japanese scientists in an area of research that, despite a lackluster showing in the past, had the potential to attain world leadership, given a different organizational configuration? A closer look at the organization of those scientists' efforts – in particular, the ways in which individual scientific careers are rewarded – would tell us something about the makings of an internationally competitive science community as well as the place of the individual in Japanese society.

The life sciences now account for some of the most profound and far-reaching developments in the sciences today, making them a good candidate for a closer examination of the organizational state of Japanese science as the century ends. Japan's 128,000 bioscientists are part of an exciting and important worldwide quest. Thanks to techniques for replicating and connecting portions of DNA molecules in new combinations, it is now possible to analyze the properties of a wide range of genes and proteins and their relationships with each other, affording detailed insight into such grand processes in the evolution of life as speciation, growth, maturation, and death.

Although most of us will have little contact with these questions, the laboratory tools devised to investigate them are spawning new technologies. Among basic science fields the life sciences have a particularly close connection to applications. Some are still on various drawing boards, others are in widespread use already, and many will exert profound influences on the way we live. Human genes have been inserted into bacteria to generate proteins for medicinal purposes. Many genes controlling susceptibility to

1

major diseases have been identified, aiding prediction and treatment of ailments. The potential applications from bioscience are wide-ranging and surprising, sometimes delightfully so. My own favorite examples involve the genes that generate light in fireflies or luminescent squid; they are now used in biochemical assays, and inserting such genes into the DNA of various shrub species may offer an energy-efficient form of illumination for airport runways and highway shoulders.

The industrial potential of these innovations represents several tens of billions of dollars in markets worldwide, but the new knowledge generated by the life sciences also offers applications in critical fields of public concern as diverse as epidemiology, energy conservation, and ecosystems management. This potential has been recognized among Japan's science policy makers for some time. Official statements citing the importance of research in the life sciences have appeared with increasing frequency since the prestigious Council on Science and Technology (Kagaku Gijutsu Kaigi) submitted its 1971 recommendation (STA 1994: 409–10).

Upward trends and bright spots

Japan is making notable progress in the life sciences. International publications by Japanese authors show a clear increase in frequency that began in the early 1970s (Garfield 1987). Between 1988 and 1994, the absolute number of Japanese articles appearing in international journals covered by the Medline data base increased by over 60 per cent (Yamazaki 1996a: 18). Japan overtook the United Kingdom in the late 1980s as the world's second largest producer of internationally published papers in the fields of biochemistry, genetics, cancer research, and neurology (Yamazaki 1996b: 396). In 1990, the American-based Institute for Scientific Information could report that Japanese biology had displayed "robust growth" in its share of articles in the world's leading scientific journals (*Science Watch* 1990: 7).

The top medical schools in Japan are now producing, per researcher, as many international publications as their prestigious Western counterparts, according to a careful study examining international life science journals in the first half of 1993; indeed, Kyushu University's figure of 0.94 publications per year per researcher, which approached the figure of 1.01 for Oxford, nearly trebled that of the Johns Hopkins University (Yamazaki 1994: 125). As Japanese bioscientists have turned more to the international scientific community, they have also devoted less effort to domestic publication activity. Between 1988 and 1994, the number of life science papers published in Japanese decreased by 23 per cent; in that same period, output of international papers rose from a rough parity with domestic publications to well over twice their number (Yamazaki 1996a: 18).

In this same period, several Japanese biomedical researchers have attained international prominence. The most cited scientific paper of the 1980s (with

3,074 "hits" – i.e. citations by other authors) was a 1984 publication in *Nature* by Kobe University's Yasutomi Nishizuka on protein kinase C (an enzyme that plays a critical role in intracellular processes). Other well-known and well-cited scientists today include Osamu Hayaishi (the oxygenases and prostaglandins), Tasuku Honjo (molecular immunology), the late Shosaku Numa (sodium channels), and Tadatsugu Taniguchi (cellular responses to cytokines).

Individual Japanese biomedical researchers have been recognized internationally for well over a hundred years. Shibasaburo Kitasato produced the world's first pure culture of the tetanus bacterium in 1889, and by the next year had also proved the existence of the bacterium's antitoxin. These advances enabled Japan's pioneer development of serological therapy for cholera and diphtheria as well as tetanus (Iinuma n.d.; Bartholomew 1989: 122). Kitasato's student, Kiyoshi Shiga, had discovered the bacillus that causes dysentery. (Shiga was only 27 years old at the time.) Jokichi Takamine was the first to identify and isolate adrenalin, in 1900. Umetaro Suzuki discovered Vitamin B-1 and reported it in 1911, at the time that chemist Casimir Funk announced similar experimental results. At the time of World War I, Tokyo University pathologist Katsusaburo Yamagiwa devised a technique for inducing tumors in experimental animals that became an important building block for modern oncology (Bartholomew 1989: 55).

Persisting mediocrity

Despite bright spots throughout the sciences such as these, Japan's scientists have yet to claim a prominent international position. One indication of the quality of internationally published research is its "impact," or the extent to which other specialists make use of it and cite it in their own articles. Citations per published scientific paper by Japanese authors between 1981 and 1994 barely exceeded half the American rate (May 1997: 793). Citations for Japanese contributions in the life sciences were noticeably weak in proportion to their share of world papers. Figure 1.1, based on all of the articles published between 1989 and 1993 by Japanese authors, makes the point by comparing the percentage of all international scientific publications by Japanese authors and the extent to which they are cited by all authors in their fields worldwide. In most life science fields, the publications are not generating attention commensurate with their presence. This conclusion agrees with the results of previous investigations covering the late 1980s (reported in Garfield 1987: 344 and Swinbanks 1991). The figure also suggests that the most activity and recognition belongs to applied physics, an area – as its name indicates – that is oriented to industrial applications.

Comparing Japan's performance in the life sciences with the United States' has limited meaning because the United States is an unrivaled powerhouse of scientific activity, in a class by itself in resources and accomplishment. Postwar

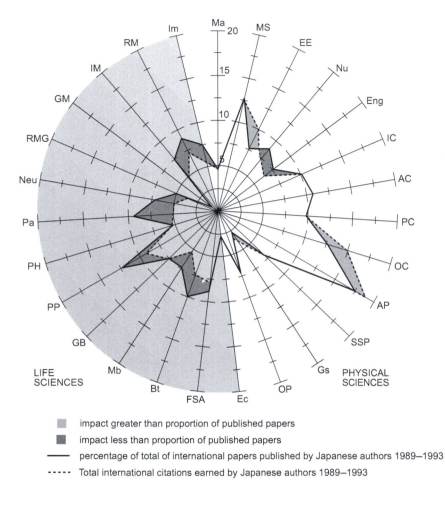

impact greater than proportion of published papers
impact less than proportion of published papers
—— percentage of total of international papers published by Japanese authors 1989–1993
----- Total international citations earned by Japanese authors 1989–1993

Life Sciences

Ec	Ecology	Pa	Pathology
FSA	Food Science, Agriculture	Neu	Neurosciences
Bt	Biotechnology	RPM	Reproductive Medicine, Geriatrics
Mb	Microbiology	GM	General Medicine
GB	General Biology	IM	Internal Medicine
PP	Pharmacology, Pharmacy	RM	Research Medicine
PH	Public Health	Im	Immunology

Physical Sciences

Ma	Mathematics	AC	Analytical Chemistry
MS	Materials Science	PC	Physical Chemistry
EE	Electronic Engineering	OC	Organic Chemistry
Nuc	Nuclear Sciences	AP	Applied Physics
Eng	Mechanical, Civil, Other Engineering	SSP	Solid State Physics
IC	Inorganic Chemistry and Engineering	GS	Geosciences
		OP	Other Physics

Figure 1.1 World publishing activity and impact 1989–93 (adapted from Barker 1996)

4

Nobel laureates in the natural sciences awarded to American scientists numbered 156 as of 1995, a figure almost four times the 41 won by the United Kingdom, its closest rival. In the mid-1990s, spending on research in the United States (calculated in terms of buying power) towered over other countries', easily doubling the amount spent in Japan. The United States' spending on research and development in 1995 nearly equaled the total of the next six largest spenders combined, a position the US has held for a decade (NSB 1998: 4–35).

We could leave the United States out of the comparison and still find room for dissatisfaction with Japan's life sciences, however. Japan's economy, second only to the United States' in size, has a Gross Domestic Product twice as large as Germany's and well over four times the size of the United Kingdom's. Japan's wealth and its high level of technoeconomic sophistication have led observers to expect more from its scientists. When *Science* magazine (1992a: 564) compared Japan's output of academic papers in the previous decade with those of the United States, UK, Germany and France, it found that Japan's total output was small overall, and output proved the lowest when controlled for Gross National Product (i.e., number of papers per billion dollars GNP). The previously mentioned 1981 to 1994 tally of citation impact placed Japan eighteenth in international rankings (May 1997: 793). A comparison with European nations in the number of Nobel Prizes in the sciences also reflects the relative paucity of great developments in any of the natural sciences. As of 1995, Japan could claim only five, all earned since the end of World War II; Germany, by contrast, had won a total of twenty-five in the same period. Only one of Japan's was in Medicine or Physiology.

Japan's scientists appraise their efforts in basic research similarly: Japan, they say, is behind the West, particularly in the life sciences. Japanese researchers surveyed by the Science and Technology Agency in 1996 evaluated basic research in the United States and Europe more highly than their own in the three fields of life science, materials, and marine and earth sciences, and placed the United States (but not Europe) ahead in information science and electronics, the fourth field surveyed (STA 1997b: 44). A 1987 nationwide survey of liaison members and organizations by the Japan Science Council typified their country's life science research as plentiful in work that builds on subjects and methods from abroad, but has "little in the way of creative research in the true sense." The report asserted that worldwide appraisal of Japanese life sciences was high "in general," but regretfully acknowledged that "there is not much in original, creative research of the kind that leads the world" (JSC 1988: 171–2). That assessment remains the same among Japan's life scientists (IHEP 1996), including the ones whom I interviewed and with whom I have worked throughout the 1990s as well.

Scientific versus technological success

The suggestion that the Japanese could be unsuccessful in their laboratories seems to contradict Japan's record of exquisite successes over the past several decades over a broad range of technologies, from transistor radios to earthquake-resistant building design to low pollution automobile engines. The problem at hand, however, is basic research as opposed to research devoted to the development of various technologies. The growing intimacy of connections between basic and applied – or between "science" and "technology" – has brought many to conclude that the two activities are hopelessly blurred. For that reason, I must beg the reader's patience as I pose a distinction between the two types of effort, for we can distinguish qualitatively different ends even when the means are identical procedures conducted in one laboratory with the same equipment.

Science is public knowledge building that formulates fundamental laws behind natural phenomena. Its practitioners make public statements about such lawful properties, in ways that allow fellow observers to test them. The more far-reaching (that is, systematically influential) the mechanism explained, the better the science. A classical (by now shopworn) example is work elucidating the structure of DNA. Technology is a product, an embodiment with a specific use, and it typically can be sold for profit. Whatever information that is provided with it is just enough knowledge to make the product work, as opposed to the exposition of a generalizable principle.

The science–technology distinction proves its viability by helping to explain the contrast between industry-based and academic researchers in their career aspirations and approaches to research, presented in Chapter 4. The evolving relationship between science and technology also helps in predicting the future strength of Japan's science, ventured in Chapter 8. Even if we were to confine our discussion of Japan's research and development track record to industrial applications, however, the pattern does not suggest a continuation of Japan's past successes. The survey of Japan's R&D specialists who placed the West ahead in basic research also compared capabilities in applied research and development. Respondents gave the United States superior marks in all six of the fields surveyed (energy and production processes and machinery were added to the four fields surveyed for basic research), and they placed the Europeans ahead of themselves in life sciences and marine and earth sciences. In every category, including those in which Japan was judged superior, the West had gained ground since the same question was posed in 1993 (STA 1997a: 39). A survey of major Japanese corporations by the *Japan Economic Journal* in 1998 also found industrial R&D specialists giving superior marks to the West in biotechnology and software, though claiming a much stronger position for Japanese industry in robotics and automobiles (*Nihon Keizai Shinbun* 1998).

Funding priorities

One well-known reason for Japan's less-than-expected showing in the sciences is the country's budgetary emphasis on commercialization of technology. Although the absolute figure for Japan's total research budget leads those of the Western European countries, over 70 per cent has come from industry, which targets applications for profit; some 20 per cent of the money spent on research and development in Japan has come from the government – about half to two thirds of the proportion that governments in other major industrialized countries spend (STA 1994: 315; NSB 1998: A-179). In the decade since 1984 about 72 per cent of Japan's research money excluding social sciences and humanities has gone to development and another 22 per cent has gone to applied research, leaving to basic around 6 per cent of the research total (MCA 1996: 43). Universities in Japan spend about 13 per cent of the country's natural science research money – lower than the United States and lower than the proportion for university research in Western European countries, though not far from their average of 16 per cent (calculated using STA 1996: 104). The proportion is higher in the life sciences, but here as well companies have accounted for half of the spending (calculated using MCA 1996: 221).

One of the hallmarks of academic scientific research in Japan has been its material poverty. In the early 1990s, Japan's spending on university research as a proportion of gross national product represented less than half the proportion spent in either the United States or former West Germany (Nagakura and Kikumoto 1994: 1189). Western visiting researchers must acclimate to a pervading dinginess. Exposed pipes and overloaded electrical sockets add to the developing country ambience. Medical school laboratories in old annex buildings of affiliated hospitals contrast starkly with the bright and well-kept main entrances for patients and visitors. Laboratory floor space per researcher is less than half that of Western countries' universities (Yamamoto 1991), so cramp and clutter lend their own tint of squalor. Visitors should not assume that their hosts are satisfied with their narrow lot; almost three fourths of the biomedical researchers polled by the Japan Science Council in 1990 stated that lack of floor space undeniably hindered their research (JSC 1991: 40, 164).

Even the most prestigious national universities offer graphic examples of the handicaps to bioscience researchers. Kyoto University's plant physiologists have used hallway space to culture seaweeds in containers salvaged from trash. One of the lecturers has become a connoisseur of vending machine sake, but his tastes focus on the size and shape of the container rather than the contents: the glass containers are used in place of beakers, which the researchers cannot afford. At Hiroshima University, a researcher who relocated from the National Cancer Center in Tokyo had to abandon using rats for his experiments because there was no space with the necessary atmospheric temperature and moisture controls (Endo and Imai 1991: 9, 11).

Scientists in Japan also lack support staff, from technicians who provide routine technical services to secretarial and janitorial helpers. The ratio of support staff per researcher in the 1990s has been less than 0.5 to 1, a figure less than half the ratio in the Western European countries of France, England, or Germany (STA 1996: 130; STA 1998: 157). In this regard, the life sciences in Japan are in worse shape than the natural sciences in general; support staff per researcher is, as of the mid-1990s, 0.23 assistants (calculated using MCA 1996: 220). The situation in the universities is the worst, with only 0.12 assistants per researcher (STA 1996: 131). The list of maintenance and support activities performed by researchers themselves runs from emptying trash and washing laboratory utensils to typing requisition forms.

As of the mid-1990s, the funding situation for science has begun to brighten considerably, if not dramatically. In the early 1990s the influential Council on Science and Technology proposed a doubling of government science spending by the year 2000, and by late 1995 their plans and negotiations bore fruit: the Japanese Diet enacted the Science and Technology Basic Law, which calls for increasing government spending on research to 1 per cent of the country's gross national product in five years. An economic analyst typified government support for research in the mid-1990s as "a picture of solid, steady commitment" (Choy 1998a: 5). Official pronouncements concerning the importance of bioscience have been backed with increased resources in recent years also. Government spending on the life sciences in the seven fiscal years between 1990 and 1996 has increased each year over the previous total at an average rate of 8.9 per cent (calculated using MCA 1996: 221; 1998: 199).

The credit cycle and its significance

Substantial increases in money beyond current levels will not automatically raise Japanese bioscience to world leadership. There is a growing recognition that the already respectable sums now spent on basic research are not yielding commensurate results, particularly in the universities (Choy 1998a). Legacies of poverty in the laboratory must be overcome, such as the practice at universities of assigning support work to students of various levels, and the mentality that accompanies it (discussed in Chapter 2). More critical yet is whether the organization of career development in Japan can realize two closely related improvements: greater mobility among researchers, in order to optimize the fit between individual scientists and their research groups, and rechanneling of resources to the most able individuals and groups.

We can approach these issues with a concept called the *credit cycle*, set forth in Latour and Woolgar's 1986 *Laboratory Life* and elaborated here for its application to Japan. If the word "credit" brings the financial world to mind, it is no accident: scientists in the West (and the United States in particular) build their careers by using their achievements in research to obtain more resources in the form of competitively allocated grants, which they then invest in further research activity – hence the "cycle."

The mobility element in this process is both figurative and literal. Based on their accumulated accomplishments, scientists enjoy the metaphorical "upward mobility" of increased authority and command of resources, as signaled by changes in titles along the way (e.g. graduate student to postdoctoral fellow to researcher or assistant professor to laboratory chief). The more literal spatial mobility involves moving from one laboratory to another. As the geographical spread for recruitment widens, the competition of course increases, as does the probability of a good fit between the candidate's configuration of interests and the recruiting institution's. Unless a researcher's home institution happens to evolve in precisely the direction that the researcher is moving, the further development of that researcher's interests and abilities will require moving to a different laboratory that shares his or her interest, and the facilities to realize it.

Social and geographical mobility merge when a researcher moves into an institution of higher or lower quality on the basis of his or her past performance. On the institutional side of the coin, individual mobility reflects a research organization's ability to reconfigure its personnel in its competition with other research groups. The institution aims for better research teams by recruiting ever more accomplished researchers who share the same or complementary interests. Thanks also to this mobility dynamic, the research institutions' administrators will respond to the prospect of losing their better researchers by providing advancement and more resources, to induce them to stay. Mobility also benefits the research institution because the incoming researchers have created bonds of familiarity with colleagues at their previous institutions that provide channels for further cooperation and information exchange. I must emphasize, though, that the ideal dynamic that I am describing does not just move researchers around like molecules, randomly expanding their networks and exposing them to different ideas and styles. It provides a merit-based reward system critical to individual career evolution as it assembles kindred spirits in the research enterprise.

The managerial nurturance of a vibrant credit cycle is perhaps as close as we can get to institutionalizing those groups that organize spontaneously, with members who can continually learn together. These "communities of practice" are defined most generally as "a group of people who are informally bound to one another by exposure to a common class of problem" (quoted in Stewart 1996: 141). In one management commentator's words,

> [these groups] emerge of their own accord: three, four, twenty, maybe thirty people find themselves drawn to one another by a force that's both social and professional. They collaborate directly, use one

another as sounding boards, teach each other. You can't create communities like this by fiat, and they are easy to destroy. They are among the most important structures of any organization where thinking matters . . . . (Stewart 1996: 141)

The credit cycle in the real world

I have been describing the credit cycle in its ideal form – a kind of frictionless machine – whereas the real world dampens the cycle in various ways or obstructs it entirely. Stagnation in the job market for scientists, for example, will leave researchers stuck in various stages of development. Another variable affecting the credit cycle is the degree of job security afforded workers by their representative organizations. Mobility, after all, requires the stressful "push" dimension of personal competition and job loss that inevitably complements the "pull" and enticement of more attractive positions. Workers as a sector of the larger society may act politically to resist the insecurity of job changing, creating rules that extend to scientists' terms of employment as well. Other impediments to the credit cycle that lie in society's larger political-economic dimension include discrimination against the ethnicity or gender of the researcher.

The study of these impediments to the credit cycle could inform debates about the relationship between science and democracy – a topic of perennial interest among students of Japanese science and society. Some elements of democracy may prove indispensable to an effective credit cycle, among them equal opportunity to compete and open access to information regarding the process of allocating rewards. Other ostensible features of democracy, such as voting, could be counterproductive; a community-wide vote to determine professional rewards, for example, could be diverted by political quid pro quos away from performance-based criteria.

Obstacles to an effective credit cycle in Japanese society

Several features of Japanese society (its political economy, if you will) severely discourage the credit cycle dynamic – indeed, some might argue that there is no credit cycle activity seen in Japan. Rather than categorize Japan as a unique (and therefore unexplainable) case, we can identify the reasons for Japan's anemic credit cycle using variables that could be applied in future studies in other industrialized societies. One of the variables is labor mobility. Long-term or "permanent" employment in one organization is nearly universal among Japan's well-educated male employees. (The Japanese term, *shūshin kōyō*, literally means "employment for life.") Americans in particular are unfamiliar with the ramifications of the practice, since the United States has an unusually high frequency of job changers; although Japanese workers fall decidedly on the low mobility end of the stasis versus movement continuum, workers in the United States occupy the other extreme. The European nations fall in between, though somewhat closer to Japan's end of the distribution. By way of illustration, only about 10 per cent of Japan's labor force in 1991 had been in that job for less than one year, compared to nearly 30 per cent in the United States, with the major European nations ranging between 13 and 19 per cent (EPA 1995: 54; see also Reed 1993: 87). Of the Americans surveyed in a 1989 multinational study of technical specialists, 38 per cent had previously changed workplaces, in contrast to 5 per cent of their Japanese counterparts (JPC 1990a: 69). So extensive is mobility in the United States that political scientist Steven Reed proposed the term "ephemeral employment" (1993: 86).

The biggest obstacle to the credit cycle from permanent employment is obvious: a researcher cannot move into a different position reflecting more substantial accomplishments and more evolved interests. Conversely, permanent employment's dark side, the protection of the mediocre and unproductive, keeps resources from going to the more deserving via the credit cycle. The shared tacit knowledge of individual and group performance in an immobile community also subtly discourages systematic evaluation. As science policy specialist Fumio Kodama explained from firsthand research experience: "The lack of mobility ... means that the research community is homogeneous and people know each other well. Everyone is aware of who is the best scientist, but it is never explicitly stated" (Evered 1989: 31). The political walls built around permanent employment in Japan also complicate project-related hiring and dismissal of technical support staff; expanding technical assistance requires a far more serious, long-term commitment to employees from the administration than it would in countries with more mobility. The United States contrasts starkly in this regard.

Another feature of labor management in Japan that frustrates credit cycle dynamics is seniority, the allocation of rewards on the basis of how long an individual has been in the organization (*nenkōjoretsu*), as opposed to individual performance-based contributions. Seniority practices reinforce permanent employment because workers cannot transfer their number of years with one company or government organization to another workplace. Throughout the years since the end of World War II, Japanese employers have hired young people at salary rates below their contributions to the organization, and raised them predictably with years of service – to the point, arguably, of overpaying them in the years just before they retire out of their regular jobs. In 1993, middle-aged white-collar males were earning over three times as much as men under 25 (EPA 1995: 62).

The practice of pegging career stages and rewards to age has helped stimulate a very evident age-consciousness in Japanese society. Ages invariably accompany names in newspaper articles. As a Japanese journalist friend explained, seniority allows one to surmise roughly from age what a person's status is, such as section chief in a corporate or government office. Hotel registries and various applications require customers to state their ages.

Terms of address are age-graded as well; I have heard a 72-year-old former national university president addressed by his own elders with a diminutive term (*-kun*).

Permanent employment and seniority may look like the stuff of contract terms for auto workers, but they do apply to scientists' careers as well. Science historian Shigeru Nakayama summed what the permanent employment and seniority configuration means for mobility among Japanese scientists:

> Japan is a society in which moving invariably means losing. I know many people for whom jumping ahead impulsively, taking on hardship and moving about from here to there, has left them with bitter regrets, barely scraping by in their retirement years. (1996: 317)

Seniority may take a more subtle toll as well. Age among scientists, regardless of their nationality, poses a liability to progress in several respects: older scientists have more of a vested interest in approaches and concepts that they have developed and with which they are familiar, and they have less to gain from radical shifts in thinking (Stephan and Levin 1992). In Japan, according to the scientists themselves, scientists (particularly academic scientists) become authoritative figures and wield substantial resources when they enter their fifties. Here as well, the credit cycle suffers when authority and resources are allocated on the basis of a consideration other than performance.

Japanese science policy makers and commentators have been discussing the need for more researcher mobility since the latter half of the 1980s, using terms like "fluidity" (*ryūdōsei*) and "personnel exchange" (*jinji kōryū*), along with calls for more opportunities for younger researchers. This is not mere obligatory hand wringing for foreign consumption: the concerns are genuine and the contexts are varied, including a round table of eminent university professors discussing problems in university research (Takeuchi 1990), a government-funded proposal to create alternative employment structures for R&D personnel (Iinuma and Iinuma 1990), and a high-level position paper on the promotion of structural biology (AETDC 1996: 33). The Japan Science Council's 1987 survey of the sciences also called for introducing mobility among university and research institute researchers to improve the quality of research (1988: 173). The calls for more "flexible" and "competitive" research environments have crescendoed in the late 1990s, resulting in laws for universities and national research institutes intended to facilitate term employment. (The measures are discussed in Chapter 8.)

Power and hierarchy

Another feature of Japanese society that obstructs the credit cycle is less easily quantified – and less easily named – than "permanent employment" or "seniority," but it, too, is influential. The power of the state in Japan is more

strongly centralized and is exercised more hierarchically through its bureaucracy than in the West. The tendency is less severe than authoritarianism;
more apt labels include "culture of paternalism" (Leflar 1996: 14) and "soft
authoritarianism" (Johnson 1995: 46). There are more powers exercised by
bureaucratic officialdom than by elected decision makers, and the ministries
are more insulated from reform than in most Western countries. Japan does
not have guarantees of access to government information, as in the Freedom
of Information Act in the United States and similar laws in Europe, nor are
there laws to protect individuals such as informed consent requirements for
research subjects.

A hierarchical authority pattern extends to the scientific community as well.
Academic positions and research money flow more through hierarchical
institutional and personal channels in Japan than through open competition
among individuals based on clearly applied, impersonal criteria of ability and
performance. Hiring practices for R&D personnel in the private sector rely
heavily on introductions from academic advisors and other university
officers. In the 1988–89 multinational study of technical specialists mentioned
above, over half of the Japanese respondents with graduate degrees (and
nearly three fourths of those holding PhD degrees) reported that they relied
on their advisor's introduction for their jobs, in contrast with well under half
that proportion among advanced degree holders in the United States,
Germany, and England (calculated using figures in JPC 1990a: 71; JPC
1990b: 73; JPC 1990c: 61).

These phenomena certainly occur in the West as well, but they are
particularly strong in Japan. (Reference letters from academic advisors are
an important element of the Westerner's job search, for example, but the
advisors function more as evaluators than as manpower brokers.) Hierarchy
undercuts the most basic condition for effective credit cycle dynamics. Also,
more egalitarian, less regimented social environments encourage the
cultivation and sharing of original ideas, and are more likely to reward their
proponents while protecting them from more powerful established scientists
whose own knowledge (often received) is devalued in the process. Susumu
Tonegawa, Japan's only Nobel Prize winner in Medicine or Physiology,
surely had these problems in mind when he criticized Japan as an
"administrative society" (*kanri shakai*) that hinders the development of
original research (1994: 2). Tonegawa's own Nobel Prize was only an
apparent exception to the problem of Japanese research creativity: he had left
Japan at the urging of his advisor at Kyoto University before he was 25 years
old. "Had I stayed in a Japanese university" he told the *Wall Street Journal*, "I
may not have been able to do this kind of work" (Yoder 1987).

A 1996 article in *Science* aired the opinion that the greatest challenge to
improving academic research careers in Japan would be to "introduce real
competition and tolerance of debate and nonconformity into a society that
cherishes stability and harmony" (Kinoshita 1996a: 49). The challenge is both

easier and harder than that. There is no impenetrable culture-wide preference for the status quo: as you will see, the breadth and frequency of objections to current practices, and the attempts to reform them, argue against explanations invoking deep-rooted national character. Reform will not come easily, however, because it will require some sensitive trade-offs involving authority, control, and security. Effective change must take place on several fronts at once, and no change will take place without cost to someone.

This study

One way to study the issues surrounding career development in Japanese science is to go to the scene of the action and learn about them from the ground up by experiencing researchers' everyday lives over an extended period of time. The approach is usually labeled "participant observation." It involves winning the cooperation of the people studied by becoming a familiar element in their lives, while learning about their interests and concerns and observing their behavior first hand. This approach also opens up a frankly inductive opportunity to discover important facts and dynamics after arriving on the scene, as opposed to first formulating a set of questions for testing before making observations.

The intensive field work portion of my research in Japan began in late 1990 and lasted one year. Preceding the year in Japan, I spent three months as an observer in the von Hippel laboratory at the University of Oregon's Institute of Molecular Biology. There I observed daily life and discussed career-related issues with graduate students and postdoctoral fellows. While reminding myself not to regard this first extensive exposure to laboratory life as the norm from which Japan's was the deviation, I collected observations for comparison and contrast.

Over two-thirds of the year in Japan were devoted to two new organizations featuring term (as opposed to permanent) employment: the Osaka Bioscience Institute (OBI), a metropolitan biomedical research facility, and the Protein Engineering Research Institute (PERI), a government-sponsored research consortium. The remainder of the year went to field work at a private school of medicine in Kansai (the region that includes the Osaka–Kyoto conurbation) which I will refer to as the Medical College, a brief field work stint at the Ministry of Agriculture, Forestry and Fishery's Food Research Institute (FRI), and visits to several universities for interviews.

My choice of field sites was far more a matter of serendipity than perspicacious, theory-inspired planning. (Coleman 1996 describes in detail the methodology of access to the field sites.) The project as conceived in 1989 was to study the effects of social hierarchy in the laboratory through participant observation, and I had only a budding interest in the issue of researcher mobility. The advice and assistance of a few influential Japanese science administrators proved crucial to identifying target organizations and then gaining access. My lead contact, Genya Chiba of the Japan Science and Technology Corporation (at that time the Research Development Corporation of Japan), was the originator of the innovative and successful Exploratory Research for Advanced Technologies (ERATO) projects begun in 1981, which brought together academic, government, and industry researchers for projects of limited duration (Anderson 1992a).

When I told Chiba I wanted to spend a year doing an intensive study of a life science laboratory, I mentioned as candidates a first-tier national university and a prestigious government research institute. He replied, first, that one year was a long time: lab heads would probably balk at having someone around that long, particularly since I was coming in with a rather vague agenda. How about two or three places, with stays of several months each? "And why do you want to go studying organizational dinosaurs? I could suggest some places that are much more interesting." He briefly described OBI, PERI, and a research consortium in Tsukuba. "You want to see what Japanese labs of the future will look like? Go study those!"

Before I knew it, Chiba had given me the telephone number of Osamu Hayaishi, a former ERATO project leader, who had become OBI's first director. I met Dr Hayaishi soon after, and he suggested I also approach Dr Morio Ikehara, then PERI's director. Both men were well-known and highly placed, but they were also critical of the prevailing organization of Japanese science, and they were deeply involved in creating alternative organizational structures.

Despite Chiba-san's sanguine suggestions, I was worried about not having a more representative sample of Japanese bioscience organizations for the sake of contrast and comparison. With Dr Hayaishi's help, I approached the president of a private medical college in the Kansai region and added it as a third site. I later supplemented my research activity there with a visit to the Ministry of Agriculture's Food Research Institute, again with the indispensable help of one of its administrators, Dr Shoichi Kobayashi.

Both OBI and PERI stood out from the more typical Japanese laboratory research institution in several respects. They were affluent, affording their researchers state-of-the-art equipment, ample materials, and a more favorable support staff ratio than other laboratories. Neither offered its researchers permanent employment: OBI, as we shall see, had a very explicit set of limited term appointments, and PERI was a project with a ten-year life expectancy.

My command of the Japanese language allowed me to negotiate entering Japanese laboratories and interact with the researchers and technicians without depending on an interpreter or confining my discussions to researchers who would speak in English. My study, however, was not destined to become a classical ethnographic monograph that describes daily life in detail. I was dealing with sensitive issues in well-known laboratories, where detailed descriptions of individuals would reveal their identities. Individual career successes and failures are a sensitive topic in any industrialized culture, but criticizing the system and specific individuals within it poses more serious liabilities in Japan. Valid or not, there was a palpable fear of retribution among my informants who were critical of the status quo. I conducted interviews under terms of complete anonymity and confidentiality.

By the end of my year of field work, I had conducted 110 structured interviews with researchers and technicians. In the same period, I conducted interviews and discussions with some twenty-five other Japanese professionally involved in scientific research, including policy makers, journalists, and academics. I also interviewed twelve foreigners then doing research in Japanese bioscience laboratories. Before leaving the field, I conducted self-administered questionnaire surveys at OBI and PERI. (A brief methods appendix (see Appendix I) provides a description of field work conditions, the total interview sample and the questionnaire surveys.) During the field work year I also gathered a wide range of materials in Japanese on bioscience and related areas, from government reports to articles in popular magazines. I have returned to Japan at two-year intervals since then for updating, including brief visits to my major research sites, most recently in the summer of 1998.

Before discussing the PERI and OBI experiments in career shaping in Chapters and 4 and 5, I have provided two chapters depicting the world they were meant to supplement – or replace. Chapter 2 explains the obstacles to dynamic career formation posed by hierarchical organizational forms and practices in Japan's universities. Chapter 3 examines the tension between organizational priorities and basic research career trajectories in a government research laboratory. Chapter 4, devoted to the Protein Engineering Research Institute, studies the differences between industry and academic researchers' professional reward structures, and the constraints on the credit cycle in the consortium recruitment process. Chapter 5 looks at the Osaka Bioscience Institute as an unprecedented opportunity for younger researchers, and studies both its radical reforms and continuities with more traditional organizations. Field work at OBI piqued my interest in relations between scientists and lay administrators. Government policy and practice affect Japanese scientists profoundly, and government initiative provides the fulcrum for change in scientists' careers; Chapter 6 relates and analyzes that dynamic of officials' relations with scientists using firsthand observations.

Since political (non merit-based) criteria of inclusion and exclusion hamper the effective operation of the credit cycle, sex-based discrimination creates a barrier to the production of better science in any country. This factor is particularly relevant in the study of Japanese bioscience not only because of the country's legendarily high level of gender-based discrimination, but also because there are in fact so many women currently involved in bioscience research there. Roughly 20 per cent of the 12,000-plus membership of the Japanese Biochemical Society is female. Data from field work at OBI and

PERI, combined with an analysis of larger social trends influencing women, indicate that the chief barrier to women's full contribution to science resides in an unresolved conflict with domestic work and child raising.

If compared with the rest of Japan's scientists, the OBI and PERI interviewees and informants would be located near the ambitious end of a motivation continuum. They could also represent the tip of an aspiration iceberg. Chapter 8 presents survey statistics and other material indicating widespread discontent with the status quo among Japan's scientists, particularly the younger, and their desire for more independence. The question is whether Japanese society will nurture or discourage the restless chance takers, for only with encouragement will their numbers grow. Chapter 8 also lays out the obstacles to the spread of reforms represented by OBI and PERI.

Chapter 9 anticipates a criticism. The case of Japanese scientific creativity in world fora is so unusual, and the problem so chronic, that it has generated a welter of explanations involving Japanese mentality or other supposedly unique circumstances. A close look at Japanese social psychology finds nothing wanting in creative potential, but an examination of key points in Japanese geopolitical history does find very real obstacles to scientific accomplishment unknown in the West. None is insurmountable, but their solution depends on understanding and responsive administrators.

Positioned for world leadership?

The litany of weak performance indicators in Japanese science hides the fact that Japan contains some critical ingredients for preeminence in basic research. The country's wealth and technological sophistication are prodigious, reflecting the efforts of a highly educated populace. Japanese elementary school education inspires students' curiosity about science and a desire to learn more (Lewis 1995). Mathematics and science instruction at the primary and secondary levels has long enjoyed international praise, and its current performance is still impressive. The Third International Mathematics and Science Study (TIMSS), hailed by the United States' National Science Board as "the largest and most ambitious undertaking of its kind" (NSB 1998: 1–4), found Japan's fourth grade students outperforming peers in all countries but South Korea in its science assessment; among eighth graders, Japan was bested only by South Korea and Singapore. In the study's mathematics assessment, Japanese fourth graders outpaced their counterparts from South Korea and Singapore, and eighth graders scored higher than all but students from Singapore. Another phase of the project rated the quality and practice of mathematical instruction in Japan particularly highly (NSB 1998: 1–12,1–18, 1–20).

Despite the impressive array of factors that ought to result in stellar basic science research performance, there remains a missing ingredient:

organizational features that would nurture a lively credit cycle. This book will introduce you to three bioscientists in particular who are now approaching mid-career. I chose them because, beyond their demonstrated competence, they were willing to take big professional chances and make sacrifices in order to pursue a life in basic research. I have encountered many more worthwhile candidates qualified for such a profile, too. I have come to see these energetic and talented younger and mid-career scientists of Japan as vigorous seedlings and young trees confined in pots that are too restrictive to accommodate their growth. The problem for Japan's science policy makers is not to instill a passion for science but to reward it.

2

THE UNIVERSITY STATUS QUO

The core of Japan's organizational predicament in basic science lies in the country's universities, where most basic research is conducted and where over two thirds of the country's life science researchers work – and shape the next generation of scientists.

Kōza membership and duties

Major research universities and medical schools organize research and teaching on the basis of the *kōza* (or "chair" – the term more literally means "course" or "lectures") as the fundamental personnel and budgetary unit. In natural science departments, the kōza is typically staffed with a full professor (*kyōju*) at its apex of authority, with one associate professor (*jokyōju*) and two positions for an assistant (*joshu* – a term that literally means "helper," which I have translated into "assistant" as a stand-alone term, not an abbreviated form of "assistant professor"). The poorer universities more often have only one assistant. The professor in Japan is also the laboratory head for the discipline represented by the kōza. The dual role explains the interchangeable use of the terms "Department Chairman" and "Professor" in English renditions of the Japanese title. Each kōza also contains graduate students and advanced undergraduate students who have entered the kōza to learn laboratory research skills and write graduation theses. The numbers of both graduate and undergraduate students vary. Informally, the kōza is known as "Professor X's room" (*X-sensei no heya*), and the professor is often referred to (in his absence) as the "boss" (using the transliterated term *bosu*).

The most senior kōza members must take part in university-related administration, and Japanese universities impose a particularly heavy burden of faculty committee work and related politicking compared to demands on senior faculty in other countries (Clark 1983: 113). As an assistant in the Medical College put it, the professor is "always away from the lab, waving the flag somewhere." The associate professor typically takes a position reminiscent of middle management, articulating the professor's priorities to assistants, who in turn conduct the daily experimental work of the laboratory and supervise graduate students and advanced undergraduates. Assistants assume responsibility for teaching hands-on technique. In some cases, graduate students also become involved in teaching undergraduates.

According to my informants, the heaviest proportion of daily laboratory tasks falls to graduate students, followed closely by assistants. "It's just manual labor," said one associate professor in agricultural chemistry, "and the students are paying tuition to do it at that!" He also fulminated to me about how his senior colleagues told him on several occasions not to worry about seeking funds for equipment: "just use your students."

Kōza hierarchy in funding and credit

The kōza features a strong element of hierarchy that frustrates the credit cycle. Figure 2.1 offers a schematic drawing of the kōza as research unit. The associate professor and the assistant are "under" the professor in several key respects. Although these subordinates have independent access to modest supplementary research funds, each kōza receives most of its funding for research via the university administration in fixed amounts known as "general university funds" (*kōhi*). At all of the national universities, faculty receive the same funding base as determined by the Ministry of Education (MOE or "Monbusho"), which funds the country's 98 national universities and sets policy for the other 467. (Faculty salaries have a single base also, with grades for seniority.) The authority for using the regularly allocated kōza funds for both research and operating budgets rests with the professor.

Subordinates must cultivate both a shared research interest and congenial interpersonal relations with the professor to get access to research funds. At the Medical College, the professor of a kōza having two associate professors, a lecturer and two assistants received 4 million yen a year in direct funds;

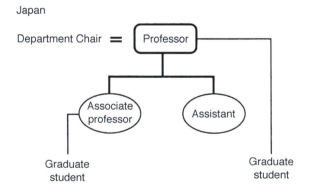

Figure 2.1 The organization of the Japanese University Research Unit (adapted from Arai 1996a)

according to another faculty member familiar with that kōza, the professor excluded his associate professors from using over three million yen because he "didn't hit it off" with them.

Kōza hierarchy also tips the balance toward the professor in the already difficult process of allocating credit in publication. The practice of including the name of the professor on all kōza members' publications is widespread, regardless of his actual role in conceptualizing and executing the research reported. A pilot study using a five-year sample of Japanese and American scientific publications beginning with 1987 found a higher number of co-authors among the Japanese. The percentage of all papers having four or more authors was 14.4 per cent for the United States sample and 31.5 per cent for the Japanese (calculated from the authors' table of cumulative percentages). The authors suggested several factors for the difference, but they identified as the "most fundamental" the tendency for the group's elder member to sign on only for his role in "editorial supervision" (Negishi and Yamada 1992: 34).

My academic interviewees and informants explained the rationale for the near-universal practice of professorial co-authorship: the research was conducted in that professor's laboratory, with "his money." A government researcher in agricultural chemistry who had been an assistant for ten years explained it thus: "Even if the assistant does a really good job, it's seen from the outside as the professor's work, and the money goes to him. That's the system." A 1990 article by Koji Nakanishi, Director of the Suntory Institute for Bioorganic Research in Osaka and Centennial Professor of Chemistry at Columbia University, took aim at the credit deficit for talented assistants. "The professor's name goes on the papers, and even if the concepts and experiments were provided entirely by assistants and students, the asterisk (for the responsible contact author) would probably be placed next to the professor's name." When invited to international conferences by foreigners who "don't know the real situation," such professors would "simply read their papers, attend the conference, go touring and then come home to Japan" (Nakanishi 1990: 363).

Work and hierarchy

Few of us outside the laboratory world know about the long hours that laboratory researchers spend on their work. An inkling comes from bioscientists' own writings, such as biochemist Arthur Kornberg's autobiography (1989), or Natalie Angier's *Natural Obsessions* (1988), the narrative of a participant observer in the Weinberg molecular biology laboratory at the Massachusetts Institute of Technology's Whitehead Institute. In the most competitive laboratories, 12- or even 16-hour days are not unusual, and six-day weeks are the norm. Among the postdoctoral fellows I studied at the University of Oregon, 45- and 50-hour weeks were typical.

Although I have no comparative international statistics on which to base the claim, I believe scientists in Japanese academic laboratories log more hours than their counterparts at all but the most intensely competitive laboratories in other countries. (Chapter 9 provides some aggregate figures for Japan.) The laboratory day at the Medical College began late, at 10 or 10:30 AM for most kōza members, but would soon be in full swing. Members would work through the dinner hour with a short break for a light meal at a nearby restaurant, or – more often – a snack cobbled together from boxes of instant noodles and other snack foods pulled out of laboratory storage drawers, and continue their work on into the night.

The long hours stem in part from the dearth of support staff in university laboratories, described in Chapter 1, and the larger Japanese society (for reasons identified in Chapter 9) also encourages long work hours. There is also a reward system for long hours that is generated by the synergy of routine work demands and kōza hierarchy. Several informants told me that many university laboratory hours are spent not in the hot thrill of discovery but out of a felt need to be seen putting in time at the workplace. A 34-year-old biochemist with a PhD from the University of Tokyo realized just that when he returned to a Japanese laboratory after a two-year postdoctoral stint at a free-standing research institute in California, where the work atmosphere was intense but the researchers' hours erratic: "In Japan, the ones who spend the most time in the lab are the ones who are the most favorably evaluated. If [scientific accomplishments] were determined by hours in the lab, Japan would be tops in the world right now!"

One other biochemist would add, from his own graduate school experience, that being seen by the Professor was the most important element in doing work for the kōza. As a graduate student, Seiji Muto (a pseudonym) had attempted to win the approval of his professor by maintaining the laboratory in earnest, alternating between all-night work binges and stints beginning at 5 AM that ended in mid-afternoon. The attempt did not win the approval he craved, though. He believed it was because the professor only arrived in mid-morning, and noticed only that Muto was not among the attentive graduate students who surrounded him.

The guaranteed position and amputated careers

All of the positions in the kōza, from entry-level assistant on up, are tenured – that is, they carry the guarantee of employment until retirement age. The problem of "dead wood" – an unmotivated and unproductive research group member who occupies a job slot – can thus occur at any rank, and not just at the associate professor level and beyond, as in the United States. More importantly, permanent employment in the kōza truncates researchers' careers. The pyramid shape of the kōza cannot accommodate promotion for both of its assistants at the time of the professor's death or retirement. The unpromoted assistant will remain in the kōza despite being passed over, accumulating years in the laboratory with no increase in authority or promotion to a higher pay level. (Seniority in the pay scale does provides small yearly increases in salary, however.)

Permanent employment and seniority are supposed to optimize the working group's harmony. The competition built into the system between the two assistants, however, is a perennial source of tension. During my visits to university laboratories I heard complaints that the two assistants did not help each other enthusiastically, or would even subtly sabotage each other. (The colorful expression used was to "pull the [other person's] legs," *ashi o hipparu*.)

The personnel change that allows one assistant to assume the associate professor position typically heralds a change in the research agenda, requiring the remaining assistant either to adapt or pursue an independent course separated from the main research direction of the kōza – alone and short on resources. Hence the comment from the late Tatsuo Miyazawa, PERI director and former professor of protein chemistry at the University of Tokyo: "Of course the [unpromoted] assistant can stay, but I tell my former students that if they have any self-respect they'll leave."

That latter alternative requires a growing academic job market, however, which Japan's is not. Meanwhile, the problem of the ageing assistant is a popular subject among scientists, and a source of real dread among younger academics. The average age of assistants nationwide in 1992 was 35.7 years, and nearly 20 per cent were 40 years old or over (MOE 1993: 300–1). Those figures represent a slight increase since 1986, when the average age was 35.1 (MOE 1987: 312–13), but the figures for 1995 were nearly unchanged (MOE 1996a: 288–9), casting doubt on my informants' dark image of a large cohort of assistants passing through the system in a cohort bulge.

Dysfunctional variations in recruitment

Nor must promotion take place from within the kōza, even for its one associate professor. A professor does not have to promote from within his kōza if an associate professor leaves, and the professor does not have to consult with assistants on the decision. (Professors are particularly inclined to look for an associate professor outside the kōza if they themselves came into a kōza that already had assistants in place.) In one case at the Medical College, a professor in a basic science field decided to look for an associate professor from outside because the two assistants in his laboratory were, in his words, "too young." "The associate professor," he explained, "is the professor's representative." Both assistants were in their mid-30s. (The age criterion was rather arbitrary; although the assistants were some ten years younger than the national average for all associate professors, a fourth of the country's associate professors were also under age 40.) In other cases described for me, both interpersonal relations and research performance could influence professors to turn against their own associates, or cause faculty committees to intervene in the selection of a new head.

The case of the immature assistants also illustrates the extensive (sometimes definitive) authority of the professor in kōza personnel decisions. The choice of assistants is solely the professor's. Faculty committees may intervene in associate professor and professor appointments and promotions (becoming one focus for political maneuverings), but more often than not, according to my informants, the professor's wishes are honored.

Group research interests in the kōza suffer their worst ruptures when an outsider assumes the professorship, resulting in a kōza head who has not chosen any of his subordinates. In a kōza in agricultural chemistry at a first-tier national university, the new outside professor was several years younger than the associate, which fueled their subsequent antagonism. A kōza head's retirement occasions a lot of anxiety among kōza members. Two assistants in a Medical College kōza experienced life with a professor who had not chosen them, and were bracing themselves for his retirement. "There isn't really that much communication," said one of the assistants, "so even if he is out on business there are plenty of times when we don't notice it." She was concerned, nevertheless, because his retirement was less than a year away, "and I'm uneasy about what happens after that."

A contrast with the United States

The kōza is Japan's version of the chair system (discussion based on Clark 1983). Teaching and research units in universities can be compared internationally on a continuum, with "chair" at one end and "department" at the other. (Different countries display mixes and shadings of important features that distinguish the two poles.) The chair end of the continuum concentrates authority and responsibility in each chair holder, a senior academic with the rank of professor. As the Japanese case illustrates, academic staff working in the same unit are under the chair's direction.

At the other end of the continuum, a departmental unit contains several academic researchers in the same or closely connected specialties, like "biochemistry and biophysics." Although the more senior members of the department enjoy more authority than do junior members (sometimes much more), the authority is spread among several individuals, and can more easily accommodate participation by associates and assistant professors. In the laboratory sciences, each department member has his or her laboratory that includes postdoctoral fellows and graduate students under the general direction of the department faculty member.

Departmentalism is found mostly in the United States, and the chair approach prevails in Europe and Latin America as well as Japan. Figure 2.2 schematically represents the United States configuration. The more

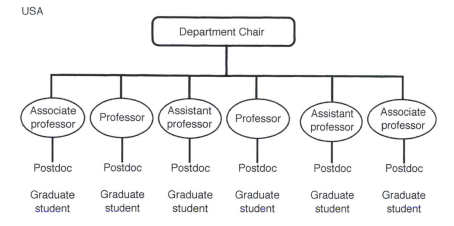

Figure 2.2 The organization of the United States University Research Unit (adapted from Arai 1996a)

horizontal arrangement gives researchers more independence, particularly since they have independent access to equipment and materials. They must seek funding for their research activity, including salaries of support staff, by submitting competitive grant applications outside the university, to government agencies, nonprofit foundations, and corporate donors. The figure's horizontal juxtaposition of department members overstates somewhat their equality, since seniority does confer more authority in American departmental decision making. The biggest dividing line (not shown in this figure) is permanent employment, or "tenure," conferred on successful assistant professors after six years of research and teaching. The criteria are explicit, and include quality and quantity of the candidate's publications, volume of grants, and the evaluations of outside reviewers and other (more senior) department members. Nevertheless, hierarchical politics at that juncture can be intense enough to corrupt the process. Unsuccessful tenure candidates get one additional year of employment.

Despite these qualifications, the fact remains: the Japanese configuration requires more time for a researcher to attain independence. Neuroscientist Shigetada Nakanishi of the Kyoto University Faculty of Medicine provided some observations on the lag in independent career building in contrast with the United States. A Japanese bioscientist can become an assistant by age 30 or so; an extremely competent (and fortunate) researcher may become a professor with complete research independence only after age 40 or 50. In the United States, by contrast, an academic bioscientist with three years of postdoctoral study after receiving a PhD could become an assistant professor with his or her own laboratory by age 32. The decade-long gap becomes evident among those Japanese bioscientists who have distinguished themselves internationally, which requires yet another five to ten years-plus: as Nakanishi noted, such luminaries as Yasutomi Nishizuka and the late Shosaku Numa were in their fifties when their work gained acclaim outside of Japan.

The narrow path of academic recruitment

Hiring practices in Japanese academia severely limit the potential of the credit cycle: Japanese universities tend to recruit from their own graduates, as opposed to a broad pool of applicants responding to public job announcements. Two thirds of my eighteen respondents who had taken positions as assistants immediately after finishing their PhD requirements stayed in the same university, and two thirds of them in turn had remained in the same laboratory. In the mid-1990s, overall a third of Japan's university faculty had graduated from the institution at which they were teaching, a proportion unchanged over the last decade (*Asahi Shimbun* 1996a). A 1994 study of assistants (joshu) in the natural sciences who had left their positions in the preceding five years found 55 per cent at all national universities moving into positions at the same university, with higher figures for private and other public universities (Kato 1995: 154). The Japan Science Council's 1990 nationwide survey of researchers found about half (48 per cent) of university faculty indicating that they hired as a rule from among their own faculty and graduate students. (Among natural science respondents the figure was 39 per cent; JSC 1991: 160, 89). By contrast, fewer than one out of ten (four of the forty-one) faculty in the Departments of Chemistry and Biology at the University of Oregon had received their doctorate at Oregon.

The more elite the Japanese university, the more frequently it hires its own graduates into permanent positions. The seven former imperial universities occupy the top level of status, with the University of Tokyo at the apex, followed by Kyoto University. (The other five former imperial universities are Hokkaido, Tohoku, Nagoya, Osaka, and Kyushu.) In some formulations, Tokyo Institute of Technology, a national university, joins this elite ring as a research institution. In the mid-1990s, some 87 per cent of the University of Tokyo's academics graduated from the same university, and the figure was 80 per cent for the University of Kyoto (Maddox 1994: 723). The same tendency may be operating in elite universities in the United States, but to a far lesser degree; in Harvard University's Department of Chemistry about one out of four regular faculty received their PhD degree from Harvard. In the Department of Biology at Massachusetts Institute of Technology (MIT), however, fewer than one in eleven regular faculty hold an MIT doctorate.

Postdoctoral researcher positions are also filled from within the kōza, as are various unpaid research assistant arrangements that aid the disappointed job seeker. Since 1986, the Japanese government has been assisting unsuccessful academic job seekers through postdoctoral fellowships that allow the junior-level scientist to continue research activity while waiting for an opening. Though commonly referred to in Japanese as "postdoctoral researchers" (*posu doku kenkyūin*), these positions differ from their Western counterparts, which are offered to researchers from different laboratories. Of my eleven interviewees who had domestic postdoctoral positions, eight had taken them in the university laboratory in which they had earned their doctorate. True to the American dictum of "move out," none of my five postdoc interviewees at the University of Oregon's Institute of Molecular Biology had received their PhD at Oregon. The research teams at major universities in the United States are truly hotbeds of turnover. A study of one such university found about 200 per cent turnover in team membership over a five-year period (Hackett 1995: 75n.16).

Also detracting from mobility in Japan are the channels through which academic scientists flow to other schools, a kind of colonization in which less prestigious universities hire the human products of their elite counterparts. The practice has been documented by critics from time to time as an exercise in tracing pedigrees; science critic and environmental activist Jun Ui provided a thorough description in his co-authored 1976 book, *Daigaku Kaitairon*. In 1996, as Kochi Prefecture established a prefectural institute of technology, I was told by local observers that planners would rely on faculty and graduating doctorates of the Tokyo Institute of Technology to fill the faculty ranks of the new institution during its first five years of existence. The Institute's first president and provost were Tokyo Institute of Technology products. As of 1998, degree holders from the Tokyo Institute of Technology accounted for 55 per cent of faculty appointments (84 out of 153) – not an exclusive pipeline, and only nine of the eighty-four Tokyo Institute of Technology degree holders came directly from positions there. Nevertheless, the disproportionate representation of Tokyo Institute of Technology degree holders signaled the continued existence of recruitment via an alma mater network. Chapter 8 discusses the factors that encourage this practice.

Japanese scientists are quite familiar with the practice of formal, public job announcements that canvass the entire professional community to effect impersonal, merit-oriented academic job searches. The Japanese word *kōbo* denotes the process of open recruitment nicely. According to informants' accounts, however, if the position is not filled by a graduate of the hiring university, it will be taken by someone backed by an "influential" advisor, through established collegial networks, via "introductions" (*shōkai*). Their accounts were corroborated by a nationwide study of mid-career academic researchers conducted by the Japan Science Council in 1990; only 33 per cent of respondents in natural science divisions (and an even lower 22 per cent of all respondents) indicated that their divisions' academic appointments were made entirely or "nearly all" through open recruitment (JSC 1991: 33, 160). My informants also believed that openly announced positions were actually filled through influential networks, and the cynicism was remarkably widespread.

Recruitment and professorial power

The predominant hiring-from-within pattern and the importance of introductions for recruitment to academic positions have given professors a pivotal role in securing employment for their students after graduation. My respondents believed that the kōza head's part was indispensable for finding a job at any academic institution. Said one, "In Japan, if you don't have a boss's introduction you can't get anywhere." Those who had conflicts with their professors would grow anxious about finding a subsequent position, if not simply assume that their chance for finding an academic position in Japan was entirely lost. Masamichi Maeda (pseudonym) had lost his professor's good will by taking a research direction other than the one that his professor had prescribed. In the late 1970s, Maeda was a graduate student in an agricultural chemistry kōza. As an undergraduate he had studied agricultural chemistry at a prefectural university, but relocated to a first-tier national university because his undergraduate prefectural school did not offer a doctoral course in that field. His master's research, chosen from a "smorgasbord" (baikingu) of topics in metabolism, did not keep his interest. Maeda regarded the "smorgasbord" of PhD dissertation topics proffered by his professor as "leftovers" from a largely completed project in metabolism; he wanted instead to conduct his doctoral research in membrane biology, relying on an assistant in the kōza who had been studying the subject.

Maeda prevailed in an argument with his professor over the issue, but at the price of a cordial relationship; their interactions are limited today to civil greetings at academic meetings. At the time of his doctoral research, Maeda was concerned that his advisor would resent him so much that he would be denied a degree, since the professor becomes ultimate arbiter in his role as the dissertation committee's chief investigator (shusa). Maeda's fear of such reprisal was so great that he began studying for English language placement exams, which he knew he would need to apply to a degree program in the United States. Maeda did survive, professionally; his first job came via a professional network from his undergraduate university.

The professor also plays an important role in nonacademic job placements for students with advanced degrees. As mentioned in Chapter 1, an international study of industrial R&D workers conducted in 1988 and 1989 found over half of the Japanese respondents with graduate degrees reporting that they had obtained their job through their instructors' introductions. Among PhD holders, the figure rose to 73 per cent (JPC 1990b: 73). The figures for German, British and American R&D employees with advanced degrees were 22 per cent, 20 per cent and 8 per cent, respectively (JPC 1990b: 73; JPC 1990a: 71; JPC 1990a: 61).

My interviewees' experiences formed a continuum, from professors who provided recommendation letters (and nothing else) to those who literally assigned the student to a job. Kaoru Shirogane (a pseudonym), a 32-year-old protein specialist with a PhD in pharmacology, experienced the latter; his advisor committed him to a job offer from a major distilling company without asking him about it. "Later I realized it was good. If it really were disagreeable I would have declined." His first interest was a university career, but there were no positions on the horizon at the time. Jun Hosokawa (also a pseudonym), who ended his education with a master's degree in biophysics, was frankly relieved that his advisor did no more than suggest a few places. "There are faculty who have to send someone to a certain company every number of years, and it's like getting an order [when you're told to go]. Fortunately I didn't have that. I'm glad he didn't help!" A few industry-based researchers whom I interviewed sounded apologetic. "I've had an extremely close relationship with my advisor," said Osamu Yorozuya (pseudonym), a 30-year-old biochemist at a foreign pharmaceutical firm in Japan. "That's how I got into my company, but in a bad sense, through his connections" (*kone*).

Anemic vitae

In the life sciences, a long-standing bulge in unemployed researchers has further reinforced the tendency to rely on predetermined channels and the professor's good offices. An oversupply of PhD holders relative to demand hit young Japanese scientists with particular force between the mid-1970s and early 1980s, and persists today. The result is *ōbā dokutā* (a direct transliteration of "over doctor"), or "OD." (More precisely, the term is used for PhD holders who are not yet regularly employed but are continuing research in some capacity or other; Tsukahara 1996: 25.)

The weak demand for PhDs has further depressed mobility among scientists. It has also reduced any incentive among Japanese academic researchers to use the curriculum vitae as a way of telling the rest of their professional world about themselves. The curriculum vitae (or "vita," or "cv") epitomizes the workings of the credit cycle because it organizes and presents credit-related information in competitive bids for academic positions and research grants. A fully developed cv identifies the researcher's specialties and interests, relates his or her professional accomplishments, and chronicles the researcher's progression of institutional affiliations and positions. Japanese scientists are certainly familiar with cvs, but only half of the 40 academic researchers from whom I requested a cv had one on hand. (A few thoughtful interviewees responded by offering to write one up for me.)

Nor does the typical Japanese cv provide the declarations of professional interests and accounts of accomplishments contained in American bio-scientists' résumés. These portions of larger statements from two American postdoctoral fellows in their mid-30s are typical:

Professional Goals: To develop an academic research and teaching program concerning biophysical and biochemical aspects of RNA-Protein interactions

and;

Research Interests: Chromatin: ... I am interested in studying the physiological instabilities of nucleosomes and chromatin, especially under transcriptional conditions.

With few exceptions, the vitae I received from my Japanese interviewees were written on two-page forms sold at stationery shops. (The term in Japanese, *rirekisho*, is best translated as "personal record," and there is no term to distinguish it from an academic cv.) The main body of these forms was dedicated to an "academic and work chronology," with columns for year and month. There were spaces also for a photograph and the listing of "licenses and other qualifications." Some forms devoted separate blocks to personal information such as favorite hobbies and sports, health status, and a listing of family members' names and ages.

This type of cv focusses on institutional affiliation as an account of one's whereabouts at different points in one's life. "It's all one set form," said a mid-career microbiologist at the Food Research Institute. "They're very official, you know. An individual, private face doesn't become very visible." Said a PERI biophysicist,

It doesn't really ask what you've done, just where you've been – where you graduated from, what company you joined, what year, what month. In that space there's hardly any room for writing in what you did. So unless you ask someone to write a cv on their own, you can't get anything out of it.

When I showed him my own cv, he said, "Yours is activity-centered and a Japanese cv is organization-centered." The Japanese version also hints of social control. An OBI researcher in her mid-30s with a PhD in biophysics contrasted the American and Japanese cv: "The spirit behind the cv in the U.S. is, 'These are my most appealing points.' In Japan, it's 'Look, I haven't done anything bad.'" A few of the cvs did display an older convention of the Japanese résumé, the category "rewards and punishments" (*shōbatsu*), with the somewhat reassuring entry "none." In any event, Japanese bioscientists do not regard their cvs as pieces of personal professional advertising. My interviewees typically had a proprietary attitude toward their cvs, and some specimens came to me with the name blackened out.

The apprenticeship element in education

A 1996 overview of the life sciences in Japan commissioned by the Science and Technology Agency identified a "difference in thinking" between Japan and the United States in the nurturing and career formation of young researchers.

> ... In the United States the methods for forming a career are clear, and the basic stance in which young researchers themselves design and build their own careers differs from Japan's. The Japanese researchers' career formation is, to use the oft-mentioned term, an "apprentice system (*totei seido*)," in which the master's wishes and the influence of academic cliques play a greater part in the shaping of the disciple's future than do his own intentions or plans. (IFT 1996: 56)

My descriptions of the kōza hierarchy and the channeling process for employment corroborate the assertion that Japanese science education smacks of an apprentice–master relationship. The education of a researcher also discourages the development of independent thinking. Surely one of the most difficult challenges of education in science is to cultivate the student's ability to choose a research topic independently. If students receive that responsibility too early in their training, they will either choose a topic that is trivial or flounder in one too difficult to execute. But if graduate education does not eventually confer such authority, students will later have trouble formulating innovative and imaginative topics.

The experiences of my respondents suggested a decided tilt in the Japanese system toward a top-down approach to creating new researchers. Among the fifty-three respondents who told me how they had chosen their master's thesis topic, twenty-seven stated unequivocally that the topic was assigned by the kōza head, more than twice the number of those who claimed a clear personal initiative in choosing. (This subset excluded graduates of medical schools, who do not submit master's degree theses.) The remaining fourth or so of the fifty-three respondents explained their choice of thesis subject as a selection from two or more choices offered by the lab head, sometimes referring to the process as a smorgasbord. Among the forty-two doctorate holders who discussed their choice of dissertation topics, about one out of five had been assigned his or her topic by the professor in charge of the laboratory.

Japanese graduate students do not experience a curriculum designed to expose them to a full range of subject and subspecialty options. Their commitment to a particular research area has actually already taken place, during their undergraduate days. Although academic degrees in Japan progress in stages familiar to Americans, with four-year bachelor of science degrees followed by master's degrees (requiring two years) and doctorates (three years), students in Japan who major in most sciences enter one kōza – and perforce, one research area – for their instructional needs by the end of their third year of undergraduate study. By contrast, such a choice takes place among more seasoned students in the United States, during the early years of graduate work after a rotation among the department's laboratories.

There are some mitigating factors to the Japanese case. In eighty interview accounts of kōza choice, some four fifths of my respondents indicated that they had based their decision on their interest in the kōza's research topics; the professor's personality or treatment of students (e.g. job placement ability) was either secondary or irrelevant to the decision. Some of my interviewees came from laboratories in which the professor varied each student's degree of independence in master's research topic choice on the basis of his perception of the student's ability. Respondents also believed that undergraduate students today exercise more independent power of choice than did past cohorts. Some departments facilitate the process of choosing by providing a faculty cameo lecture series or special briefing event (literally an "exposition gathering," *setsumeikai*) designed to introduce the students to the different laboratories. Chiba University's Akikazu Ando, now a professor of biochemistry, has invigorated the process by requiring his thirty or so third-year undergraduate students to visit labs and then present their findings in terms of their personal interests to their fellow students, with a prize for the best presentation style.

The medical schools' ikyoku

Japan's eighty medical schools are indeed major players in life science research, providing 70 per cent of the country's contributions to international life science journals (Yamazaki 1991: 547). The organizational features of Japanese science that frustrate the credit cycle in academia occur most potently in the medical school variation on the kōza, however. The chair system in Japan's medical schools takes the form of the *ikyoku* (literally "medical bureau/office") kōza, or "clinical department." Ikyoku are divided up by clinical specialties familiar to the West, such as internal medicine or thoracic surgery. Like other kōza in the sciences, they provide undergraduates with lectures and laboratory instruction, and supervise graduate research. The core staff, known as "department members" (*ikyokuin*) or "teaching staff" (*kyōshitsuin*) are the familiar professor, associate professor and assistant(s), joined by lecturers (*kōshi*) who assume a rank between the assistant (joshu) and the associate professor (jokyōju). As in other kōza, research topics are determined by the professor's specialties and interests, but the ikyoku may have research subgroups known as *han* (squads or teams).

Undergraduate medical school students in Japan, like undergraduates in the natural science curricula, choose an ikyoku kōza in which to spend the last year before receiving their degree. Unlike natural science degree programs, however, medical schools in Japan require a six-year course of study that confers a "master's degree in medicine" (*igaku shūshi*) degree. The first two years or so are devoted to general education, as in natural science curricula, and the curriculum then moves into more science courses, followed by clinical specialties. Students spend the last one or two years in assignments (*haizoku*) to hospital wards and laboratories, with some electing assignments in laboratories conducting basic research (*kiso haizoku*) in kōza dedicated to fields like biochemistry or physiology.

Participation in the ikyoku after graduating is indispensable to a medical career. Although graduating students take a national medical examination at graduation that legally entitles them to practice medicine, newly minted medical doctors (*ishi*) undergo at least a few years as residents (*kenshūi*) in an ikyoku before beginning independent practice as a physician. They need subsequent years in a department not only for more specialized training and supervision but to develop an affiliation with a professor's group as well. That ikyoku membership, purchased with some two to seven or more years of labor during residence, will yield job placements and an enduring guild-like affiliation that also provides identity among fellow professionals.

These residents sustain themselves and earn their ikyoku membership by virtue of a critical function of the ikyoku beyond teaching and research: the dispatching of medical expertise, both to the university hospital and to affiliated hospitals, either on rotation or as a placement service. (Long 1998 offers an insightful account of the funding, patient referral, and medical manpower distribution dynamics that give the ikyoku its resilience.) The only members of an ikyoku who are regularly salaried are its teaching faculty core (the ranks of assistant through professor) and a secretary: some eighty or more other members, among them residents, graduate students, adjunct instructors and assistants of various stripes, earn money while affiliated with the ikyoku through part-time and full-time jobs provided by the department via its position in the university hospital and – more importantly – the professor's networks with affiliated hospitals.

Gatherings of the ikyoku in its office lounge for lunch or on patient rounds in the hospital represent only a third or a fourth of its actual membership: the rest are at their assigned jobs at other hospitals, either in rotations or on a more permanent basis. The affiliated hospitals depend on this arrangement for part-time labor, some of it critical to their own functioning. The pay is attractive for the more accomplished ikyoku resident; by one account, going rates are 60,000 yen a day or 500,000 yen a month.

Medical schools' narrower recruitment channels

Prominent medical school faculties as of the early 1990s had recruited all or most of their members from within. All of the clinical faculty at the University of Tokyo and University of Osaka medical schools were graduates of the same medical school; among the basic science faculty, insiders comprised seventeen of nineteen members and seventeen of twenty-one members, respectively. Similarly, some nine tenths of the clinical faculty and three fourths of the basic science faculty at Kyoto University and Keio University medical schools were home grown (Sankei Shinbun Shakaibu 1992: 60). Over 60 per cent of the respondents in the Japan Science Council's 1990 nationwide faculty survey who belonged to medical, dental and pharmacy schools reported that their organization hired from within, making them the JSC's most incestuous section (against a figure of 48 per cent among all respondents), although the medical section respondents also reported open recruitment practices that registered somewhat above the mean (JSC 1991: 33, 122).

The political dimension of academic hiring and promotion is particularly intense in medical schools. "They call it open recruitment for professorial positions," said a graduating medical student at the Medical College, "but it doesn't really add up to it." He related what he and his classmates had heard about hiring for a professorship in anatomy: "When it was all said and done there weren't any serious contenders. We here at the bottom don't know much, but we heard that there was some money changing hands." Several students and instructors referred me to *The White Tower* (*Shiroi Kyotō*, by Toyoko Yamazaki), a 1965 fictionalized account of the struggle that precipitated when a medical school professor about to retire decided to back an outside candidate for his position rather than promote his own associate professor. Among the resources enlisted by the professor and his associate professor opponent in their bids for faculty votes: hospital bed allocations, alliances for votes in future promotions, memberships on boards of professional associations, and research grants. The portrayal in *The White Tower* was fictional. My informants, however, believed it reflected hiring and promotion dynamics that they had seen and heard of.

The academic medical career as someone else's bargaining chip

The medical school professor's role in personnel decisions affords him considerable sway over his subordinates' current and long-term well-being. Hitoshio Kanda (pseudonym), an associate professor at a Tokyo area private medical college, was a non-physician in one of the basic science specialties. He and others in nonclinical specialties, he said, had found the individual professor's power in personnel-related matters to be the hardest aspect of medical school professional life to live with. He had been promoted to associate professor, he said, as a "prize" for allowing his kōza's professor, a particularly influential figure at his medical college, to assume first authorship in the published results of Kanda's research. Kanda did not seem concerned about the misallocation of credit, but he was ambivalent about the way in which he was promoted. "Objectively [the promotion] was a good thing, but I don't know if it really was."

One of my interviewees provided a detailed example of medical school career politics from his own experience. Mikio Takezawa (a fictitious name, as are the others that follow) was an assistant in biochemistry at a major national medical school in the late 1970s. The head of Takezawa's kōza, Professor Gen-ichi Nomura, was on very bad terms with his associate professor, Hiroshi Maehara. Maehara was directing the assistants (of whom Takezawa was one) to work on research projects of Maehara's own choice, thus openly rejecting Nomura's research agenda. Nomura was all the more incensed because he had chosen Maehara for the associate professor post. Takezawa's sympathies were divided. Maehara's treatment of the person to whom he owed his position was "scandalous." Nomura's health was failing, though, and his research was not garnering the interest and respect of colleagues, whereas Maehara presented a full and lively agenda.

Matters embroiled Takezawa even more when Maehara was given the opportunity to leave and head his own kōza in the same medical school. Maehara wanted to take both the assistants with him. Promotion to full professor would require Nomura's approval, though, and Nomura made it known that he would back the nomination for full professor only if he could keep Takezawa to work for him. Enter Professor Keizo Tamura, a fellow faculty member at the school of medicine who wanted to see Maehara become a full professor but was also sympathetic to Nomura. Tamura suggested to Takezawa that he take a two-year postdoctoral researcher position with a colleague of Tamura's at a university in the midwestern United States. In the course of two years, Tamura reasoned, the situation would be resolved. "At that point," Takezawa recalled, "I was in complete despair." By leaving, he was risking losing his job altogether. The story had a happy ending, for when Takezawa returned to Japan he was promoted to an associate professorship. Years later he remained appalled by the process, though. "Could you Americans ever conceive of such a thing? It was trade in human flesh (*jinshin baibai*)." There was certainly no room for credit cycle dynamic in Takezawa's case.

The basic research career in medical schools

Japan's medical schools confer a doctorate in medicine (*igaku hakase*), but the degree does not represent a commitment to a career in research. By one estimate (based on subtracting the number of practicing physicians from the total number of physicians), fewer than 3 per cent of the holders of the PhD degree in Medicine are actually conducting research (calculated using figures in MHW 1992: 108–9). Japanese physicians may view their degree with cynicism, as a kind of useless appendage or something "inedible." A popular simile likens the degree to a grain of cooked rice stuck to the sole of one's foot: irritating if left there, but too dirty to eat.

A few observers said that the degree increases patient confidence, but doctors' advertisements (as in telephone directory advertisements and billboards) do not mention the degree. Several medical school informants also said that the Ministry of Health and Welfare requires the degree for financially rewarding and prestigious positions in top-level administration at large hospitals. A representative of the Ministry, however, denied that the Ministry either makes the degree a statutory condition for hospital heads or otherwise takes a position on the desirability of the degree. One point on which everyone agrees, however (including the Ministry of Health and Welfare representative), is that a medical doctor without the degree would feel left out, or lacking in "status" or "appearance."

The degree is also the physician's receipt from the professor that confirms full ikyoku membership, paid for by the physician-in-training through years of work in hospital wards and the laboratory. Residents earn their PhD degree as "research students" (*kenkyūsei*) who spend somewhere between five and seven years in that status to complete research leading to the degree, as they support themselves through part-time jobs and hospital rotations. The PhD may be formally indispensable only to those aspiring to an academic career, but to turn it down would be to repudiate the professor–student relationship that is indispensable to attractive jobs: every major hospital in the country falls under the purview of a university hospital, which means that a medical university professor will play a decisive role in filling directorships and chiefs of staff, as well as influencing lesser appointments. Unfortunately I did not ask residents at the Medical College how it was determined that they would be working in the laboratory, or for how long. (I naively assumed at the time that their laboratory stints were purely elective.) Kyoko Imamura, a critic of medical school research, observed that professors tend to spread out the clinical and laboratory work among all residents, leading sometimes to "the collapse of a research project" (Imamura 1993: 280).

The image of the MD-PhD researcher-physician poses an appealing possibility; empowered by experience in conducting research, clinicians could add an intellectual dimension to their work and report from the grassroots to the research community. The reality, however, is an apprenticeship arrangement in which research activity serves as conduit to a better job outside of research and not a component for building better researchers in a basic research credit cycle. Also, the time required to learn increasingly sophisticated research techniques is only partly accommodated in the present resident system, risking the creation of what critic Imamura called "a half-trained scientist and a half-baked clinician" (1993: 280).

Training through hierarchy in the ikyoku

A Japanese resident's training, according to its practitioners and observers, emphasizes hands-on experience and tacit learning, as opposed to the more text-based and conceptual approaches found in natural science departments. Doctors occasionally use an expression that literally means "stealing a craft" (*waza o nusumu*) to describe learning, which is structured in varying degrees on individual pairings of new residents with more senior residents, replete with terms that designate the older/younger superior/inferior relationship (typically *senpai* and *kōhai*, terms also used in Japanese schools and clubs).

The tendency to learn by following permeates laboratory research as well. A 23-year-old fourth-year student at the Medical College found his biochemistry lab rotation to be what his friends had said:

> Half or more of it is physical labor. Professor K told my lab mates, "Right now rather than think, use your body while you're young." He wanted us to work from the results we see, not from reading in a book. . . . I feel what I study is all based on the professor's experience.

He voiced a typical concern regarding the intellectual dimension of his laboratory research training,: "Doctors have a 'make-an-object' mentality, a workman (*sagyōin*) aspect that is stronger than you'd find among basic scientists." As a result, "the room for thinking and acting on your own is pretty limited."

My basic research respondents' perception of medical school training was top-down and regimented, capable of exacting a highly efficient division of labor for "factory" production but short on conceptual learning. An assistant in biochemistry at the Medical College gave me this perspective:

> Cloning is the kind of work that benefits from skilled armies. The big famous medical school labs don't teach students the entire process, but regiment them for parts of a bigger job. A lot of the students are MDs; they could go into private practice, but the economics of the small private practice are less and less favorable; the best jobs are in administration at big hospitals, and those jobs go to PhD holders. So such students don't care about becoming full-fledged researchers. I don't think natural science graduate students would come to a lab where they were treated that way.

In a quip that was circulating in the early 1990s, one graduate student in biochemistry at an elite national medical school asked another, "By the way, what *is* this gene we're cloning?"

Physician and PhD careers in medical schools

Enrollment in a medical school doctoral degree program does not require an undergraduate medical degree; students are also admitted by examination to a four-year program at medical schools from the ranks of natural science master's degree holders. Like their natural science counterparts, they are then known as "graduate students" (*daigakuinsei*). Hence the life scientist with a PhD in medicine who, to a Westerner's surprise, cannot practice medicine. The degree title may be identical to a physician's PhD, but the natural science background dooms its holder to eternal second-class status in any subsequent career as a medical school faculty member. The nonphysician holders of the PhD in medicine degree that I had interviewed said that they had entered their graduate programs because the research subjects interested them, and because the entrance requirements were easier than for natural science PhD programs at universities on the same prestige level.

There are status fault lines between clinical and basic science credential holders in the American research laboratory as well, in which a medical degree brings in a higher salary. (In the case of the National Institutes of Health, investigator MDs enjoy salaries a fourth higher than their PhD colleagues; *Science* 1993: 868.) Nevertheless, the career differences between research PhDs and medical degree holders pose an unusually deep and wide chasm in Japan, and the disadvantages to a non-physician make the medical schools unattractive – if not downright inhospitable – to non-physician PhD holders. The differences begin during graduate school; residents are rewarded for their rotations in and out of the ikyoku with seniority-based increases in status and income, but the system does not apply to other graduate students in the ikyoku.

The starkest separation appears in promotion policy among medical school teaching faculty. Unlike the US, nonphysician PhDs are, with few exceptions, barred from promotion into the ranks of full professors. Kazuo Watanabe (pseudonym) had left his assistantship in biochemistry at a prestigious first-tier national university medical school to join a national research institute when he was in his late thirties. His original goal had been teaching and research in medical biochemistry, but his professor offered him two options for relocating because, "of course I could not be promoted where I was." In addition to the research position that he took at the national research institute, his professor had offered him an associate professorship at a medical college that was clearly less attractive to Watanabe because it would eventually pose the same problem of promotion, and it was "in the countryside" at that.

A senior administrator at the Medical College defended the practice of limiting non-physician promotions by contending that only a physician can teach certain courses such as human physiology or anatomy to undergraduate medical students, given the physician's training and experience in those areas. Medical students aiming for a clinical career also want basic courses taught by MDs as a reassurance that the course material will be useful in a clinical practice (Satō 1998). My stay at the Medical College was neither long enough nor intimate enough to gather first-hand observations on the expression of the clinical–basic status divide in daily life and interaction. I did learn, though, that undergraduate students had enshrined the discrimination in a myth (unfounded) that the lounge on the top floor of the twelve-story research building was monopolized by clinical faculty, who denied entry to basic science faculty members.

Researchers with medical school backgrounds complain of a lack of cooperation between the clinical departments and non-medical specialists in basic research. The lower status for basic laboratory researchers at medical schools certainly discourages collaboration between clinical and basic research specialties, exacting a lamentable toll in research progress. Medical school laboratories in Japan are deprived of the powerful tools from genetic engineering that originated in the West in the late 1970s and soon permeated American and European medical school laboratories as they revolutionized molecular biology and biochemistry. A 1996 report commissioned by the Japanese government criticized "the thick wall between medical schools and other departments" in Japan. The report noted, by contrast, that the number of MD and PhD researchers at the United States' National Institutes of Health is near parity, and that substantial disparities from medical school and non medical school differences between medicine and basic research have all but disappeared at prestigious institutions like MIT's Cancer Research Center and Cold Spring Harbor (IHEP 1996: 33). Perhaps the most articulate and authoritative critic of these problems is Ken-ichi Arai, Professor of Molecular Biology at the University of Tokyo's Institute of Medical Science (IMSUT). A master of terseness, he summed the problem in his 1996 workshop presentation: "MDs and PhDs live in separate worlds" (1996a: 16).

Differences among the medical schools

There are several ways of categorizing Japan's 80 medical schools along lines of sector (national, other public, and private) and the era in which the school was established. In any variation on the scheme, the twenty-nine private medical colleges (minus one or two star performers) offer the least desirable places to attempt a research career. The national universities provide much of the country's international publishing output, and the medical divisions of the former imperial universities are the top performers in international publications. (Chapter 1 summarized their publishing feats.) The private schools have congregated at the bottom; their publication rate per faculty member is only a third of the second-tier national universities' rate, and one seventh of the former imperial universities'. (Ratios are based on figures in Yamazaki 1996a: 115.) Particularly low in output per researcher are the large private universities in the Tokyo region, reflecting the demands on faculty of research and patient care (Yamazaki 1996a: 113–17).

My researcher informants regarded a teaching position at a regional medical school as a one-way road to professional extinction. The demands of teaching plus skimpy resources for research were their main concerns, but the overwhelming emphasis on clinical training also figured in their abhorrence.

Students enrolled in private medical schools are even less inclined to choose a basic research career than their counterparts in the national universities; a career in research, unlike a medical practice, does not easily repay the hefty sums required for private medical school tuition. At the Medical College, entrance fees and tuition came to over 12 million yen in the first year, and tuition required another 2 million yen every year thereafter.

The cost of arbitrary power in medical schools

My negative observations concerning Japanese medical school organization reflect my pointed application of the credit cycle concept for an ideal model of optimal basic research activity. The most difficult part of this analysis is to address the possibility that the political clout of senior faculty members could influence research reporting itself. There were no indications at all of such a problem at the Medical College, but a published article by surgeon Seiji Ninomiya under his actual name recounted such an experience in his first year of residence at a different medical school. Ninomiya's professor assigned him a topic – replete with conclusion – "Four Cases of Brain Tumor Effectively Treated by the Anticarcinogenic Drug M," to report to a neurological study group. After finding that all four cases were treated with surgery or radiation before the drug was administered, Ninomiya refused to present. "The professor's response" he wrote, "came one month later. I received a transfer order to Emergency Medicine, whose Professor M was feared as the most hard to please [faculty member] in the university hospital" (1993: 88).

An investigative article in the September, 1983 Japanese edition of *Playboy* recounted the fate of a promising young ikyoku member at the University of Tokyo who had strongly criticized another's research at a meeting. Unbeknownst to the resident, however, the research was a project cherished by his professor. The professor, informed by loyalists who had attended the gathering, exacted his revenge by banishing the dissenter to the headship of a medium-sized hospital in Beppu, a small city in Kyushu. The professor's vindictiveness extended to the transgressor's family; he hounded the junior colleague's father out of his position as a professor at a regional national university medical school, and arranged the expulsion of his mother, a pharmacologist, from her laboratory as well (Anonymous 1983: 91).

These stories might not merit repeating were it not for the insulation of the medical school world from outside purview. Medical school governance remains intramural; in contrast to institutional review boards in the United States, Japanese counterparts are composed entirely of in-house members, or ostensible outsiders who nevertheless share an affiliation with nonmedical divisions of the same university (Leflar 1996: 81). The flow of honoraria, reimbursements, and lucrative consultation fees is far from transparent also. Science journalist Tsutomu Tanabe of the *Asahi News* complained that "it's difficult for the outsider to comprehend the movements of money in the medical world. Sometimes some wondrous things go marching brazenly past the eye of the general public." His article criticized the "shady remunerations" that pharmaceutical companies give medical school faculty for drug trials (Tanabe 1996).

In the course of my field work I heard a refrain both within and outside the Medical College: "This [the Japanese medical school] is the closest thing to *yakuza* (criminal gang) society that you'll see." Different individuals said it with different degrees of humorous sarcasm, dismay, or rancor, but they all had in mind money and power politics, the professor–trainee relationship of obedience in exchange for protection and succor, and the personal control that professors exercised over subordinates' lives. The refrain may reflect an exaggerated image of impropriety. As long as the rewards for a research career are not allocated transparently on the basis of merit, however, we cannot rule out the possibility that power relations could contaminate the research process itself.

An element of competition in university research funding

The methods for allocating research money among Japanese universities sustain the hierarchy status quo in the kōza and among universities. The majority of research-related expenses comes from equal allocations (kōhi) among kōza. University laboratory space is also limited to equal allocations among professors; even prominent researchers can only look with envy at the ability of entrepreneurial American colleagues to expand their laboratory space. Until recently, funds that were allocated on a project basis could not be used to pay support staff salaries, either. (Chapter 8 explains this stricture in terms of the politics of permanent employment.)

Practices in the United States, though always open to improvement, illustrate measures used successfully at the institutional level to encourage the performance-based resource allocation essential to an effective credit cycle. First, most research projects in American universities are funded by external sponsors. This feature removes decision making from local politics and widens the pool of competitors far beyond one university. Grants for conducting research include overhead money (or "indirect costs") that pays for utilities, building upkeep, and administrative expenses. This mechanism increases the research investigator's fiscal independence and rewards the more competitive university, which in turn makes the effective grant-getting researcher more dear to his or her institution. (An overhead system would also benefit OBI and other free-standing research institutes, as discussed in Chapter 6.) These grants also typically have provisions allowing researchers to take grants with them if they relocate to another university. Postdoctoral fellows can enter a university laboratory "bringing" their own research money from independently initiated proposals, or join a laboratory where they receive their stipends and expenses from a grant earned by their laboratory head. Postdocs at the University of Oregon said the former arrangement allowed the visiting researcher more research independence.

The largest research grant program for Japan's university researchers is the Ministry of Education's Science Research Fund (hereafter SRF; in Japanese it is the *kagaku kenkyūhi*, known more popularly as *kakenhi*). The SRF has a competitive element since most grants are awarded through open competition, but it does not provide awards large enough to confer credit cycle dynamism to the kōza system. Nor was it ever intended to; the grants are officially identified as "supplementary funds" (*hojokin*), and most awards to individual bioscientists average less than 3 million yen (Yanagida 1990; see also Matsuo 1995). In aggregate, SRF moneys represent about a fourth of the research funds available to national university laboratories (Kobayashi 1993: 236).

If Japan's Ministry of Education were to increase substantially the size and number of awards to individual researchers, the SRF could help move the kôza system into a genuine credibility dynamic – which is probably why there has been so much discussion of the SRF program among Japanese academics and science commentators in recent years. As in other areas of Japanese science, however, increased injections of money will not produce optimal returns without several changes in the way the program is conducted. The fund favors the elite universities. As of the late 1980s, the former Imperial universities represented 14 per cent of the country's teaching staff, but accounted for 43 per cent of successful grant applicants and 58 per cent of the SRF's big-ticket grant winners (Kato 1992: 7). My scientist discussion partners in 1998 perceived the pattern as unchanged.

The SRF award selection process lacks clear-cut merit review criteria. Most importantly, reviewers do not justify and explain their evaluations to candidates, as in the United States' National Science Foundation and National Institutes of Health system. The practice promotes reviewer accountability while it gives applicants the valuable chance to improve their research strategies – not only from criticism, but from encouragement regarding features of their research that reviewers may have found strong, along with reviewer suggestions for further improvement. Japanese researchers would welcome reviewers' critiques. Scientists' attitudes toward this and other issues relating to the SRF were measured in an opinion survey that was conducted and reported by the Japanese Biochemical Society (JBS) in 1997. (There were 244 respondents among the 300 members between the ages of 40 and 60 who were polled. This was a select group of professionally active members that included full professors and other laboratory heads.) Over 80 per cent of responses favored receiving comments from reviewers (JBS 1997: 1306–7). A field work vignette corroborates the results. When I offered to show a neurophysiologist at the Osaka Bioscience Institute the reviewers' comments from my own recent National Science Foundation grant application, he read it avidly – even though the field was social studies of science, some distance from his specialty – and he discussed it with me afterward. Several of his lab mates requested a copy and circulated it among themselves.

Some of the criteria for successful selection of an SRF award may be inferred from the questions in the application form or application instruction booklet, but such information is limited to terse, one-line statements that point to such dimensions as the "social significance" and the "special features" of the research, explained as "original and pioneering points with a view to trends in technical development" (MOE 1991: 3). In the absence of more information, applicants are not sure of the criteria for success either. In a 1990 survey of bioscientists under age 40 conducted by the JBS, 65 per cent of the 539 academic researchers qualified to compete for SRF funds claimed "absolutely no knowledge" of the criteria used for selection. (Only two respondents claimed to know the criteria well; Sekimizu 1991: 46.)

Another problem in the current system is simply that reviewers have too many proposals to evaluate. Reviewers are assigned several hundred research proposals, and deadlines are tight; one professor in biochemistry from the Medical College was assigned 300 applications to evaluate in one month. (There is only one application cycle per year.) Here lies one source of bias toward more funding for the established elite: since the volume discourages careful consideration of each proposal, elite names provide a short cut for ostensibly safe decisions with less effort. Scientists also recognize that the work load per reviewer must be reduced if reviewers are required to write comments (JBS 1997: 1307).

My own interviewees and informants believed that success in getting SRF grants resulted from the number of times one applied, or that hierarchy and political factors in one form or another were at work. One informant told me he had received a grant after resubmitting the identical proposal that had been rejected the year before. Others believed that affiliation with an influential figure was the key to getting money. Said a 30-year-old PhD holder in pharmacology, "Let's say you're working under someone like Professor Ikehara (introduced in Chapter 1). If your relation with the boss is good, you can get a lot of money immediately. That's comfortable . . ." A mid-career biochemist at a prefectural university told me he applied regularly but,

> It's futile . . . One out of five [chances for success]. And on top of that, the bosses are clutching the money . . . the bosses take turns [as reviewers], and since it comes around by turns, the groups [beneath them] will have a relatively steady source of funds.

A few of my informants believed that there were high-level trade-offs by region, in a tug-of-war between the Kanto (which includes Tokyo) and the Kansai regions.

Reviewers for SRF grants in biochemistry are selected by vote of the entire membership of the JBS. (The ballot for 1992 elections had seventy-six candidates in five categories.) Although reviewers for SRF may not evaluate their own applications, there are no other restrictions to discourage conflict of interest (JBS 1997: 1305). In the United States, major governmental funding agencies have assembled explicit measures aimed at minimizing conflict of interest in the relationship between reviewers and applicants. To help identify bias in reviewer selection, the National Science Foundation requires grant applicants to list academic advisors and all research collaborators and students over a specified period of years. Prospective reviewers receive guidelines enumerating the relationships that would disqualify them, such as having served as the academic advisor of the project's principal investigator. Although these measures do not guarantee an end to political machinations, they provide the kind of precaution that Japanese researchers would welcome. Respondents to the 1997 JBS survey saw extensive conflict of interest problems in the SRF reviewer selection process; 84 per cent of responses agreed with the statement that conflict of interest should be reduced, and similar proportions identified members of the same research group, advisors and subordinates as relationships that should be excluded from reviewers' purview (JBS 1997: 1306).

The system for selecting reviewers in Japan is not widely understood, and that in turn invites cynicism and suspicion. Only 6 per cent of the respondents in the 1990 JBS survey said they understood the reviewer selection process well, and that the process was electoral; another 36 per cent said they understood it "by and large," leaving the majority to claim either that they didn't know about it at all (30 per cent) or "just a little" (27 per cent) (Sekimizu 1991: 46). Bioscientists whom I interviewed told me that few members of the JBS actually vote. The JBS did not respond to my repeated requests for figures on voter turnout. A respondent to the Society's 1997 opinion survey concerning SRF wrote, however, that "With a voting rate of 10 per cent it is easy for boss influence to develop" (JBS 1997: 1304–5). Two assistant-level faculty at separate schools told me they handed over their unfilled ballots to their kōza head, who had said he knew best how to vote for everyone's sake. If the darker view of subterranean deals is in fact accurate, he had a compelling argument.

3

A GOVERNMENT RESEARCH INSTITUTE

Japanese government laboratories devote a little over a fourth of their expenditures to basic research (MCA 1996: 192). Since basic scientific research takes place at government life science laboratories, we can ask about careers and the nature of credit cycle dynamics there as well. Government laboratories in Japan do conduct less basic research activity than universities, however. Government laboratory researchers polled in a 1990 study devoted one third less of their time to basic research than their counterparts in public universities (IFT 1990: 50). The difference reflects institutional supporters' agendas; just as universities must blend research with teaching functions, government laboratories must relate to decision makers who want answers for questions of policy, and to constituencies who seek applications with tangible returns. That certainly means more applied research and development activity for the Food Research Institute as well.

The Food Research Institute's applied research mission

The Food Research Institute (FRI), an interconnected complex of eleven ferroconcrete laboratory buildings and offices, belongs to a Ministry of Agriculture, Forestry and Fisheries (MAF) research complex located in Tsukuba Research Park, 60 kilometers northeast of Tokyo. Several amenities give the complex the feel of a small, self-sufficient town. A cafeteria with several hundred seats offers full meal service. Also in walking distance are recreational facilities, a post office, and a variety of shops. At the time of my observational visit in 1991 there were about 110 full-time research personnel at FRI.

The Food Research Institute's mission is to improve the technology of food production, through "post-harvest" research and development for edible agricultural products. That makes FRI the furthest from academic basic research among my field work sites. The main consumers of FRI's information and knowledge are food processors and manufacturers of food processing equipment. FRI's laboratories were dotted with displays of scientific and technical models and photographs – the carbohydrate

45

laboratory featured a colorful cyclodextrine molecule model – together with various packaged commercial products.

The Ministry of Agriculture has twenty-seven other research and testing institutes, also dedicated to technologies of production, but they focus on pre-harvest processes. The distinction has placed FRI the closest among the Ministry Institutes to "real need," according to its then director, Keiji Umeda. His written statements adroitly connected food research to larger social policy concerns such as the rising health care costs of Japan's ageing population (Umeda 1991).

True to its applied research priority, the administration at FRI, like the rest of the Ministry, has not developed a system of professional rewards for publication activity. Director Umeda explained that although researchers' publications were noted in evaluations,

> it's not that severe, and if publications did become an issue, how many points would we give for different journals? For example, '*Nature* or *Journal of Bacteriology* gets ten points, but a domestic publication like *Chōri Kagaku* (culinary science) or *Kukkingu* (cooking) gets one point' – we'd have to designate points, and we aren't going that far.

His choice of contrasts was instructive, for it pitted high-status international journals in English with homely but practical publications in Japanese.

Another clear indicator that FRI gave basic research no particular priority lay in its recruitment process and pay policy for PhD holders, which was the same throughout MAF. FRI did not have a separate examination, hiring, and promotion track for doctorates. Entry-level pay at FRI for those who completed PhD course and examination requirements equalled that of a researcher with five years of service, with an additional year of seniority for having completed the dissertation. (As Chapter 2 described, the graduate curriculum for a natural science PhD degree in Japan requires five years of study.) A researcher at FRI who was considering getting a PhD degree also told me that getting it would not make any difference to his status in the Institute.

Some aggregate statistics suggest that PhD holders do not receive higher salaries at government research institutes nationwide, either. When a 1992 study of four cohorts of science and engineering graduates compared yearly incomes of PhD holders and classmates with less education among national research institute employees, only the PhD holders in the oldest cohort (1965) showed a clear advantage in income (some 15 per cent higher). In the youngest (1986) cohort, those who had gone on to receive PhD degrees were earning 16 per cent *less* than cohort members with less education (IFT 1993: 24).

Director Umeda identified the problems of hiring PhDs: "Lots of people come out of [universities with] molecular biology, but it has to have a related technology goal or it won't be of use to anybody [here]." He also related FRI's perspective on the kōza system PhD:

> They're too locked up in a specialty. In Japan a doctoral course is five years. Before that, four years of undergraduate study. So for as many as seven years this person is attached to the same teacher. For good or bad, they've got the stamp of that one teacher.

Cultivating greater professional expertise at the individual level without a new set of goals would detract from organizational coherence. An FRI laboratory head summarized the Ministry's rationale for PhD entry-level pay: "What has the new PhD done for *us* in those five years?"

Basic science toehold

None of the Food Research Institute's informational literature in either English or Japanese claimed basic science objectives and themes among its goals, although its ten-page glossy review brochure did include "basic research" in the Institute's spectrum of activities. The Institute's Division of Food Physics and Chemistry, in which the carbohydrate laboratory was located, featured research projects that would be familiar to basic bioscience researchers elsewhere, such as soy protein gene analysis, analysis of starch structure through enzymatic decomposition, and physiological functions of peptides. Most of my interviewees and conversation partners among researchers were decidedly on the basic end of research at FRI, since I approached them through a "snowball" of introductions that began in the Division of Food Physics and Chemistry. The resulting observations do not apply to all of the researchers at FRI, but they do offer us a glimpse of the problems of basic researchers' careers in government laboratories.

There was certainly nothing reprehensible in FRI's promoting applied research and development, especially since neither the Institute nor the Ministry of Agriculture, Forestry and Fisheries has claimed otherwise. Of the five research objectives set forth by the Ministry in 1991 (MAF 1995), only one referred to "fulfilling base-type (*kibanteki*) research" that underlay R&D for agriculture, and the rest were clearly application oriented. FRI's study of mundane, grass-roots agricultural problems and their dissemination of the solutions to producers continued an important tradition begun in Japan of the 1700s. Those first systematic efforts in technology transfer provided the skills and wealth that enabled Japan's industrialization (Smith 1988a). Nor were my subjects at FRI any less interested in their research than the members of other bioscience laboratories. Their shop talk at dinner parties ran a lively gamut from abstract properties of polysaccharides to the pros and cons of different beer manufacturer's fermentation methods.

According to Director Umeda, FRI was taking on more basic research subjects; in the emerging division of R&D labor, regional research centers and prefectural research facilities were assuming research previously undertaken by FRI, such as canning and pickling techniques. The issue had its tensions. "We're looking for a balance," he added. Everyone agreed that interest in basic research was increasing. One source of the interest was younger researchers. On the other end, however, were administrators at the division chief level and above, who tended to question researchers about the benefits and immediate applications of particular research topics. An administrator fairly near the top at FRI suspected some faddism in basic approaches, particularly regarding molecular level research. The director regarded basic research as a costly option for FRI and its researchers' careers.

> If you keep calling for 'basic, basic' indiscriminately, young people will flock to 'basic, basic' and take on difficult academic subjects. That work has to take place in universities and research institutes that encourage that kind of work. This place is different. If [our young researchers] do an academic job for ten years, by and large they're going to hit a wall. Only one out of twenty researchers is going to break that wall down. The remaining nineteen researchers are broken in the process. This organization has to use all twenty people.

Fiscal constraints

FRI did not suffer from the kind of material deprivation so graphically evident at some national university laboratories, but my interviewees were not entirely satisfied with the state of their resources. One laboratory head in a highly applied area said that there was an unfavorable trend that was leading them to "the university level." When I asked one upper-level administrator his dissatisfactions, he mentioned his inability to get analytical research equipment, but he was quick to add that there were other compensations. I myself could literally feel administrative parsimony; at the time of my visit, the oppressive July heat was peaking at 33 or 34 degrees C every mid-day, causing two lab heads to wonder out loud with irritation when the air conditioning would be turned on. ("Not until mid-July." "Who knows *when* they'll turn it on?") There was a sense of time lost that sharpened their exasperation: July and August were a lull in the yearly rhythm of reports, meetings, and industry visits that opened the longest uninterrupted stretch of time to focus on research.

The resource press that bothered my interviewees was personnel: there were simply too few people to accomplish all of the project work. Each laboratory had an official staffing of three regular researchers, but, as the Institute's table of names and telephone numbers attested, ten of the thirty-nine laboratories did not have their full complement. "The Food Research Institute may ask [the Ministry] for a certain number of graduates in Agriculture or Agricultural Chemistry, but we may not get them," said one division head. There were also open laboratory head positions. Nor did laboratories have a technical assistant category; the lowest rank was "researcher" (*kenkyūin*) which included the job description of "technical staff" (*gikan*). A visiting researcher from the United States' Department of Agriculture warned tactfully in his site report that, "Each researcher is expected to perform all aspects of his research, including routine analysis. Visiting scientists should be aware that this is a hands-on assignment" (Weber 1992: 9). Some of my informants felt the shortage intensely; a 29-year-old fermentation specialist with a master's degree in engineering adamantly asserted that his research would progress twice as fast if he just had a technician.

The Institute's two-birds-with-one-stone response to the problem was to host visiting research personnel as "trainees" (*kenshūin*), creating more hands to accomplish project work while sharing expertise with other public laboratories in agriculture and constituent companies. (My informants' statements emphasized the former, "hands" benefit.) Much of the variation in the laboratories' actual number of members came from lab heads' ability to attract industry personnel. In 1998, by one division chief's estimate, industry visitors outnumbered regular staff by two to one.

Researchers in Japan's government laboratories log somewhat fewer hours on the job than their academic counterparts. In the IFT study, self-reported hours were 8 per cent lower than the average for university researchers (calculated from figures in IFT 1990: 46). I did not try to determine work hours at FRI, either by structured observation or through systematic questioning. One of my interviewees with a university assistant background said that the hours were the same as academics'. Laboratories began work at 8:30 AM (the designated time for beginning work) or soon after, but a few informants pegged quitting time at 6:30 or 7 o'clock in the evening, which matched my own limited observation, and Saturday work took place on alternate weekends, in line with officially prescribed work hours. The pace of work appeared less concentrated than in the Medical College. Mid-morning and mid-afternoon snack breaks in the multipurpose room were longer and more well-attended.

There was no forgetting that this was a laboratory, however. As at the Medical College, researchers wore stop watches like pendants when doing timed processes, and their forays into the multipurpose room were at the mercy of their timers. The front door of the laboratory bulletin board next door was emblazoned with a sign exhorting all who entered: "Think hard! Work hard! Write up! Publish!"

Recruitment

Unlike the kōza's veiled and particularistic recruitment process, entry-level hiring for national government laboratories took place through open, merit-based recruitment. Researchers at FRI were hired through a national examination system (*kokka kōmuin shiken*) in two parts, the "general education" (*ippan kyōyō*), and "specialized knowledge" essay examinations (*senmonchi*) in fields such as agricultural chemistry or pharmacology. A 28-year-old master's degree holder in plant pharmacology explained her path to the Food Research Institute as a matter of wanting to do basic research but not having the personal connections needed to get an academic position: "If I joined a company I couldn't continue such basic research there, and there was no one I knew at a university, so I went for a place where I could take an exam and enter on my own, so . . ." with a short laugh she summed, "here I am!" Nor did a network of MAF officials who had graduated from the same university (a first-tier national university) guarantee entry for a 33-year-old microbiologist with a PhD in Agricultural Chemistry; they did give her job-related information, but "It's not that they were able to get me in," she said. She then described the examination process.

In addition to entry-level hiring, FRI recruited laboratory heads via mid-career recruitment. A senior administrator explained the practice of mid-career hiring as a response to a very recent problem of internal demographics: heavy hiring in the postwar years had resulted in an inverted pyramid age structure, with too few qualified candidates in-house for administrative positions in the middle level. The three cases with which I was familiar had come from basic bioscience departments at first-tier national universities, and their recruitment represented an injection of advanced basic science skills. All three were refugees from kōza: none had advanced beyond assistant at his university, and every one had been in that position for ten years or more. For their part, they had wanted more independence in determining their subjects of research, and they had found it. The greater latitude was qualified, however. Said one, "there are many times when [the administration's] sense of direction (*hōkōsei*) and the direction I've thought about do not match up 100 per cent. This place is very application oriented. That consciousness is strong."

Three laboratory heads whom I interviewed were hired at mid-career from universities, and they were selected on the basis of their credentials and several interviews. The recruitment process for mid-career hires is less transparent than entry-level hiring. A former FRI researcher said, "They announce the positions, but they usually have someone picked beforehand." All three of the mid-career entrants I interviewed said they had been recruited via introductions. Criticizing the process, another laboratory head said, "It's like mushroom picking (*kinoko-tori*); there are some better ones deeper in the woods but they don't want to walk that far."

Putting together working groups

Although entry-level hiring practices were performance-based, the assignment of laboratory positions frustrated the formation of research groups based on common interests. Every year, representatives of the Ministry interviewed the new employees that were allocated to them by the National Personnel Authority (Jinjiin) from the pool of applicants who had passed the specialized examination. The Ministry then divided the group into administrative and research tracks. Unlike kōza heads, laboratory heads (*kenkyūshitsuchō*) had no say in the assignment of researchers to their group. Said one exasperated head, "I've been assigned someone who doesn't like the area we work in. It's terrible! Nothing gets done!" The laboratory heads did have authority over invitations to industry trainees, however, which increased the trainees' value as research team members.

Laboratory career cut-offs

FRI's researchers between the ages of 35 and 40 faced the requirement of moving out of laboratory research at FRI in order to qualify for promotion. Promotion required a rotation out of FRI to a regional Ministry of Agriculture research station or, in a few cases, headquarters in Tokyo. (The Ministry's home office has had, as a rule, two staff members with FRI backgrounds.) The next grade above laboratory head (*shitsuchō*) at FRI was division chief (*buchō*), reserved for those who entered FRI after stints in other MAF laboratories and offices. The position offered more administrative authority, but FRI's division chiefs did not have their own laboratories or research budgets, which effectively severed their participation in research activity. Nor were the scientists hired at mid-career immune to this separation from research.

The laboratory heads hired from universities were in a contradictory position to begin with; they enjoyed a latitude of research topic choice resembling a professor's, but they lacked a professor's authority in a number of areas, among them personnel recruitment and mundane matters like choosing suppliers for reagents. The "move out to move up" option made them acutely aware of the gap. My question to one of the mid-career laboratory heads of where he would like to be ten years hence precipitated a thinking-out-loud monologue that reviewed all the contradictions and ended with the hope of finding a position somewhere that would provide both the authority of a division chief with the research activity of a laboratory headship.

Although administrators' justifications of the rotation practice had a "freshen up the organization" rhetoric, these migrations were not intended to introduce fresh scientific ideas from outside the Ministry: research stints in overseas laboratories did not qualify as extramural stints. Rather, it was knowledge diffusion and technology transfer to regional facilities (and their constituencies) that kept the practice alive. When the director warned that promoting basic research would break "nineteen of twenty" young researchers, he then described how their eventual assignments to prefectural experimental stations and farmers' cooperative plants would instead fill a pipeline of FRI knowledge regarding post-harvest food processing to complement local specialization in the pre-harvest phase of production. Rotations also served the organizational interests of the Ministry. Assignments to MAF Headquarters in Tokyo helped create administrators conversant in Ministry culture and priorities. The top-down nature of the assignments also reasserted MAF's centralized authority.

FRI's researchers did indeed perceive the mid-career transfer as an obstacle (if not a death blow) to developing a laboratory research career. Certainly none of the regional research facilities could claim the resources or talent that FRI held. When I asked the director a hypothetical question about a researcher who felt his research would suffer if he were transferred out, he interjected, "That's just about everybody." At the Ministry, I asked a mid-career PhD holder in microbiology about the effect on his research career of his assignment to headquarters. The softness of his voice only dramatized his terse response: "A waste." He went on to say that he had learned a lot about the extent of the Ministry's activities, and had received valuable insights about the project application process, but the challenge of returning to his own field of specialty and making contributions after a gap of five years appeared insurmountable.

Larger organizational needs do not necessarily require such a sacrifice of individual interest in research. The Agricultural Research Service (ARS) of the United States Department of Agriculture has devised mechanisms for promotion that appear to better protect research skills. According to the ARS officer responsible for classification of research positions, administrators of research units, known as "Research Leaders," are required to conduct personal research. The directors of large, multiple research units ("Laboratory Directors" and "Center Directors") are not required to conduct research – and are unlikely to – simply because the administrative demands are so great. Nevertheless, the ARS "dual-track system" attempts to accommodate individual skills and preferences; scientists can be promoted into the highest pay ranks (the "supergrades") via their personal research activity without becoming managers because ARS has formulated a position classification system that is based on personal research contributions, scientific impact, and the professional stature of the individual. (Scientists who prefer a management role, however, must rely on a mix of opportunities as they arise and top management's appraisal of their administrative talents as well as research ability.)

Seniority and evaluation

Rewards in pay and qualification for promotion at FRI were determined by seniority. The calculation of PhD salaries at entry against years of service reflected this more general managerial principle. Although I have no survey results for determining researchers' attitudes, the arrangement had at least one detractor among the laboratory heads. I asked him about seniority using the Japanese term *nenkō joretsu* for seniority; nenkō (年功) means years of service, but the two characters for years of service mean literally "years," *nen*, and "meritorious deeds," *kō*. (Joretsu (序列) means rank or order.) His tart reply, with an irritated wave of the hand: "We have nen-joretsu here, not nenkō joretsu."

Less witty but just as earnest was the government research institute head who wrote these comments in a 1991 survey:

> Management of ranking and promotion is paralyzed by restrictions. The real situation is that almost all ranking and promotion are decided only by past credentials, academic degrees, and seniority ... at this rate, I think our excellent young researchers are going to give up and rot. (Muto and Hirano 1991: 67)

This highly standardized, seniority-oriented approach is a mark of bureaucratic management. One other source of support for seniority, however, lay in the union. FRI's staff belonged to a union affiliated with the National Civil Servants' Federation (Kokka Kōmuin Rōdō Kumiai Rengōkai), and these organizations have consistently supported seniority and across-the-board yearly pay raises. The Institute was heavily canvassed, and 98 per cent of its researchers had joined during the time of my field work. (Membership was voluntary, and extended to the laboratory head level.) In 1998, all but 2 of the 130 regular staff at FRI were union members. "The researchers aren't enthusiastic members," said one senior administrator, "but there is a lot of union activity in regional offices." The Ministry of Agriculture has had the highest unionization rates among the national ministries and bureaus; in 1997 it stood at 95 per cent. The average across all ministries and bureaus was a hefty 58 per cent, however (Nihon Kokka Kōmuin Rōdō Kumiai Rengōkai 1998: 69). That figure represents roughly twice Japan's unionization rate in industry, suggesting that unions should be considered when analyzing career building in government laboratories.

Differential salary rewards for individual expertise and accomplishment have posed a problem for the union. Such individualized rewards complicate the task of negotiating workers' interests, and could even pose a managerial divide-and-conquer strategy. The union intervenes to modify individualized reward schemes for researchers. A "special pay increase" (*tokubetsu shōkyū*) program, originally designed by the administration to reward outstanding researchers, was blunted through union negotiations to become a modest acceleration in pay scale based foremost on when the deserving researcher first entered the Ministry. According to a senior administrator interviewed in 1998, the union also opposed a special pay increase formulated by the National Personnel Authority in 1997 based on accomplishments like papers published in major international journals.

The Institute did conduct individual evaluation exercises. Unlike the kōza members I had interviewed, interviewees and informants at FRI were able to identify evaluation activities. "At the universities everyone knows what each individual is doing, I suppose, but there is no system – unless someone's taking notes on the sly," said one of the laboratory heads who had come from a faculty position in a national university. "Here, everyone writes down their presentations and journal articles so it can go on their records." None of the individual evaluations relied on a cv format. (Only one of the nine interviewees whom I asked for a cv had one on hand.) The Institute also held an annual "results discussion meeting" (seika kentōkai) that required researchers to present 30-minute summaries of their research.

Despite the recognition of evaluation activity, no one gave me a clear statement of how the various procedures influenced their own status. According to a division chief, the main function of evaluation activities was to assess the appropriateness of research topics and move, in extreme cases, to terminate the least satisfactory ones. The lack of a credible evaluation and reward system may have been behind union opposition to merit-based rewards, as a division chief suggested to me in 1998. By then, however, the Institute's director, agricultural chemist Hajime Taniguchi, was seriously involved in systematizing an evaluation and reward system for individual researchers. The move to reform was pressed by a government-wide administrative initiative to turn national research institutes into "agencies," which would give them more latitude in personnel regulations while exposing them to wider competition for research funds.

Unlike university research budgets, a substantial portion of the research money spent at FRI came from competitively submitted grant projects in addition to regularly allocated funds (known as keijōhi). The latter, by my own calculation, represented somewhat under half of all research money spent at FRI at the time of my research. By 1998 project funds per capita represented 4.7 times the regular allocation (a statistic provided by FRI). The competition was remarkably severe for project approvals; according to the director, the Ministry-wide success ratio was 5 themes in 100 submissions. The administration's efforts to explain rejections to unsuccessful applicants looked thin. According to the director, the Ministry had provided comments since 1990, but "if we had to respond to questions about why certain proposals failed, one by one, it wouldn't be worth it"; budget limitations prevented the funding of all good proposals, he explained. One of the researchers had a very different experience a few years before, when he had written to inquire why his proposal was rejected: the written response from above, he said, informed him that no one had asked such a question before, and rebuked him for his "insolence."

Among their administrative tasks at the Institute, the scientists liked least their reporting on projects to MAF headquarters for evaluation. The dislike was predictable, but it was particularly onerous to them because it came on top of report writing for constituents such as trade associations and companies. The latter exercise, at least, benefitted laboratory work by providing a means for recruiting industry trainees. The amount of paperwork involved in reporting research to nonspecialist Ministry officials had vexed the laboratory heads with whom I talked. "I have to write the same kind of thing over and over again a number of times," said one head. "In order to send it here, I have to change this part slightly. In order to send it there, I have to revise another part just a little." Said another, "our work is being parceled out to little domestic targets here and there. Lots of reports for limited groups. It's not synchronized, either."

The form of reporting did not bolster critics' confidence in the worth of the exercise. "I can only write this much (his hands forming the shape of a B4 size paper) about the research," said an agricultural chemist, "so I can't write a very substantial statement." He suspected also that the mechanical formality of reporting for a lay Ministry audience invited bolder claims of accomplishment from researchers than did published findings or presentations to professional societies. Like other researchers with whom I discussed the problem, he believed that evaluation by specialists in the same field through professional channels would have more validity.

Careers, creativity, and bureaucracy

Articulation between scientific specialists and the people who administer their programs is no easy proposition in any government or industrial organization. Ultimately, institutional priorities will precede specialized expertise in all but the most specialized of organizations. Although FRI's scorecard of career cultivation for basic scientists surpassed Japan's universities in several respects, researchers' various comments indicated a gap with the administration that went beyond the tension between basic and applied research.

There were research specialists who felt the administrative apparatus rewarded generalist administrators with "no serious errors" (*taika nashi*), as opposed to administrators equipped to evaluate their research and take some risks in promoting it before the larger Ministry apparatus. A laboratory head – and one involved in a highly applied area at that – complained that Japanese officials "get promoted by sitting quietly at their desks and bowing their heads in apology. That's how they stay out of trouble; it goes whizzing past their ducking heads!" He was more sadly reflective than angry, though.

I think that it's too big a problem for us researchers to solve on our own. It's so frustrating. Why do we exist? Why are we here? To make copies of revised reports with the correct seals and stapled together? And what also worries me are the younger researchers getting discouraged. The field won't be attractive to them with conditions like this. You know, I ask my friends, "What was the most enjoyable time in your career?" And they tell me, when they were doing research overseas. No telephone calls, no meetings, no dumb paperwork.

Is my presentation of these discontents unfairly slanted against administrators – particularly since my stay at the Food Research Institute was brief (ten days), and my sample biased toward basic researchers? Take these grains of salt, but be sensitized nonetheless to the dynamics of when and how careers in science in Japan have been relegated to larger bureaucratic agendas.

4

THE PROTEIN ENGINEERING
RESEARCH INSTITUTE

Government-initiated industry consortia that recruit academic researchers hold one possibility for new career patterns in science. Government initiatives for joint research with industry are not new to Japan; the government has been experimenting with them for well over one hundred years (Choy 1992). The early 1980s witnessed a new direction, though, when the Japanese government decided to apply consortia to the R&D needs of high technology industries by emphasizing basic research (NRC 1989: 20). The move drew inspiration from the weak state of academic research.

One product of the policy shift was the Protein Engineering Research Institute. PERI provided an important career alternative for basic researchers from academia, but its organization also illustrates the limitations of industry involvement in basic research careers: there is still an important distinction to be made between "science" and "technology," reflected in the approaches and aspirations of the industrial and academic cultures that came together there. The authority patterns and prerogatives found in large business and government organizations also limited PERI's ability to realize the full benefits of a credit cycle dynamic.

The case of protein engineering

The ultimate goal of protein engineering is to design proteins or portions of proteins that do not occur in nature, with particular attention to enzymes (proteins that catalyze biochemical processes). Some of the tools for modifying naturally occurring proteins and creating new ones are already available through gene-altering technologies (in particular, site-directed mutagenesis). As of the early 1990s there were some thirteen research organizations in various parts of the world dedicated to protein engineering.

Protein engineering has several features that favor a consortium approach involving industrial participation and support. First, the field offers terrific industrial potential if it can solve problems of a generic order. Duplication and enhancement of enzymatic processes on an industrial scale would yield a bonanza for the pharmaceutical, food, and fine chemical industries, electronics (one example is high-sensitivity biosensors), and pollution control (as in biodegradation of pollutants). Second, a single funding source would be hard pressed, since the methods used in the investigation of protein structure and function are expensive. One mid-1980s estimate put the operating cost of equipment and expertise for a protein engineering research facility at 3 million dollars per year (Fox 1986: 516). In addition to formidable financial barriers, technological bottlenecks call for a pooling of resources. There are still few methods available for analyzing proteins' three-dimensional structure at the atomic level, and they are costly and time-consuming.

To realize its many industrial possibilities, the protein engineering quest must produce some major conceptual breakthroughs. As of this writing, however, researchers have yet to produce a successful commercial application. Creation and production of proteins for industrial processes would require an understanding of the ways in which proteins assume their forms based on instructions contained in DNA, as well as more knowledge concerning the relationships between protein structure and crucial biochemical properties such as stability and solubility. The complexity is daunting. Protein molecules are chains composed of anywhere from fifty to hundreds of thousands of amino acids; in addition to intricate secondary structures occupying some portions of the chain, proteins exhibit a tertiary structure assumed by the molecule's entire amino acid chain. It is this tertiary structure that determines the protein's biochemical function, but as yet it cannot be predicted simply from the knowledge of an amino acid sequence. Tertiary structure formation, known as "folding," has been occupying the attentions of academic protein chemists, biophysicists, and other life scientists for decades. This, in short, is the stuff of basic science.

PERI's origins and scale

The Protein Engineering Research Institute was established in 1986 as an initiative of the Japanese government's Key Technology Center, also known as "Key-TEC." The government solicited the participation of PERI's corporate sponsors and asked them to share a portion of the project's expenses, an approach typical of Japan's government-initiated research consortia. Key-TEC's financing methods were new, however. Their projects involved two or more companies providing 30 per cent of the total investment funds for a joint-stock research company, with public funds constituting the sizeable remainder. In PERI's case, five core companies provided the most substantial stock commitments, and they were later joined by nine others. (Their names are listed in Appendix II.) PERI's charter gave the Institute a life expectancy of only ten years from its inception: as of 1996 it was reorganized under a new name, the "Biomolecular Engineering Research Institute," with the acronym BERI – hence my use of the past tense throughout in discussing PERI.

PERI was an unusually large consortium; it was the largest of the Key-TEC investments, with a total commitment of 17 billion yen over the period of its existence. It was also unusual among Japanese research consortia in having its own building, built specifically for its research activity. Research projects were first conducted in six separate corporate laboratory locations, but in August of 1988 PERI researchers moved into their own research facility on the northern edge of Osaka, a spacious and elegantly appointed new building with an interior decor described in *Nature* as "more reminiscent of a plush hotel than a research institute" (1992: 577). Common areas outside laboratory and office areas were tiled and painted in gray and blue pastels, and the dining area, lounge, and first floor reception area afforded ample space for quiet and relatively secluded discussions and – happily for my case – interviews.

PERI's material circumstances were blessed. The research facility (including a separate structure housing micron spectroscopy equipment) boasted 7,340 square meters of floor space, of which about 5,800 square meters were devoted to research activity for its sixty or so researchers and technicians. The computers, microscopy, and other laboratory equipment were state of the art, with ample supplies. PERI's researcher–assistant ratio was a little over 0.4 assistants per researcher – certainly better than the national average in bioscience, and also of high quality. All sixteen technical assistants had bachelor's degrees, and among them were three MS holders, a PhD recipient, and one with work toward a doctorate completed (an "all-but-dissertation"). PERI's researchers, including foreigners, rated the technical staff's performance very highly.

Organizational structures and groups

PERI's operating staff fell into three types, based on their professional backgrounds, recruitment, and contractual relationships with the Institute: academic researchers with PhD degrees, hired from university positions for the duration of PERI's existence; industrial researchers and administrative staff from the participating firms, assigned as temporary transfers of two to three years' duration; and technicians, typically recent graduates, hired on one-year renewable contracts. PERI's staff members themselves universally recognized these categories, and used them frequently in their discussions. Academic researchers were called "proper" (*puropā*) researchers, since they were hired directly by PERI, or were called "researchers from universities." Industry-based researchers were typically called "industry temporary transfers," "temporary transfer company members," or simply "temporary transfers" (*kigyō shukkōsha, shukkō shain*, or *shukkōsha*, respectively). Technicians were referred to as "research aides" (*kenkyū hosa*).

The Institute's formal organization consisted of five divisions or "departments." (A table in Appendix II summarizes their separate tasks and specialties.) The variety of specialties, ranging from computer science to biochemistry, made PERI a decidedly interdisciplinary effort. When I began field work at PERI there were fourteen academic researchers, including a Japanese postdoctoral researcher and a graduate student, and twenty-six researchers from industry, in addition to the sixteen technicians. The director was an academic, as were two of the four division heads (*buchō*), the other two from industry. All of PERI's six on-site administrators were seconded from participating corporations. I interviewed forty-four research staff: twenty industry-based researchers and twelve academic researchers, including two department heads in each group; and twelve technicians. I also interviewed four department heads (two each from academia and industry) and two graduate students, yielding a total of fifty Japanese members involved directly in research activity as well as three foreign postdoctoral fellows, four of the on-site administrators, the director and both of his successors (in 1996 and 1998). Before leaving Japan in 1991 I conducted a self-administered questionnaire survey among PERI's researchers and technicians which yielded forty-six responses.

The terms of competition

An English language brochure for PERI briefly presented its rationale: to catch up with and hopefully surpass the United States and Europe in protein engineering, despite the "sporadic" efforts of Japan's academic sector. The goals were indeed academic, as my informants and interviewees at PERI saw it. Their evaluation of the Institute's performance focussed on publication in major international scientific journals; these publications were providing the main forum for information exchange and argument surrounding the fundamental problems encountered by protein engineering. Whatever intellectual property PERI had produced was not a salient issue for its administrators and most of its researchers. A research planning officer mentioned that a few patents had been generated, and one was finalized for licensing, but "we are more interested in results (*jisseki*) than money." A senior administrator from industry who acted as liaison with Key-TEC said that a substantial part of the government's evaluation of PERI was based on the Institute's publication track record, and publication activities made up a large part of his reports to Key-TEC.

Most of the competitors whom PERI's researchers identified were university-based. Although some researchers did not know of specific competitors or were reluctant to name them, eleven interviewees named among them nine universities and three nonprofit research institutes, and only three corporate competitors. Researchers polled in the questionnaire survey agreed that publications should serve as a source of evaluation for the Institute (see Table 4.1).

Table 4.1 Opinions concerning publication as a criterion for evaluating PERI (Likert scale) – "PERI's achievements should be evaluated in terms of the quality and quantity of international publications"

Subgroup	Agree	Agree somewhat	No opinion	Disagree somewhat	Disagree
Academic	10	1	0	0	1
Industry	8	8	0	3	2
Technical	5	3	4	1	0
Total	23	12	4	4	3

Subgroup	Subtotal	*Mean
Academic	12	+1.58
Industry	21	+0.71
Technical	13	+0.92
Total	46	+1.04

Note
* A mean score of 2.0 would indicate unanimous agreement; a score of −2.0 would indicate unanimous disagreement.

Academic recruitment and career trajectories

The academic researchers at PERI were produced by the finest research and educational institutions in Japan; most had come from first-tier national universities, and Kyoto University graduates held a plurality. Their narratives and their ages, however, indicated that they were escaping from the problems of the kōza system described in Chapter 2, in particular the lack of opportunities for promotion and choice of research topic. Of the thirteen academic researchers there, seven came from lowly assistant positions, as did both of the academic department heads. Half of the twelve academic interviewees said they had come to PERI because of problems typical of kōza such as lack of independence in the choice of research topic or the retirement of the current laboratory head. The other academic researchers came from postdoctoral positions, with the exception of two newly minted PhD holders. One of the new PhDs said that he had decided against applying for a university position because opportunities for advancement were too limited; he noted that one assistant he knew had been in that position for eleven years.

The average age of the former assistants was a little over 39 years at the time of entry. (The youngest was 33, the oldest, 44.) Their ages reflected the problem of promotion in Japanese universities, and they attested to PERI's acceleration of their careers; assistants in a university would not be entitled to either the resources or degree of discretion in determining research topics that PERI afforded them (particularly as department heads). The ages of these former assistants were important in another respect as well. There is an age cut-off of 35 for job changing without suffering palpable downward mobility, reflected not only in popular perceptions but in want ads. (For example, one major recruitment magazine runs a special section entitled "Opportunities for those over 35"; Beck and Beck 1994: 200). Although the deadline age has risen by ten years since the 1970s, Japanese professionals under 35 including research personnel are very concerned by it. (The average age of the other academics at PERI was 32.)

PERI's academic recruits were not part of a larger researcher exodus from universities, although the media were devoting coverage at the time to defections to industry, as when two faculty from the University of Tokyo's Institute of Applied Microbiology left for Japan Steel and Toa Synthetics. The academics' move to PERI contrasted with the migrations of American academics to bioindustry since the late 1970s; consulting academics in the United States were lured with high salaries and positions in innovative small start-up firms, often without leaving their university posts (Kenney 1986). PERI's salary levels were based on industry pay in first-tier companies – respectable but not particularly remarkable. Like their industrial counterparts, just over half of the academic interviewees expressed satisfaction with their salaries. The arrangement was one reason for the modest 30 per cent of PERI's budget devoted to payroll, in contrast to 50 to 65 per cent in other countries' research facilities (Ikehara 1991: 2). Better income did not figure as a motive among academic researchers for joining the Institute, and a few expressed misgivings that their term at PERI would be a financial setback, figuring in the severance pay (*taishokukin*) offered in lieu of the retirement benefits in a university position.

Although PERI provided the means for academics to repudiate the kōza system with their feet, PERI's recruitment methods for academics represented nothing new in academia. None of PERI's academic researchers had been recruited through open job announcements; all had been invited by their current division heads, or were introduced by advisors who were in the division heads' professional networks. The practice was not universally accepted among PERI's researchers. A few interviewees suggested that academic recruitment should take a more impersonal form, and respondents to the questionnaire survey called for more open recruitment (*kōbo*, discussed in Chapter 2) as well.

Recruitment from industry

PERI's recruitment of industrial researchers and its place in their careers did not provide the mobility or motivation to garner basic research credit seen in the treatment of academics. Industry placements were, after all, rotations from the company laboratories and were slated to return. Moreover, the authority to select industrial researchers lay with the participating companies, not PERI. One division head acknowledged that he had returned an industry assignee whose knowledge of proteins was insufficient, and two other division heads discussed attempts to make use of industry researchers who were only marginally useful. According to another division head, it was not unusual to get information on new individual industry researchers until only one or two weeks before their arrival.

The participating corporations did not take pains to select interested participants; industry researchers who had requested assignments to PERI were a distinct minority. Most of the industry researchers (excluding division heads) responded to my question of why they had become researchers at PERI by first observing that they were told by their companies. The very question struck three of the interviewees as amusing: with a laugh, each had explained that the Japanese employee had no choice but to do as told by the company. "The company's word is a command," said one. Others paraphrased the company's order, "Go to PERI" (with commands used to inferiors such as *iki nasai*). There were four interviewees who said they had requested the assignment, and six others said that they were pleased when they learned that they had been chosen. Two of the latter said that they had dropped hints to their superiors that they wanted to come to PERI. On the other end of the continuum, however, two industrial researchers expressed dismay at their assignments.

Career rewards for industry researchers

The few industrial researchers who did request assignments to PERI were not motivated by salary considerations, since PERI paid them the same salaries and fringes received by their cohort who remained behind (which, incidentally, created something of an accounting headache for the PERI managers). Nor was a stint at PERI a pathway to faster promotion or other rewards at the home company. Industry researchers' assessments of the effects of their rotations on their status in their home companies were varied, but few were optimistic, and those who felt that coming to PERI would benefit their standing in their companies were clearly in the minority. One said it was a conditional plus, and the statements of several others indicated either that they did not feel it was a demotion, did not know, or at least did not worry about it as a potential liability. There were two who believed it was a "demerit."

Industry interviewees said they could not hope for credit for their work at PERI in their home companies because they were doing basic research that would not contribute to corporate profits. One young industry researcher had been particularly disappointed in his hopes of doing applied research at PERI, having taken too literally the "engineering" in protein engineering. A conscientious worker, he said he enjoyed "research that asks 'how do we make this?' more than 'what's going on here?'" He criticized himself half-jokingly; "Ever hear of a salary thief (*gekkyū dorobō*)? They're people who ask for a salary without showing results. I'm still a thief." The few industry interviewees who did identify advantages to their companies from their assignments talked in terms of their "networking," the "image" value of their publications ("as decorations," said one), or specific skills they had learned.

Evaluation of industrial researchers by their home companies based on regular reports was not possible, given the ground rules of participation at PERI: researchers were enjoined from reporting individually the specific contents of their research to their home companies. When asked if they reported their progress to their companies, many pointed out that they didn't because they were not supposed to. ("That would be a mess if someone used this as a 'pipe' to one's own company," opined one.) One company had a "Self Report" as part of its career development system for its researchers at PERI, a two-page form with such subheadings as "This Year's Duties" and "Development of Abilities," but none of the boxes provided room for more than three sentences' worth of information.

Publication activity, perforce, did not hold the professional currency for industry researchers that it did for academic researchers. Table 4.1 shows that industry researchers were also less inclined than their academic counterparts to advocate measuring PERI's performance in terms of its international publication record. One interesting exception to industry-based researchers' attitudes was an interviewee who said that publishing meant more than supervisors' evaluations or reports for in-house consumption, which he called "self-advertising"; journal articles, by contrast, were more significant because they were judged by "a completely separate third party." Publications in the major Japanese and international journals would mean that "no matter where I go, a third party will be able to evaluate my work." Go he did: within a year of our discussion, he had left his company for a faculty position at a major Japanese university.

Although I did not conduct a systematic study of work outside of regular hours, my impression, corroborated by statements from technicians, was that industry researchers were less likely than academics to work after regular hours. The odd-hour weekend and late-night style fit with university laboratory culture, and reflected the pressure on academic researchers to produce publications. According to a personnel manager, industry researchers who worked after regular hours were also more likely to request overtime pay than their academic counterparts.

A typical concern of industry researchers was falling out of step with research groups in the home company. Older researchers were more likely to express concern about placements on their return to the company, fearing that personnel officers would not know where to place them on their return. A few industry researchers in their twenties, however, said that assignment to PERI would not harm the careers of those new to their companies because evaluation would not take place for the first few years after entering the company anyway. (Their assessment fits with Takagi's 1984 findings for engineers.) One researcher said placement at PERI could be a boon, but would handicap him if there were a "gap" between his work and developments at his company. (Only one researcher expressed the fear that he could be competing with his home company's research effort.)

Setting research agendas

In a perfect world of credit cycle dynamics, researchers would have the authority to choose their own research topics, to which they would tie their professional fates. The selection of research subjects at PERI fell short in that dimension. About a third of both the industry and academic researcher interviewees who discussed their roles in research topic selection indicated that they had effectively negotiated the research subjects of their choice, with an equal proportion of both groups claiming no role. (The remainder said they had carved out supporting roles, or were continuing the work of someone preceding them.) Much of the direction for research strategy resided among the division heads and the director, according to a research planning administrator, and that description fitted accounts in casual discussions at the Institute and comments written in the questionnaire survey.

The desire to see changes in the research topic selection process was quite evident among the questionnaire respondents, particularly among industry researchers, as shown in Table 4.2. An industry researcher's written comment on the questionnaire form captured a popular sentiment: "It is essential to have selection of subjects that aren't just follow-on imitations but have originality. PERI should build a system in which the researchers themselves, and not just 'above to below [communication],' determine research subjects."

Table 4.2 Opinions concerning the selection of research topics (Likert scale) – "PERI should change its methods of selecting and determining research topics"

Subgroup	Yes	No opinion	No
Academic	8	0	4
Industry	17	0	4
Technical	10	1	2
Total	35	1	10

Subgroup	Subtotal	*Mean
Academic	12	+0.33
Industry	21	+0.62
Technical	13	+0.61
Total	46	+0.54

Note
* A mean score of 1.0 would indicate unanimous agreement; a score of −1.0 would indicate unanimous disagreement.

Others commented that the goals were too vague, or that efforts were too scattered. Division heads were familiar with these sentiments. One, from industry, expressed his own frustration: "I've asked for people's opinions and suggestions. They just don't give them to me." A few informants suspected that the turnover in industry people prevented them from taking a greater role in determining research strategy.

Incomplete liberation

The academics had sacrificed the security of permanent employment to pursue research that interested them (along with the resources to do it). When asked what kind of work they would like to have ten years hence, their answers made research content uppermost; nine of the eleven academic interviewees said that they wanted to continue their current research or have the right to choose their own topic. (The other two stated specifically that they wanted academic positions.)

There were indications, though, that the academics were not taking complete advantage of their freedom. An academic researcher said he was disappointed that his colleagues entered PERI with their own projects which they continued because they were "safer," despite a larger logical line-up of research specialties offering interdisciplinary approaches. Academic researchers were anxious about post-PERI employment opportunities; in the face of limited mobility within academia, professional life after PERI posed a big question mark. The uncertainty could well have encouraged conservatism in their choice of research topics. Since publications constituted a major asset for finding another position, those topics that were more familiar, easier to publish, and easier to get evaluated by domestic academic colleagues were more appealing. That hypothesis found agreement among my researcher informants at PERI, and a department head had mentioned the problem as well; one of his researchers, a biophysicist, was particularly worried that his work at PERI would not help him in his subsequent job search.

Industry backgrounds and credentials: The MS–PhD divide

Another source of trouble in research topic selection was the lack of basic science training among industry people, who outnumbered academics by nearly two to one. Despite PERI's orientation to basic research, most of the industry participants had less experience in basic research than their academic counterparts. Researchers from industry had typically ended their university educations at the master's level. Of the twenty-six industry researchers, four held baccalaureates only, and seventeen were MS holders; only five had PhD degrees. They were also some three years younger, on average, than the academics; the industry interviewees' average age was 33, and their ages clustered in the late 20s. Division heads generally agreed that there were discernible differences in research approaches between MS and PhD holders. The PhD-level researchers, according to one head, were more skilled at writing (in Japanese as well as English). Another department head said, the MS holders have technique, but "the PhDs have research know-how."

There were other signs as well that having a PhD made for a more appropriate fit at PERI. Among industry researchers, the PhD holders posed an exception to the industry researchers' tendency to worry about credit for their work back at their home companies; rather, they welcomed the chance to do independent basic research without the pressure to think in terms of a marketable end product. Industry researchers who had requested their assignment to PERI – either directly or indirectly – were PhD holders, or had hoped to earn a PhD based on their research at PERI (through an option known as the "thesis degree," explained below). The one exception was the particularly disillusioned researcher I had described, who had thought the work would have an engineering element.

The PhD in industry

These observations about PhD holders will seem altogether fitting – or even banal – to Western eyes. After all, the PhD represents the quintessential "research degree" because it is awarded for the ability to generate new knowledge. The PhD is a rather insubstantial credential in Japanese industry, however – hence the criticism from prominent senior scientists such as Saburo Nagakura that PhD holders aren't taken seriously enough in Japan. In terms of initiative in research, the PhD may indeed be relatively unimportant; according to one nationwide survey conducted in 1989, less than a third of the PhD respondents in industry indicated that they could choose a research topic independently (IFT 1990: 65, 67).

As in government practice described in Chapter 3, the income advantage to a PhD holder in industry is nearly nil. Statistical surveys have found an advantage only among researchers in their forties, who in the early 1990s were reaping somewhere between 4 and 15 per cent more in income than nonPhD holders (calculated from figures in IFT 1990: 57 and IFT 1993: 23). The youngest group of PhD holders in the private sector, according to one 1991 nationwide study that included engineering majors, was receiving some 22 per cent *less* than fellow college graduates in industry who did not have the PhD (IFT 1993: 23). These were graduates of the top national universities, but they were evidently penalized by a seniority system in which their years in graduate study had not counted as much as years in the company. The four interviewees from industry at PERI who were pursuing a PhD expressed their motives as a matter of personal achievement rather than as a career investment; one had said his friends were telling him it would be useless.

67

(Their desires were not irrational, however; one of them was the defector to academia, and the others were anticipating a nascent credentialism that Chapter 7 discusses further.)

Previous chapters described several institutional features of the PhD in Japan that lessen its usefulness to the research world outside of academia. Recall the reservation about hiring PhDs raised by the Food Research Institute's Director, in Chapter 3: having entered one kōza in their last year of undergraduate work and studying under one professor for several years afterward, their graduate education makes Japanese PhD holders "narrow" in experience and interest. A division chief in drug development for a major Japanese pharmaceutical firm, whom I interviewed in 1996, made precisely the same criticism. The PhD in Medicine is in worse shape, given the role of laboratory research work as servitude for medical students, as described in the section on medical schools in Chapter 2.

The industry approach: grow your own

Japanese industry hosts the variation on PhD production that waters its value most: the "thesis degree" (*ronbun hakase*), occasionally referred to as the "paper doctor" (*pēpā dokutā*). In addition to PhD degrees for matriculated students (*katei hakase*), Japanese universities award PhD degrees for research conducted in corporate laboratories – hence the attempt of four industry researchers to earn a PhD while at PERI. In the bioscience pattern, an industry bioscientist with a master's degree submits his or her published research (typically from internationally recognized journals) to a committee chaired by the candidate's former academic advisor. Although engineering doctorates are more likely than scientists to hold thesis degrees, well over 40 per cent of the science doctorates awarded in Japan since the early 1960s have been to nonmatriculating researchers who submitted papers (based on figures in Nishigata and Hirano 1989: 6). Several informants told me that, within the sciences, the closer an academic specialty to an industrial application, the greater the proportion of thesis degrees among PhDs.

Cast in its best light, the thesis PhD affords candidates the use of facilities in well-equipped corporate laboratories, and a chance to obtain an advanced degree while earning a living. The thesis PhD also cancels out a university faculty role in obtaining research skills, however, since recipients need not spend time in university laboratories to receive their degrees. It short-circuits academic validation of research ability because conferral rests on articles that have already been peer reviewed in international journals. When I asked one candidate for a thesis PhD in biology from a major national university if he was anxious about his upcoming oral exams, he replied that his journal articles practically guaranteed his committee's approval.

The thesis PhD subordinates an individual's research training and credentials to the corporate culture's priorities, by providing training once within the organization. The result is a PhD with a corporate stamp of approval, and research content that reflects company interests. Science policy specialist Fumio Kodama wrote that Japanese employers prefer hiring engineers with master's degrees over PhD holders because the firms "believe that masters [degree holders] are more flexible in adapting to their needs" (1989: 43). One industry researcher at PERI used the evocative expression "reared from youth" (*kogai no*, used otherwise for apprentices started early in life, or captured wild animals) to describe his company's preference for hiring researchers with only bachelors or masters levels of education. In at least one major pharmaceutical company (not represented at PERI), cohorts of masters degree entrants are evaluated competitively, and the top performers are encouraged to pursue thesis PhDs. One industry-based informant at PERI told me that superiors used the thesis degree to groom researchers at his firm for promotion; another industry informant said that the degree was good to have on a name card "when dealing with foreigners."

Given their grow-your-own preference, corporate managers would find PERI an attractive source of training for basic science expertise. The President of PERI, Yoshikazu Itoh, the President of Toray Industries, said as much in a 1996 article, although he posed it as a matter of limited resources: "The basic research that the companies themselves can do is limited by talent and capital. So we send employees to universities or places like PERI where they get education and training" (*Tsūsan Jānaru* 1996: 24). Industry transfers included several new MS holders sent straight to PERI. PERI researchers, however, including industry transfers, rejected the idea that PERI should be judged in

Table 4.3 Opinions concerning industry training for evaluating PERI – "PERI's achievements should be evaluated in terms of the techniques and knowledge that corporate participants can take back with them to their own companies"

Subgroup	Agree	Agree somewhat	No opinion	Disagree somewhat	Disagree
Academic	1	0	1	6	4
Industry	3	5	2	5	6
Technical	0	1	3	6	3
Total	4	6	6	17	13

Subgroup	Subtotal	*Mean
Academic	12	−1.08
Industry	21	−0.29
Technical	13	−0.85
Total	46	−0.63

Note
* A mean score of 2.0 would indicate unanimous agreement; a score of −2.0 would indicate unanimous disagreement.

terms of what industry researchers took with them on their return to corporate laboratories, as shown in Table 4.3. They knew that PERI was not organizationally equipped for that function, and that the work was often far afield of what their own companies were doing.

The industry way

PERI's orientation to basic research made it a decidedly difficult place for industry researchers. Younger industrial researchers felt that they were being cast adrift in an environment without structure or direction. One particularly critical researcher from a major fine chemicals company said PERI was "irresponsible." His own company, by contrast, had a drug development system with a highly defined course for channeling substances having patent potential, and clear consequence – up or down – for the careers of research team leaders who succeeded or failed. The criticism that PERI's administration did not provide sufficient concreteness in research goals is very difficult to interpret and evaluate, though, in light of the frequent criticism that subject selection was "top-down." The sense of a lack of direction could stem from several sources: the subjects' unfamiliarity with an environment offering a measure of individual freedom; compromises between physics-oriented and biology-oriented division heads; and the ambiguities of protein engineering as an emergent interdisciplinary field.

Perhaps most fundamentally, recruitment patterns hampered effective research topic definition because they resulted in fewer like-minded researchers with experience and academic sophistication. An academic researcher commented with some irony on the lack of these capabilities in a young researcher from industry (pseudonym Tabuchi) with whom he was working: "Good research has three components: one, grasping a research problem; two, executing it thoroughly; and three, reporting it in an elegant way that will interest others. Tabuchi's real good at number two."

PERI's consortium arrangement also presented an authority problem in the motivation of its industry researchers. The Institute's administration did not have the power to allocate or withhold rewards to its researchers based on their performance. Researchers from academia were motivated by the need for publications. As mentioned, however, industrial researchers' home companies were not evaluating their performance at PERI. An academic researcher wrote on the questionnaire survey form: "It would be better to keep as few industry researchers as possible, and recruit from universities, etc. ... in an environment without [their company] supervisors, they lack a *hungry* eagerness for research; the work they do is *minimal effort*." (Italicized words were emphasized in the original, and were written in English.)

Life without industry hierarchy

Managers from any company would be vexed in this situation, but the contrast with their home companies would be particularly stark for Japanese research managers, coming as they did from large corporations where considerable effort went to cultivating discipline, cooperation, and a sense of group membership. (See Rohlen 1974 for a classic account of corporate socialization.) Said a division chief from industry in a discussion of PERI's researchers' mix of backgrounds, "You can order these people and they won't listen. It's because they aren't evaluated by us." Similarly, a division chief with an academic background observed that senior researchers from industry too often assumed that they could direct researchers from other companies in their team with the same authority they exercised over their own subordinates. The carefully cultivated hierarchy in large Japanese corporations also exacerbated problems of communication and research topic selection; the division chief who said he asked for ideas but received none felt that his industry researchers were "too used to taking orders."

PERI's heterogeneity also posed a challenge to its administrators, coming as they did from the carefully cultivated homogeneity of large companies. When I asked one of the administrative officers the least favorite aspect of his work at PERI, he paused for a solid 30 seconds, and then replied that it was trying to get cooperation among the different "cultures," particularly the academics, with their different concepts and goals. "If this were within one company we'd have agreement, but [here at PERI] it takes a lot more time to get everyone going in the same direction." At the highest level, corporate partisanship had left its mark on PERI's organizational structures. A senior academic researcher involved in the Institute's formation said that originally the five major corporate participants wanted that structure as an assurance of their representation – a kind of turf claim, with each company providing its own department head. (The configuration at the time of my field work was a *de facto* compromise, with two industry division heads, two academic heads, and one division, the fourth, headless.) Corporate parochialism did not extend to the ranks of researchers, however, in their horizontal relationships with one another. PERI society had at least two groups forming occasionally around leisure activities – horse racing and motorcycles – that cross-cut specialties and departments, as well as corporations; the former group had some eleven participants from all five departments and administration, among them an academic researcher, a technician, and industrial researchers from six different corporations.

Scientific communication across the two cultures

Another indicator of organizational fault lines at PERI was the extent and quality of communication. The administration had structured some substantial activities geared to keeping members of different specialties from industry and academia abreast of developments, and educating them in advanced concepts and techniques. The most effort on everyone's part went into monthly Institute-wide meetings for departmental progress reports (*geppōkai*) that blended educational functions with interdisciplinary critiquing. Research team members and technicians presented 25-minute summaries of their work at these meetings, prepared in advance with printed synopses and visuals. The effort paid off: researchers and aides unanimously identified monthly meetings when I asked them how they learned about work in other divisions. Institute-wide "in-house educational lectures" (*shonai kyōiku kōza*), journal clubs, and occasional invited speakers also provided education and updating.

Nevertheless, there was a felt need for more effective discussion. One of the researchers wrote in the questionnaire survey that more open discussion would improve the selection of research topics as well: "We should want [research topic selection] decisions that include the thought and hopes of everyone involved, made in a context where anyone can make statements a little more openly. If not, there'll be no connection with interesting research." Foreign scientists with postdoctoral experience at PERI also said that more discussion was needed to generate high-quality research. One (whose term at PERI had ended before my arrival) had exhorted his PERI colleagues to that end at one of his presentations, in late 1989.

The discussion problem stemmed partly from a passivity inherited from the larger Japanese culture; audience members were conditioned to remain silent by past experiences of top-down, one-way lecturing styles and other strongly hierarchical teaching practices endemic in Japanese high schools and universities. The audience seating pattern and status order of comments from the floor at these meetings reminded me of presentations at the University of Oregon's Institute of Molecular Biology: the most senior, highest status faculty sat in front and were the first to make comments and ask questions after a presentation. At PERI, questioning and comments were typically initiated by the division chiefs or the director, who sat at the front of the room. Of course, in neither country was anyone prescribing this pattern, and the Americans would probably deny its existence. The drop-off in participation with declining status was more severe at PERI than at Oregon, however. More junior members, sitting a greater distance from the podium, rarely continued a dialogue with presenters.

Active sessions were not totally alien to PERI. When Tatsuo Miyazawa assumed the director's office (midway in my term), he exhorted presenters at the monthly meetings to simplify their material for optimal understanding, and called repeatedly for enthusiastic discussion. The first monthly presentation afterward was more lively, but researchers were not optimistic about how long the effects would last. A sizeable proportion of research staff found company affiliation a problem for communicating about research; their

Table 4.4 Communication with industry researchers (Likert scale) – "I have good communication with researchers from (other) companies concerning research activity"

Subgroup	Yes	Yes, rather	No opinion	No, rather	No
Academic	5	0	1	5	1
Industry	6	5	4	3	3
Technical	1	7	0	4	1
Total	12	12	5	12	5

Subgroup	Subtotal	*Mean
Academic	12	+0.25
Industry	21	+0.38
Technical	13	+0.23
Total	46	+0.30

Note
* A mean score of +2.0 would indicate good communication among all respondents; a mean score of −2.0 would indicate no communication among all respondents.

responses to a question in the written questionnaire survey on the issue appear in Table 4.4. Mid-career academics were particularly likely to express some dissatisfaction with their industrial counterparts' ability to communicate. After suggesting that I study the problem of communication at PERI, one academic researcher said, "The company people aren't quite as good at discussion as university people. [They have] different ways of thinking what research is all about."

Everyone involved would agree that the knowledge required to discuss highly specialized subjects across disciplines posed a major difficulty for discussions. The professional youthfulness of the industry researchers must have exacerbated these knowledge gaps. An industry researcher with a PhD also suggested a link between academic preparation and communication:

> At the National Institutes of Health [in the United States, where he previously had held a postdoctoral position] almost everyone was a PhD ... Here, if anything, there are more people without PhDs. Company transfers. Not the same level of understanding, so there are flaws in doing something in collaboration ... There are only about three or four people I can talk to freely.

A youthful industry researcher who always sat among his age-mates in the back rows at monthly meetings also illustrated the role of the PhD in encouraging discussion: despite his position (figurative and literal) he was a conspicuously active discussant. He was also a PhD holder.

Evaluating the "jewel bug"

I have cast PERI's organization in a particularly critical light because I use an ideal model of credit and mobility. An accurate picture also requires looking at some extremely solid accomplishments. By mid-1993, PERI could claim fourth rank among all of Japan's bioscience research institutes for per capita international journal article production (Yamazaki 1994). PERI researchers' accomplishments included international recognition for clarifying the structure and function of RNase H, an enzyme that plays a crucial role in retroviral infections. In its ten years of existence, the Institute also contributed half of Japan's input to the worldwide protein data base of information on protein tertiary structures, a national contribution that trebled during that period (*Tsūsan Jānaru* 1996: 22). Formal departmental lines did not pose a barrier to cooperation, either. Over a third of the seventy-three articles published by PERI researchers (sampled between February, 1990 and March, 1991) were co-authored by members of two or more divisions. At the time of my field work there were two interdepartmental study groups, one each devoted to *de novo* protein design and protein stability.

PERI was, after all, a well-equipped, elite institution, and its members, drawn mostly from elite research institutions, were buoyed by the realization that PERI was a unique experiment. They were also sobered by the high quality of foreign competition. Most of the interviewees reported that their original expectations were satisfied completely or in large part. Their animated discussions of organizational issues and their high degree of cooperation with my research (as described in Coleman 1996) reflected their identification with PERI and its potential: this was no alienated gathering.

PERI's researchers called their organization an iridescent "jewel beetle" (*tamamushi*), an ambiguous creature that displays different colors depending on one's angle of view. They had, after all, only two types of organization for comparison, universities and industry. Evaluating the participants' criticisms of the organization requires some jewel beetle perspective also. Although there is no doubting their frustration, the pungency in their expression may have represented a "pop-out" phenomenon of overstatement that comes from a sudden opportunity to speak anonymously. It was difficult to express opinions more openly because much of policy had already been cast.

Hiroyuki Toh

PERI has provided a precarious stepping stone to several basic science researchers' careers, but one in particular sets in sharp relief the liabilities as well as the rewards of individually crafting a career path. Bespectacled, heavy-set and soft-spoken, Hiroyuki Toh did not particularly look his part as PERI's youngest academic researcher (see Figure 4.1). He had joined in 1989 at age 28, right after completing his doctoral research. Toh's career had been

Figure 4.1 Hiroyuki Toh, 1998

unfolding in a restless but logical pattern. As an undergraduate in biology at the University of Kyushu he read books on evolution, and one in particular (Susumu Ono's *Evolution by Genetic Duplication*) had left a strong impression. His interest also developed by elimination: by the end of his third year of undergraduate study, when the time came to choose a kōza, he had realized that his hands were too awkward for experimental work.

He would find his tools in mathematics instead. He knew that he wanted a kōza that dealt with evolution, and he had the choice of a kōza in population genetics or one in mathematical biology. He assumed some initiative that was unusual among my respondents. "I went and did interviews – I said I wanted to do mathematical biology, and the one who had the more interesting discussion was the one I chose."

The mathematical biology kōza offered a variety of specialists that appealed to him, including a theoretical population geneticist who was applying the very latest findings from molecular biology. Toh stayed in the same kōza for his master's research, which he conducted on the evolution of reverse transcriptase structure and function. Two years later he took an unusual step for his PhD dissertation research. To satisfy his growing interest in quantum chemistry, he negotiated a move to Hiroshima University. The process was conservative, though, in its interpersonal execution; rather than simply apply to a university having the configuration of expertise that he wanted, he negotiated the move via his advisor, who acted as "intermediary" (*tsute*). Toh preserved his affiliation with his kōza, and labeled the move a "domestic study abroad." (His official status at Hiroshima was auditor.) In the period between his college graduation in 1983 and his move to Hiroshima University he had authored thirteen publications, five of them in the prestigious international journal *Nature* with first authorship.

The move to PERI also took place through Toh's advisor, who provided an introduction after the advisor received an inquiry from one of the division heads at PERI. Toh was eager to go. As someone who had been doing computer modeling, the prospect of working with experimentalists appealed to him strongly. He envisioned using a computer to generate predictions that could be tested by experimentalists under the same roof. The reality was more difficult, since the proteins selected for his computer-based models differed from those studied by in-house experimentalists. With his department head's tacit approval, he engaged in extensive extramural collaboration. While at PERI, Toh also took some personal initiative to collaborate with a next-door neighbor at OBI after reading one of his articles. (Despite the stone's-throw proximity of the two institutes there was no structured cooperation or exchange other than PERI's arrangement for use of OBI's laboratory animals.) The effort yielded knowledge of the synthesis of prostaglandin D involved in the sleep/wake cycle, and highly acclaimed insights regarding the evolution of the prostaglandin D synthesizing enzyme.

In our discussions Toh had expressed a deep desire to do original work. The key to PERI's survival, he felt, would be in doing research that was "novel" (*zanshin*), but he expressed his concern to me that neither his research nor PERI's was novel enough. On two occasions in his graduate research career, Toh had found that researchers in the US and Europe were conducting the same research – in one case, just after his first *Nature* article was accepted, in another, just as he was preparing to submit to *EMBO Journal*. As he related those incidents to me, he wondered out loud, half-amused, if his lack of originality had exposed him to such direct competition. His 1983 *Nature* paper still stands as his proudest accomplishment nevertheless, because it placed him at the forefront through a fusion of computation and experiment that defined much of his subsequent research approach. The paper was also based on a problem he had defined himself as opposed to taking an advisor's directive. In the following decade he built on those achievements in research and publication. Colleague Russell Doolittle, Research Professor of Chemistry and Biology at the University of California's San Diego campus, recalled Toh from his 1992 collaboration at Doolitle's laboratory: he was "clearly a serious and gifted scientist" who gave as much as he received intellectually in the visit.

In 1993 Toh made a difficult decision. He left PERI for an assistant position at a regional technical university in Kyushu. He was feeling hemmed in by his then current research subject, which he felt had become "clichéd" but did not afford him the time to strike off in a new direction. More importantly, PERI was a project having a limited life expectancy, and he, like the other researchers from academia, had no guarantee that he would be included in any subsequent organizational reincarnation. He applied to a few universities through open recruitment, and the technical university was one of them.

The transition to the regional university was a shock. The university job required numerous teaching and administrative duties, including maintenance and repair of computers. At PERI, Toh had been in a full-time researcher position with considerable freedom to follow his interests. The new situation resembled nothing so much as a Japanese basic researcher's nightmare vision of a corporate job: "I felt like a new company member," he later recalled.

The problem posed a classical syndrome. (Chapter 2 could have predicted it.) Nevertheless, Toh laid most of the responsibility for his difficulty in adjusting on himself, perhaps unfairly.

> I think my own research style created much of that situation. There were many others on the faculty there who had more duties than I, and many were doing research. And I had come from an environment that was like a researcher's heaven where I could just conduct research.

He did his best to adjust, but he acknowledged experiencing considerable stress. He could take some consolation from the knowledge that his acquaintances from industry at PERI who had a strong bent toward working on their own research topics had also experienced severe stress when they returned to their home companies and found that they could no longer conduct research. A few, in fact, were quitting their home companies to pursue careers as basic researchers.

Three years later, PERI's successor organization provided a career option for Hiroyuki Toh that the academic Japanese bioscience community could not. On the invitation of a different division head, Toh returned to PERI in its newly reconstituted form, BERI, in the spring of 1996.

> I had come to the university on a day off to do some work when I got the telephone call from a division chief offering me a researcher position at BERI. I figured he knew my research style since he was also a PERI division chief when I was there, but I just wanted to make sure that I could work there even though I can't do work that's outside my research style. Once I had that confirmed I was determined to go.

At that time Toh had learned that his bid to enter another research institute had not worked out. "The call from BERI was my boat ride back to research," he observed.

Three years was also the minimum term that his graduate advisor had told him he should endure at his university post. Japanese academics may not universally recognize three years as a respectable duration, but it would at least afford the advisor some protection from losing credibility as a reference for his students. Then as now still single, Toh did not have to consider the problem of relocating spouse or children. Unlike men of the last generation, he does not regard a wife as a career helper. He has seen married colleagues either sacrifice their lives with their families to preserve an active research career or lose out on a lot of time in the laboratory to be with their families, so married life seems to him a formidable challenge to the researcher's career.

Toh is no more professionally secure at BERI than he was when he first joined PERI. His income has not suffered from his move out of the university, but the term limitation on BERI's researchers, like PERI's, has caused him an anxiety that he would not have if he were still in Kyushu. Nevertheless, his move has kept his research career intact. He has found having more time to do research extremely satisfying, and Japan has preserved a bioscience researcher who managed to construct his own unusual constellation of knowledge and interests. Toh's intellectual quest fits in the newer field of "bioinformatics," which is the application of computers to the study of cellular functions at the molecular level, in particular modeling and prediction of protein structure and function based on amino acid sequences. Toh has formulated an analytical framework that integrates evolutionary theory with questions of structure and function as well as sequence. His approach has yet to be widely adopted in the field, which he accepts with some wit: "Maybe I can claim it all for myself," he chuckled in our most recent discussion. Meanwhile, however, he has to guard against a subsidiary role in collaboration with experimentalists whose main goal is simply to generate new sequences for comparisons without exploring first their structural or functional significance.

In 1998 I asked Hiroyuki Toh if he had considered doing research abroad. With a laugh he said, "If they let me do what I want I'll do it anywhere." Although his concern with the time he can devote to research appears to eclipse any consideration of the institution in which he works, his future aspiration embraces both the discovery of scientific principles and new "base technologies" in biomolecular engineering as well. BERI appears to have chosen well.

The price of a government-led consortium scheme

From the credit cycle perspective, PERI's biggest organizational problem was political: the research teams did not have the authority to select their members from a pool of competing candidates. In an ideal credit cycle world, the teams would have chosen from among researchers who were garnering professional resources to build individually crafted careers. Some researchers' casual comments and hallway joking accused the companies of sending underachievers and misfits, and one of the division heads expressed the same suspicion. Students of industry R&D organization have long suspected that corporate consortium participants use a "minimax" strategy of sending researchers competent enough to gather important information but not competent enough to generate new knowledge of benefit to competitors.

PERI was not a dumping ground, though. There were some highly motivated individuals from industry who made solid contributions, and industry researchers were among those mentioned by department heads as their best and brightest. Indeed, one of the industry-based researchers was universally regarded as a "star." He and another former industry transfer had gone on to prestigious laboratories in the United States for postdoctoral research. One previously critical division chief, speaking from the perspective of a 1996 discussion, saw an improvement in the capabilities of the researchers sent from industry. PERI had won them through greater respect, he said, based on its accomplishments. The increased representation of large pharmaceutical companies among participant corporations (see Appendix II) also augurs well; division heads generally agreed that the companies with the most sizeable research efforts in the life sciences were more likely to send capable and appropriate researchers.

Another painful price of bureaucratic initiative was the name change that accompanied PERI's ostensible reorganization. The 1996 reformulation of research interests, which shifted some attention toward cellular functions and issues in structural biology, may prove a beneficial move. The name change, however, meant unqualified calamity for the Institute's hard-won efforts to establish an international profile. (Think of it as an institutional credit cycle issue, or imagine the response at Cambridge University if its researchers were told that it would have to change its name.) The new name reflected a hope in Japan's government that a cosmetic name change would shield officials from accusations of creating an eternal albatross. Ironically, PERI's resources and research accomplishments gave it a right to keep its name that few universities in Japan could claim.

5

THE OSAKA BIOSCIENCE
INSTITUTE AND NEW CAREER
PATTERNS

In 1987 a new research institute arrived to attack several problems in Japanese bioscience at one stroke: it was well-funded, it had a mandate to pursue basic research, and it pledged term employment for every member of its research staff, from technical assistants to its director, Osamu Hayaishi. The Osaka Bioscience Institute (Osaka Baiosaiensu Kenkyūjo), also known as OBI (pronounced Oh Bee Ai in Japanese), was initiated by Osaka's metropolitan government. OBI is a valuable vision of the possible and a glimpse of what Japanese scientists want, but OBI also illustrates the problems associated with isolated efforts at organizational reform.

Affluence in the service of basic research

The official statement of OBI's objectives in its 1987 Articles of Association would fit any university biomedical institute:

> The purposes of the Institute are to conduct bioscientific research and investigation and to train researchers in that field, thereby promoting the progress and development of bioscience, ultimately contributing to the advancement of academic research and scientific technology.

The same document began with a definition of bioscience as "the science that clarifies life phenomena through physical and chemical approaches using DNA and protein molecules, etc. as its foundations." As an admonition, it added: "we must not ignore the accumulation of steadfast basic research that lay behind the glorious achievements of biotechnology in the medical and chemical industries."

The Institute's home is a handsomely appointed facility in Suita City, which abuts the northern edge of the City of Osaka. Given the state of the laboratory life sciences in Japanese universities described in Chapter 2, OBI's arrival resembled an oasis springing up in the desert. The building's 6,560 square meters of total floor area afforded an uncramped working environment that was luxuriously spacious by Japanese university standards, and its ventilation system, lighting, and emergency facilities were state of the art. American biomedical researchers might take these features for granted, but nearly half of a nationwide sample of Japan's biomedical scientists had registered clear dissatisfaction with those aspects of their laboratories (JSC 1991: 40, 164). OBI's planners had sunk resources into aesthetics, also. They enlisted the famed architect Kenzo Tange to design the edifice, and its main lobby was walled with marble. At ¥3.3 billion ($US 22 million at the time), the cost per unit of floor space was twice that of the neighboring Protein Engineering Research Institute, also spacious and elegantly appointed.

OBI's equipment, which cost ¥1.7 billion (over $US 11.3 million), drew the praise and envy of international and Japanese visitors alike, and division chiefs used it as a major draw when inviting collaborators. Only one out of ten of their colleagues in biomedicine nationwide had access to pieces of equipment worth ¥30 million or more (JSC 1991: 41). The ratio of technical and secretarial support staff to researchers at OBI was also quite favorable.

A small package promises big reforms

OBI had four departments, one each in molecular biology, enzymes and metabolism, neuroscience, and cell biology, with several ongoing projects in each department. The single largest project involving the most inter-departmental cooperation concerned the role of substances called prostaglandins in sleep regulation, continuing the previous research pioneered by Osamu Hayaishi. At the time of my research there were seventeen research scientists (*kenkyūin*) and twelve research associates (*tokubetsu kenkyūin*, less formally referred to as postdoctoral fellows, *posudoku*) under four departmental chiefs (*buchō*). In two of the departments, chiefs were assisted by vice-chiefs (*fukubuchō*). All of the scientists and associates held PhD degrees. The two categories were distinguished by quality of research experience and performance, as judged by the chiefs. When generalizing about both scientists and associates I will use the term "researchers."

There were twenty support staff with the technician title (*kenkyū joshu*, literally "research assistant"), but one in each department provided secretarial rather than technical services. There were six foreign researchers among the staff (STA fellows), and one foreign technician. One of the department chiefs, Fred Tsuji, was a foreigner as well (a Cornell PhD, he came to OBI from the University of California at San Diego). Given his professional socialization in the US, I shall exclude him from my discussions of department chiefs, unless indicated otherwise. The City of Osaka provided a secretary general and eight staff members for administrative assistance.

The Institute's staff size would be deemed quite modest by any standards. The Institute work force was expanded, however, by thirty or more "research collaborators" (*kyōdō kenkyūin*). That category covered joint researchers with outside affiliations with universities and drug companies, but also included individuals with government and other nonprofit fellowships. I interviewed thirty-eight research staff (and an additional six foreign researchers), six City of Osaka administrators (including two secretaries general) and, on several occasions, the Director. Before leaving Japan in 1991 I conducted a self-administered questionnaire survey among OBI's researchers and assistants which yielded thirty-two useable responses. (Appendix I contains more information regarding both interviewing and the self-administered questionnaire.)

Term employment at OBI stipulated an annual renewal for all researchers based on the results of a formal evaluation, and eventual termination of employment in one's position after a specified period. Technician/secretaries were required to leave their positions after two years; associates also had two-year terms, but with the option of one-year extensions under "special circumstances." Scientists were allowed three years. Promotions that would lengthen one's stay (e.g., from associate to scientist) were also possible, however. There was no permanent tenure at the higher levels, either. Department chiefs and the director himself were allowed ten-year terms, and vice-chiefs, five years. Every year in January a formal two-day event involving outside reviewers was scheduled for individual evaluations. Department chiefs, postdoctoral fellows and researchers made individual presentations in a formal evaluation that determined their contract renewal.

The publicity surrounding OBI's establishment highlighted the review system, with article headlines like "Term Contracts for All Researchers" and subheads that announced "activation" for younger researchers or the inclusion of foreign researchers in OBI's ranks. The requirement that presentations for the annual review be conducted in English also caught the eye of the press. (Chapter 9 discusses foreign language issues.) Although OBI's regulations did not call for replacing introductions with public recruitment, an optimistic Osamu Hayaishi told a *Nikkei Medical* reporter that "we're not considering academic cliques (*gakubatsu*) at all. We're not asking about race, and even somebody who hasn't completed college is OK" (Kozaki 1992: 38).

Actual recruitment

Open recruitment claimed only a small proportion of the research staff hired by OBI. Among thirty-seven interviewees who described their recruitment, only four (a technician, a postdoc and two scientists) had entered by responding to position announcements in journals. The rest described entering OBI via introductions from professors or other seniors, or joining along with their department chiefs, all of whom came from academic positions. The single greatest channel for assembling OBI's research talent was an unusual project that Osamu Hayaishi had completed just before he assumed the directorship at OBI. In 1981 the Science and Technology

Agency's Research and Development Corporation had created a series of five-year grants under its Exploratory Research for Advanced Technology program, known by the acronym ERATO. In 1983 it invited Hayaishi to create a team from academia and industry to explore prostaglandins under the "Hayaishi Bioinformation Project."

The ERATO project involved about sixty researchers and assistants from academia and pharmaceutical companies, and it ended just as OBI began operation. Some twenty ERATO staff emigrated to OBI with Hayaishi (a few of them completing work at OBI under the ERATO grant). An STA official observed that after the five-year ERATO project had ended, Osamu Hayaishi "had to find jobs for his researchers," about half of whom were not returning to permanent positions in industry. Director Hayaishi himself said it was more complicated than that.

> I told them at the beginning they were on their own. I told them I'd write letters of recommendation but if they didn't do good work, no letter. It would be like the US. Not all wonderful letters resulted. I said, 'everything is up to you. You have beautiful equipment, plenty of materials. If you can't do well in this situation, then maybe you should be a high school teacher or a farmer or something.' That's what I tell them here, too. But in Japan we have *tatemae* (an official line) and *honne* (what we actually feel), and I felt a moral obligation to them. Fortunately, as you know, there is a shortage of people for jobs now. Companies are making deals to get students eight months before they graduate. There were many I invited with me to OBI, but others whom I felt were doing mediocre work.

(Informants who had come to OBI from the ERATO project were divided in their opinions about whether Osamu Hayaishi was obligated to place them in their next job, and some, like Hayaishi himself, expressed ambivalence toward the idea of obligation.)

Selection authority at OBI went to the department chiefs, who were very skeptical of an open recruitment process involving advertising. Their biggest objection was that it wasn't attracting sufficiently high quality candidates. By late 1990, one department chief was describing advertising in domestic journals and the elite international journals (such as *Nature* and *Science*) in the past tense.

> We got a load of responses, but when we looked at them we asked, what has this person actually done? Out of a huge pile of applications, more than one hundred, we just took one into our lab. There were one or two that were actually good but in the end we decided to call on various professors at various universities.

Another said that the people responding to the advertisements were "older" individuals who did not work out well in their past positions, either in publishing record or in interpersonal relations.

A rather marginal yield from open recruitment could have been predicted from Japan's scientific employment system, which offered little mobility and relied heavily on placement through introductions. Also, Osamu Hayaishi's multi-tiered professional networks in biochemistry and related fields offered an attractive resource. In the three decades before OBI opened its doors he had trained hundreds of graduate students and postdoctoral fellows, and his students (among them Shosaku Numa and Yasutomi Nishizuka) comprised a who's who of accomplished Japanese biochemists. His own postwar career transcended cliques when they were at their most virulent as well. Although a University of Osaka product, he joined the faculty at the University of Kyoto, and during his professorship there he had received concurrent appointments at the schools of medicine at the Universities of Osaka and Tokyo – remarkable feats. His was a singularly good position among Japanese scientists to begin the job of defying cliques.

Nevertheless, the OBI chiefs' readiness to dismiss open recruitment did not fit OBI's reformist potential, and those researchers who had come via advertisements had performed admirably. There was one other factor that favored laboratory chiefs to select their staff through personal networks, though no one at OBI mentioned it. According to a high-level ERATO administrator, OBI's selection process "had to be very careful," in order to screen out the kind of individual who would agitate for permanent employment. Introductions helped to prevent that. Fears (however subterranean) about employee bids for permanent positions would also help explain the inclusion of technicians in the non-renewal rule. Their inclusion made no sense for stimulating scientific excellence through mobility (they did not participate in the annual review), and it meant sacrificing some competent technicians and secretarial help after two years. It did help preserve a clear definition of term limits for the Institute's staff, however, with turnover to reinforce it.

The appeal of OBI

Two thirds of the OBI researchers and postdocs that I interviewed had come from temporary positions such as overseas postdoctoral fellowships, or positions in ERATO. The remainder of the interviewees had left permanent positions in regional medical colleges or, in a few cases, drug companies. The regional medical colleges were undesirable berths for basic researchers for reasons presented in Chapter 2. They featured the kind of top-down research directions that PERI's academic researchers had rejected, and posed a more generally inhospitable environment for basic research, such as onerous "chores" (*zatsuyō*) and heavy teaching loads in areas removed from research interest. As for perceptions of industry research, a researcher at OBI who had originally been dispatched to the ERATO project from a pharmaceutical company said he was escaping from "manual labor" at the firm.

With few exceptions, researchers themselves described their channel to OBI as their professor's suggestion, or that of a department chief or assistant chief with whom the respondent had worked before. The responses fit with the recruitment of researchers and assistants from their participation in ERATO, as well as the classical pattern of placement dynamics in Japan. Interviewees' expectations of OBI revolved around features that would enhance their productivity; some interviewees referred explicitly to OBI's equipment and money, others a more general expectation that they "could get out publications" or "get a lot done here." Another "expectation" was knowing the research subject before signing on. These expectations were not disappointed. The few whose expectations were not met had entered hoping for "collegiality" and an "interdisciplinary" experience.

With these themes in mind from the interviews, I composed a closed-ended question concerning research staff's reasons for choosing OBI for the self-administered questionnaire survey. The results appear in Table 5.1. At the suggestion of an informant, I added an item to the survey that

Table 5.1 Reasons for Selecting OBI – "Why do you come to work at OBI? From the answers below, please choose three appropriate reasons, and number them in order of 1 to 3 from the most important reason."

Reason Given	First reason	Second reason	Third reason	(No priority given)	Total
The research facilities are good	2	4	4	5	15
Research funds are plentiful	–	1	4	4	9
I can choose my research subject freely	–	–	1	3	4
There was a project that fitted the research subject I wanted	1	5	1	–	7
It was recommended by my advisor/professor (boss)	6	2	1	3	12
There are foreign researchers here	1	–	2	–	3
My experience, credentials at OBI will help in finding future work	1	2	–	1	4
It was the only place at which I could continue research	8	2	2	1	13
I wanted to do research with my current lab head/assistant head	3	2	2	–	7
Other	1	1	1		3
No answer	1	8	10	–	19
TOTAL					96

Note
32 respondents, 3 responses per respondent; "no priority" refers to three answers without priority designated

proved to attract the most first-priority responses: "It was the only job opportunity that allowed me to continue research." The "research" must have meant something more than a minimal definition of working in a laboratory, since at least two of the respondents did have the option of staying longer in their previous positions in university laboratories. Nevertheless, the frequency of this response represented a "this was the best I could hope for" situation for most of OBI's researchers, a sobering reminder of the job market's anemic offerings to PhD bioscientists. Answers relating to individual preferences in research topic made a pale showing by comparison. (Note that none of the thirty-two questionnaire respondents had chosen the "freedom of research subject" selection as his or her most important reason for joining OBI.)

The frequency of the response "recommended by my professor/advisor" corroborated the chiefs' descriptions of OBI's recruitment method. One of the postdoctoral fellows explained his own first choice of this answer by claiming that the personal character and abilities of the "boss" generated a constellation of conditions desirable to researchers ("working for someone having superb research skills and good character, ample resources and equipment, and few chores"). That respondent's favorable view of the introduction system must have reflected his own experience and pedigree; he was a product of the University of Tokyo's Institute of Medical Science, and his original "boss" was indeed a highly effective researcher and administrator.

Hard work and the OBI atmosphere

One of my first impressions of OBI was the long hours that its postdocs and researchers were devoting to their work. Official workdays, according to the OBI rule book, began at 9:15 AM, with weekday work ending at 5:30 PM and Saturday work hours ending at 1:00 PM. Actual work hours went well beyond the totals, though. OBI also had a well-used overnight bedroom with bath facilities, and it was booked through much of my time there. Of course, Japan is the land of long hours and hard work (Chapter 9 discusses the "work ethic" in Japanese bioscience), and the laboratory life sciences are, in the United States as well, specialties that exact long work hours from their devotees.

OBI, however, was located at the "long" end of the work hour continuum for researchers in Japan. Self-reported figures in the questionnaire survey for researchers averaged 58 hours of work a week. The figure was about 10 per cent higher than the average for all research workers nationwide. and exceeded the averages for R&D workers at all institutions but private universities (IFT 1990: 46). The self-reported figures were probably conservative, as well. The questionnaire item asked respondents to exclude "rest time," and my own rough estimates of researchers' time spent at OBI based on randomly recorded observations of their comings and goings was 20 per cent higher than their own reported figures. OBI's next-door-neighbor researchers at PERI perceived them as putting in unusually long hours also. When I asked OBI's participants in the questionnaire survey if they believed that OBI researchers worked longer hours than researchers at other institutions, a slight majority (seventeen out of thirty-two) agreed. (Of the rest, twelve said no.)

These long work hours can be explained by two of OBI's features that give research there a janus-faced "carrot and stick" quality. First, for carrots, OBI has provided first-rate equipment and materials, which generate a "can-do" atmosphere, reinforced by the director's "it's up to you" message. On the stick side, OBI's term contract employment means professional insecurity about the future that can only be alleviated by garnering accomplishments while at OBI; publications, in particular, would constitute the currency for negotiating the subsequent job hunt. Statements by Hayaishi and the chiefs at intramural gatherings stressed publication output by regularly announcing the number of articles by OBI researchers that were accepted by international journals.

Researchers' explanations of long hours favored positive motives but did acknowledge the pressure element from professional insecurity. I posed the issue of "exhilaration versus stress" in the questionnaire to those seventeen respondents who had indicated that OBI researchers did indeed work longer hours than counterparts elsewhere. The questionnaire form provided a 12 centimeter-long rectangular figure in which respondents could graphically indicate the proportion of long hours resulting from the "challenge" of interesting research or the "worry" about where they would be working next. The item also offered the option of "other," for individual explanations. On average, "challenge" won with nearly half the space allotted, and "other" explanations slightly edged out "worry" for the remainder (in percentages, the three options were 48, 29 and 23, respectively). The "other" explanations (written in by thirteen respondents) referred, in roughly equal proportions, to the effects of OBI's atmosphere (such as "habit" or "enthusiasm"), a sense of personal responsibility (individual or, in one case, to a group), and indications that the lab chiefs were exerting pressure ("In the name of merit [literally, 'achievement-ism'] the division chief hints to me that I should be writing lots of articles").

The explanations that I garnered from staff through impromptu discussions were likely to focus on the theme of laboratory chiefs demanding harder work, and an undercurrent of aggressive competition among postdocs and researchers. There were, at one point during my period at OBI, two postdoctoral fellows in different departments attempting to clone the gene for the same prostaglandin. Osamu Hayaishi justified the apparent race by noting that the postdocs were using different systems, which meant they could both publish their results without direct competition. Informants perceived the choice of research subject as a result of competition between the chief of one division and the assistant chief of another; since both were students of Osamu Hayaishi at Kyoto University and roughly the same age, informants suspected a kind of sibling rivalry.

One very important but elusive dimension of any research institution is its atmospherics; morale and *esprit* are crucial elements of a fulfilling research career, but their assessment is difficult because it easily degenerates into quibbles about style. I had come to OBI directly from an American university institute whose students and faculty prided themselves on an informal atmosphere featuring cooperation and enthusiastic debate. OBI seemed quite somber by comparison. I missed seeing the artifacts of "cartooning" of experimental concepts on the nearest section of chalkboard during animated spontaneous chats. Here and there, in little anecdotal outcroppings, I sensed that the chiefs were prodding and disciplining, too. I was struck by a postdoc's account of his vice-chief's response to his musings: "Don't think, work." It fitted with one scientist's complaint:

> There's a Severo Ochoa quote about good science coming from 'constant devotion, comradeship and curiosity,' but the only part they repeat here is the constant devotion. As for me, I feel like just one more piece of machinery, an interchangeable part.

Another postdoc summed his view of OBI as a "beautiful little bonsai tree, in the miniature image of Tokyo or Osaka [universities], carefully pruned by the chiefs."

The price of a career in science

OBI's researchers were making a variety of sacrifices for their dedication to research. Although scientists' salaries were roughly equivalent to academic salaries at OBI (they were paid on an Osaka City University scale), associates' stipends were a third below wages for researchers in public universities. Predictably, the postdocs did not express satisfaction with their salaries. During one interview, when I asked a 29-year-old biochemist associate if he was satisfied with his salary he grabbed my tape recorder with a puckish grin and announced into its microphone, as if to appeal to the outside world, "If I were in industry I'd be making twice as much money!" Putting the tape recorder down, he became more serious.

> Of course, I've just gotten out of graduate school recently. Looking at someone who graduated from college with me and worked at a company during those years, well, there's no comparison in pay (literally, 'clouds and mud'). But they all say, 'You're doing what you want to, so isn't that good?' I tell them, 'Well, the pay I get for the parts I don't like is low!' But I can agree with them. And I turn it

around when they complain about working hard at something they don't like – I say, 'But isn't it nice that you're getting all that money?'

That last sentence brought back his puckish grin. A few postdocs at OBI either felt that they had no control over the issue of pay, or had some trouble reconciling their incomes with their elegant surroundings. One mused bitterly about how many postdocs one of the marble wall sections in the lobby could pay for.

In response to their precarious career positions, OBI's researchers were delaying marriage and family formation. (I take up the case of men here, but discuss the issue for women in Chapter 7.) The average ages of the unmarried and married male OBI researchers in my interview sample were 31.6 and 34.7, respectively; in 1990, average age at first marriage for Japanese men was 28. (One postdoc told me that, at his interview for his job at OBI, Hayaishi advised him to delay marrying. He was nearing 30 at the time.) Similarly, when I looked at marital status among PERI researchers, I found that only one of the nine married men age 35 or under whom I had interviewed was under term contract: the remaining eight were safely ensconced in permanent positions.

An industry-based biologist at PERI, then 29 years old, explained simply why he had rejected an academic career for industry. "I got married. I looked around for some way of doing research and getting paid, and couldn't find it." He dropped out of his PhD program at the University of Osaka and joined a major distilling company. A married biophysicist from a chemicals corporation gave the same reason for joining industry instead of pursuing a PhD after he received a master's degree at age 25. (Both of these men sought and received thesis PhDs while at PERI.)

Term employment at OBI and PERI aggravated the already problematic image of scientists as marriage partners in the larger society. The semi-humorous depiction, "The men who suffer from 'nobody-will-marry-me' syndrome" (Takahashi 1991) described basic researchers' spouse-finding problems and blamed them on both delayed career formation and eccentric interests. The labels in the accompanying cartoon, reproduced in Figure 5.1, leave no doubt that here is a profession vulnerable to a nerdy life style image. (There are two slang terms in Japanese for "nerd," *otaku* and *senmon baka*.)

OBI's researchers also had to cope with prestige deprivation as term employees. *Science* magazine could impress an appreciative international audience by writing that OBI was "without precedent in Japan" (Kinoshita 1994), but an international institutional profile did not alter perceptions closer to home. A 33-year-old postdoc at OBI who had come from an assistant position at a regional medical school (via ERATO) told me he felt as if he had "fallen off the conveyor belt." When I related his statement to an informal gathering of industry specialists in biotechnology and chemical engineering, one of the younger members shot back, "He did." A division chief at the City

Key
(From top right, clockwise) inflexible; boring talk; can only use specialized terminology; member of four arranged marriage circles; wears bell bottoms; children run away when he goes to the park; everything is dutch treat; lab coat a dirty brown; academic hair cut. Illustration by Take'emon Sato, from *Bessatsu Takarajima* 137, "*Kenkyū suru Jinsei*," p. 103, Takarajimasha, Inc.

Figure 5.1 This is a researcher!

of Osaka's Institute of Public Health and Environmental Sciences found the idea of hiring former OBI researchers problematic in more than one respect; OBI was new and its researchers highly specialized, but on top of that they were "real strange people" (*yoppodo kawatta hito*). The variety of terms that OBI researchers themselves used at times to refer to long-term positions, such as "a secure position" (*antei shita pojishon*) or even a "decent job" (*matomo na shigoto*) did not help their self-esteem, either.

The role of the annual review

The annual review attained its stated goal of inspiring rigor and energy among the researchers. Preparation for presentations gave the Institute a particularly brisk atmosphere, although most interviewees said the annual review did not make them more busy than otherwise because they were always working on more than one project at a time. Some of the researchers became very nervous as the review approached, and one gave a presentation at the review session that was obviously stilted by his nervousness. I have no data regarding dismissals resulting directly from unfavorable reviews. Two researchers who had drawn borderline evaluations in their review during my field work had already found their next positions.

It would be difficult to find unqualified support for the annual review among the researchers. The evaluation of scientific research is a controversial subject to begin with, and the process was long on penalties and short on rewards, since there were no bonuses or other awards attached to favorable reviews. Informants felt that 15 minutes to summarize a year's work was too brief, and they were concerned that the three-person review panel would not have sufficient expertise in some of the topics presented. Several PERI informants contrasted their own multiyear project term favorably with the OBI system, and conjectured that the annual review would press researchers to opt for subjects offering quick results, but one of the OBI division chiefs said that he and his fellow chiefs encouraged reporting work in process. The deadline aspect of the review process appealed to one energetic postdoc, who said it forced him to set his goals more explicitly and meet them.

Life after OBI

OBI's success as an organizational innovation hinges on the ability of its former researchers to find positions offering a step up in some dimension – salary, degree of authority or resources, or, foremost in many minds, permanence. That is an extremely difficult criterion to meet, since OBI was not established as part of a larger system of research institutions that hire on a term basis or seek applicants other than the newly graduated. The latter type of position is especially important, since an array of receiving institutions that only offer postdoctorate and associate positions would only create an under class of perpetual nomads. In the early 1990s only two other research institutes in Japan had set up term employment for researchers (Sagami Chemical Research Center and the Physical and Chemical Research Institute) besides the postdoctoral fellowships offered to outsiders by the Mitsubishi Kasei Institute of Life Sciences and a handful of other research institutes under the direction of the Ministries of Education or Health and Welfare. Some thirty years before OBI appeared, Nobel laureate in physics Hideki Yukawa had seriously considered instituting term employment at the Research Institute

Table 5.2 1987–90 OBI cohort employment status as of mid-1996

Regular academic	9
OBI position	9
Regular industry	3
Foreign academic/industry term	3
Regular government	1
Term, government	1
Term, industry	1
No information	2
TOTAL	29

for Fundamental Physics (Kiso Butsurigaku Kenkyū-jo). The absence of destination institutions was enough to change his mind, as he then related it to science historian Shigeru Nakayama (Nakayama 1996).

Nevertheless, OBI did set before itself the goal of successful term employment (earning Osamu Hayaishi the sobriquet of "Don Quixote" among colleagues). The results present a mixed picture. My own listing, based on communications with OBI staff and annual reports, has information as of 1996 on twenty-seven of the twenty-nine researchers (vice-chiefs, scientists and associates) hired in OBI's first three years. (Like too many academic departments at American universities, OBI has not kept a statistical record of its alumni's careers for public information.) The information is summed in Table 5.2.

The most frequent destinations were universities, and four of the nine cases of faculty appointments went to elite national universities. Academic jobs were definitely the first preference of OBI's researchers. A third of my researcher interviewees specifically mentioned universities in their ideal future scenarios, and the rest described research agendas requiring the kind of autonomy that only universities (and some free-standing research institutes) could accommodate. In the questionnaire survey as well, two thirds of the respondents were positively inclined toward academic jobs, the rest undecided. (Government laboratories fared nearly as favorably as the academic destination.)

The small number of OBI alumni going to industry also fit with their expressed preferences: none of the interviewees mentioned working in industry in their ideal future, and half of the questionnaire respondents rejected the proposition. The three former researchers who did go to industry all had vastly differing fates. Two had rather attractive arrangements: a position with a major distilling firm that involved conducting experiments full-time at OBI as a collaborator, and a management position at the research center of a foreign-owned drug and fine chemicals company. The third former researcher, however, found a position with a small pharmaceutical manufacturing firm in one of the rural prefectures, and only after considerable difficulty. Japanese industry's lack of interest in PhDs also makes the industry option difficult for former OBI researchers.

There were nine cases of individuals from the original cohort who still maintained positions at OBI when I returned to Japan in the summer of 1996, and their presence called into question the consistency of OBI's original rules. (All had entered as scientists or associates between the Institute's opening and April of 1989.) To some others who had left OBI, the situation looked like favoritism. Most of these individuals had been associated with Osamu Hayaishi since the days of the ERATO project (or, in one case, as an advisee at the University of Kyoto), and five of the nine had been identified by several informants in 1990 as his "favorites." Two cases presented some extenuating circumstances: one, a former associate, had left Japan for family reasons after two years at OBI and had been rehired as a technician in 1995; another, a vice-chief, had left his associate position at OBI for an industry position in 1988, and also reentered in 1995.

Mobility and OBI in 1998

As of 1998 OBI was still hosting two researchers (excluding technical support staff) from the original cohort, but the former researchers with whom I talked regarded these individuals as cases of difficult individual careers rather than as privileged rule breakers. Eyes were focussed instead on the division chiefs. By 1998 three department chiefs had left. One (Fred Tsuji) had since returned to his professorship at the University of California, and the two other department chiefs had each taken full academic appointments at the University of Osaka and a private medical college in the Osaka area.

The remaining department chief had been given an additional five-year term. The issue of an extension was mulled by a seven-member panel of senior scientists, university presidents and pharmaceutical company board chairmen that had been assembled to make suggestions about OBI's future. According to both Osamu Hayaishi and the division chief, the panel had suggested the five-year term. The chiefs may have been a particularly difficult component of OBI's policy of full mobility. The panel's written report noted specifically that a renewal of ten years would eliminate the meaning of the system, and stated it "important to make clear the basic principle of no renewal at the time of appointment" (Ōsaka Baiosaiensu Kenkyūjo Konwakai 1997: 7). Osamu Hayaishi had justified the extension in terms of needing administrative institutional memory and the career vulnerability of the younger researchers currently involved under the division chief. The division chief said that he wanted to help get jobs for his remaining research team members, but he also viewed the extension as a reasonable reward for his division's productivity that would further benefit OBI's reputation.

Of the three vacated division chief positions, one was filled by the previously mentioned former researcher who had left OBI for industry for some years but had returned to become a vice-chief. Both he and the remaining department chief were former Hayaishi students and ERATO project participants. Former researchers described the OBI personnel configuration of 1998 as "half new, half old," and I sensed that they evaluated it as "half successful" for OBI's pledge to introduce thorough-going mobility. The two new chiefs, however, have both entered from faculty positions at the University of Kyoto. The pattern does not bode well for open recruitment because OBI has always relied so heavily on introductions, and because each department chief wields so much independent authority for hiring decisions.

OBI has also chosen its new director, Hidesaburo Hanafusa. He shares an intellectual pedigree with Osamu Hayaishi, having received his doctorate from the University of Osaka with a subsequent research stint at that university's Research Institute for Microbial Diseases. Over the coming years as director, the less he relies on that pedigree for recruiting talent, the greater will be OBI's contribution to reform of mobility.

Accomplishments

Osamu Hayaishi has been reluctant to subject OBI's performance to direct comparisons with other bioscience institutes' accomplishments, and for good reason: the place is small and still relatively young. Also, Hayaishi's own research interests since OBI's inception have moved into the physiology and biochemistry of sleep regulation, an area daunting for its uncharted territory. As he had commented to a reporter, he "wouldn't have dared" that kind of research when he was younger. Nevertheless, by conventional standards OBI was doing very respectably within several years of its establishment; by mid-1993 it could claim seventh rank among all of Japan's bioscience research institutes for per capita international journal article production (Yamazaki 1994).

OBI had put itself on the map. In terms of specific accomplishments, the most international recognition has gone to division chief Kazushige Nagata and his team for their research on cytokines (a class of proteins that signal important cellular processes). By 1997 Nagata was bested only by Hayaishi himself in the number of international awards he had received. Nagata came to OBI from outside the Hayaishi network, a "Hayaishi outsider." He was an example of how OBI had gone beyond the Hayaishi circle to nurture talent, but – to several former OBI researchers, at least – Nagata's outsider status prevented Hayaishi from claiming credit for Nagata's achievements, an exquisite irony that illustrates the depth of clique mentality among Japanese researchers.

OBI had also freed its researchers from various burdens of age hierarchy. The Institute allocated "Scientist" and "Associate" titles without relying on age; the average age of scientist interviewees was only nine months higher than the average for associates. From three division chiefs on down, OBI was a youthful place, with no researchers over the age of 45. A senior biochemist had been in residence at OBI at its inception, but no one had replaced him for want of funding. (OBI's statutes designated a visiting researcher position with a two-year term of office for an eminent senior scientist, but the laboratory space created in the Institute for the visiting researcher was used instead for storage.) Organizationally, the absence looked to me and to other foreign observers like an unfortunate gap in expertise and wisdom, but OBI's researchers were indifferent or even glad not to have older colleagues about. Senior researchers, they said, only complicated "human relations" and made demands that would detract from getting research done.

My discussions over the last several years with some of OBI's former researchers about what OBI had meant for their careers yielded a fairly uniform response. In retrospect, OBI was a substantial boon. Not having to do nonresearch tasks (the roundly disliked zatsuyō) while at OBI meant a great boost to productivity. The contrast with universities remained stark in their minds. Said one former researcher, "A friend my age in a low-level university position has a guaranteed position, but he has so many tasks he can't do his own experiments. He uses data from the students he supervises." They also still appreciated the state of the art equipment. "In modern biology," said one OBI veteran, "this can decide who will win." Next in importance to former OBI researchers came the professional network resulting from exposure to co-workers who became part of their professional resources.

Yoshihiro Ohmiya

In the long run, OBI's greatest organizational accomplishment will be creating individually crafted careers in science that could not have existed otherwise. The significance of this accomplishment comes home when we look at real individuals. The researcher at OBI who most exemplified OBI's potential for individual career crafting was Yoshihiro Ohmiya (see Figure 5.2), 30 years old when I first met him in the autumn of 1990. He had put together an unusual combination of specialties for himself – in his words, "a real jumble": undergraduate study and master's research in materials science, in an engineering program, and a PhD in medicine, specializing in endocrinology. His was the only Japanese curriculum vitae I had ever seen that featured narrative sections entitled "Course of Research to the Present" and "[Professional] Aspirations" (hōfu). The latter statement explained his combination of specialties and justified them in terms of his own personal research goals.

In the engineering school I embraced an interest in materials science, more precisely rheology, and took as my research subject the kinetics

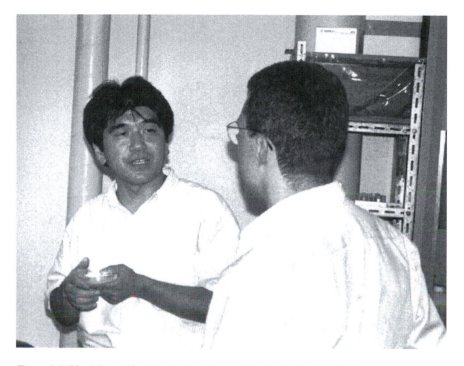

Figure 5.2 Yoshihiro Ohmiya (with colleague Vadim Viviani), 1998

and thermal properties of compound materials. In this way I was able
to master for myself the experimental and theoretical analytical rules
of rheology. While seeking answers to the question of what makes an
ideal compound material, I began to develop an intense interest in
biomaterials. I came to believe that, by pursuing an understanding
of the mechanisms of biomaterials for developing the next generation
of materials, I could know one piece of the puzzle of the phenomenon
of life. However, conducting materials science research through
living beings requires dealing with living matter itself in a serious
manner. Thus, I have chosen my present laboratory in order to study
biochemistry and molecular biology as the base of life science for my
PhD course of study.

With several publications resulting from his PhD research (among them
articles in the *Journal of Biological Chemistry* and the *European Journal of
Biochemistry*), Ohmiya was slated to stay in his PhD laboratory under a two-
year fellowship from the Japan Society for Promotion of Science. He declined
the award, however after responding to a postdoc announcement that Fred
Tsuji had placed in a Japanese molecular biology journal. The research at Fred

Tsuji's laboratory at OBI represented the chance to learn about protein engineering through the study of bioluminescent proteins, and explore their applications to endocrinology. There were other applicants for the postdoc, but Ohmiya's experience with protein chemistry and biophysics landed him the position.

OBI was not the first time that Yoshihiro Ohmiya had jumped ship from a more conventional career journey. Perhaps his most extraordinary move (at least, in Japanese eyes) came eight years before, when he attempted to enter the polymer science department at Gumma University's School of Engineering with advanced standing from a technical vocational higher school in Hokkaido. Technical schools combine three-year high school and two-year community college, and at the time were not geared to preparing students for university entrance examinations.

Overcoming a failed attempt and trying again at the entrance examination, Ohmiya entered Gumma University with advanced standing in 1981, graduated in two years, and earned a master's degree in polymer chemistry two years later. Sufficiently high graduate record examination (GRE) scores bolstered his hope to continue graduate work in the United States, but his English language (TOEFL) scores weren't sufficient. With no doctoral engineering program at Gumma to accommodate his interest in biomaterials, Ohmiya turned to the medical school for a PhD to study endocrinology and protein chemistry. Ohmiya told me he has kept his intellectual roots in engineering, which he valued as something that set him apart, a source of "inspirations and angles" lacked by others with more conventional life science backgrounds. Unlike many of his OBI colleagues, he did not express opposition to the possibility of an industry job, though he has always been intent on publishing his research and has since attained a vigorous publication record in scientific journals.

OBI represented an indispensable foothold for Ohmiya's self-formulated career, but it was not the last. At the end of his postdoctoral term at OBI, Ohmiya applied to a newly formed program (a Japan Research and Development Corporation creation) and entered a three-year term researcher position at the prestigious Physical and Chemical Research Institute (RIKEN) in bioluminescence studies. His next institutional move, in early 1996, validated his strategy: an associate professorship in biochemistry at Shizuoka University's Faculty of Education. The leap to stability couldn't have come sooner, in both personal and professional terms: while at RIKEN he had married (a friend from his high school years) and they had a child in 1995. By the time the contract ended Ohmiya had not been accepted for any of the academic positions for which he had applied, and his foothold at Riken became a toehold job of "cooperating researcher" at 40 per cent of his original salary.

Ohmiya's chances for survival in the face of all this professional risk taking were enhanced by his relentless energy. By his own estimate he worked a 70-

hour week at OBI, and he held to that work week through raging high waters – literally. One mid-September morning during my field work at OBI, the building intercom warned us of an approaching typhoon, and the prospect of a serious torrential lashing began dislodging OBI staff by mid-afternoon. Ohmiya commuted to OBI by train, but on that day he had brought a heavy raincoat and southwester, in which he trudged back to his apartment after a regular 12-hour day of work.

Lest this anecdote portray Yoshihiro Ohmiya as a compulsive plodder, by his own account he genuinely enjoyed his work, and described good science as thrilling (*waku-waku suru*):

> What's important is not the easy way of just calculating the number of papers you publish. You really have to have some way of satisfying your curiosity. If you don't, well, that's when you hit a wall and the expression on your face turns sour. When you see people walking around with those scowling faces you just know they aren't going to turn out really good, different stuff.

Ohmiya's personal outlook also gave him some resilience for his quest. "I'm something of a Buddhist, I guess. I believe that wherever I end up I'll get something good out of it ... Fact is, I'm not excellent and I know it, and that has been a help to me. The thoroughbred race horses from [the Universities of] Tokyo and Kyoto run on well-groomed tracks. Me, I'm a horse who could probably climb a mountain." At the same time, though, he has wanted very much to carve out a unique position for himself, to do something no one else was doing and earn attention for it. When discussing citation ratings for articles he said, "Instead of having an article that one hundred people cite, I'd much rather publish an article that ten people will read and say, 'Wow, I want to meet this guy!'"

As of 1998 Yoshihiro Ohmiya has adapted to the demands of teaching and research, and is thinking in terms that reflect his more established position with its greater command of resources. His most prominent contribution to teaching is a co-authored textbook on biochemistry, a field that he feels deserves a place in general science education. The book, devoted to experimental methods, illustrates concepts using bioluminescence, too. "Since bioluminescence involves light the colors are attractive and make for good educational visuals. I hope the book helps establish bioluminescence as an educational tool."

On the research side, Ohmiya is exploring novel animal systems such as bioluminescent shellfish and insects. He wants to broaden his inquiry to include issues of interest to both basic and applied bioluminescence research. To him, that means both initiating his own larger scale, interdisciplinary research projects, and participating in others' teams. "If something interests me personally, I'd like to make it more interesting and develop my own advantages by gathering people together with specialties and approaches that differ from mine. That may sound contradictory, but working against a common target with people who are different brings out some interesting results that otherwise wouldn't emerge." That orientation may have flavored his 1998 perspective on what OBI meant to his career also:

> OBI was a terrific asset, and that asset was people, relationships with people. Like Kikuko Watanabe (a research scientist). She's become my closest friend – and we've had our share of fights, too. We can talk to each other really candidly, and that includes our work. With relationships like that everyone can help each other when they face some problems. Some of my relations from OBI days are more specialized in work-related matters, but it means I can get on the phone to so-and-so and say, "What do you think about such-and-such?" ... Certainly I've remembered all the technique I've learned, and for some people learning such things was the most valuable result of being at OBI. For me, though, it's the new friends who are scientists. I'm very grateful to OBI for that.

In historical perspective, the most accomplished and internationally acclaimed of OBI's researchers will probably be Nagata, one of the thoroughbreds. A University of Tokyo product for both his undergraduate and graduate study, Nagata came to OBI from Yoshito Kajiro's laboratory at IMSUT. Since OBI gave then 38-year-old Nagata his own laboratory, it accelerated his independence – no small contribution to Japanese science, but still not the departure represented by the case of Yoshihiro Ohmiya, or the degree of risk that Ohmiya had assumed in order to pursue his chosen research subjects. Said one of Ohmiya's colleagues, "This guy is either going to be a big shot or dead in the gutter," ironic homage to the unconventional risk taker.

Yoshihiro Ohmiya's case suggests that OBI's ability to field more scientists like him will hinge on two factors, one within OBI's control but the other dependent on reforms outside its walls, at the national level. Had OBI limited its recruitment to the elite national universities there would be no Yoshihiro Ohmiya story. OBI needs to recruit broadly among the nation's universities, lest it become a colony of the elite national universities – Kyoto and Osaka in particular – that have been strongly represented there and now appear ascendant.

After leaving OBI, Yoshihiro Ohmiya was helped at two critical points: a JRDC initiative that focussed assistance on researchers his age and, more importantly, an open university search process at Shizuoka, as opposed to a comfortable berth at Gumma (where he had received his doctorate). He could no longer rely on the latter because he had chosen an unconventional combination of specialties and moves, which greatly limited the ability of his professor to provide a position for him. His bid to make a mark in world science now depends on reforms that would strengthen his chances of winning research money in open competition and assembling an internationally competitive research team. OBI also needs these larger, nationwide reforms to validate its existence. Meanwhile, OBI as a salient of professional mobility needs more OBIs to vindicate the risks its researchers are taking.

6

OBI AS WINDOW ON THE SCIENTIST–GOVERNMENT RELATIONSHIP

OBI's – and Japan's – need for more OBI-like institutions to promote career development invites a close look at how the Institute originated and how it has been administered. OBI as a municipal initiative raises a tantalizing prospect: what if OBI were the first in a series of scientific research institutes inspired by regional economic competition? Such independently financed institutes could create organizational styles that the stultifying hierarchy of the Japanese university system and national government bureaucracy could not. The proposal conjures images of the United States' state universities, a wellspring of basic research activity supported by regional economies that have benefitted from the universities' educational and extension services. These regional universities have fed talent into the graduate and postdoctoral programs at the United States' elite centers of scientific research.

The bureaucratic nature of science administration in Japan, however, has detracted from the full realization of OBI's potential. Relations between OBI's scientists and the administrators assigned to them by the City of Osaka have played out in microcosm problems at the national level. There is a mismatch between scientists' priorities and those of government administrators that arises from the administrators' lack of scientific background and their ulterior organizational allegiances. This chapter examines the price of that mismatch in the management of science at the national level in Japan, and explains the impediment to competitive funding arrangements posed by the bureaucracy's centralization of power and resources.

OBI and regional development

Regional competition did indeed play an important part in creating OBI. By the mid-1980s, policy makers in the Osaka area were looking to R&D activity to develop regional infrastructure and improve the economy. The Osaka government also needed to staunch the outflow of corporate headquarters to the Tokyo area. Centralization of Japan's information resources and corporate activity in Tokyo is remarkably disproportionate. The term "region" (*chihō*), as used in "regional development," reflects the imbalance;

it typically means "any place in Japan but Tokyo," and is even applied occasionally to the Osaka conurbation despite its sophisticated technoeconomy and population of 8.7 million. Tokyo's already swollen share of the nation's corporate activities and information resources had grown further in the 1980s, and informed analysts were saying the trend would continue.

Osaka's concern about corporate flight coincided nicely with a heightened interest worldwide in the industrial potential of genetic engineering and related technologies. Biotechnology was also particularly appealing to Osaka's leaders because the city's industries included numerous drug and fine chemical manufacturers, food processors, and distillers. Japanese biotechnology watchers also believe that the Kansai region (which includes Osaka, Kyoto, and Nara) has a stronger resource base in biotechnology than the Kanto region to the east, with Tokyo as its center. A popular phrase describing Japan's winter weather pattern, "West is high [air pressure], east is low" (*seikō fōtei*), summarizes the comparison. Osaka is indeed home to Japan's largest pharmaceutical company, Takeda, and the famous distiller Suntory, and the perception of leadership in biotechnology lent some momentum to interest in bioscience. (The popular perception of Kansai dominance in biotechnology does not stand out in fact, however; six of the ten Japanese pharmaceutical firms that grossed over ¥200 billion in sales in 1994 were headquartered in Tokyo, and Tokyo-based pharmaceutical firms' total sales exceeded Osaka competitors'; calculated using figures in Tōyō Keizai Shinbunsha 1995.)

Osaka policy makers' interest in biotechnology crystallized in early 1983, in a discussion group for the study of biotechnology under the direction of the city's mayor, Yasushi Oshima. In the same year, the study group authored a proposal for a "Bioscience Research Institute." The argument featured biotechnology's promised cornucopia of solutions to a wide range of problems, among them food and energy shortages, cancer, human senescence, and economic stagnation. A superstructural theme accompanied these more mundane concerns; Osaka had become a mature city, built on industry, but it was now coming of age, and should address science and culture. "Culture" in the sense of refinement and the arts has long been a sensitive point among Osakans, chafed by Tokyoites' jibes that Osaka's culture was raw and money-oriented.

Mayor Oshima believed that the city needed a research institution as both investment in the future and a sign that the metropolis had come of age. Three years after OBI was established, he recalled for me his guiding belief: "For the twenty-first century, a big city needs three things: an international airport, a heliport, and the latest technological research." The Mayor's vision for the research institute was also inspired by an historical antecedent, the "Tekijuku" (Tekitekisaijuku), a private academy established in Osaka in 1838. The Tekijuku provided the study of foreign medical texts to young scholars, some of whom later became illustrious figures in research policy

(Bartholomew 1989: 33). The 1983 position paper also made passing reference to the Tekijuku, along with a role for the institute in Osaka's internationalization.

Serendipities

Other factors at work in OBI's origins were a product of the historical moment. Mayor Oshima saw a newspaper article in 1983 announcing Osamu Hayaishi's retirement from his professorship in the Kyoto University Faculty of Medicine. (He then became president of Osaka Medical College that year.) In addition to bridging three national universities in his career (as described in the last chapter), Hayaishi had become a remarkable figure in several other respects. His research had won international recognition, and his administrative experience included five years as a Section Chief at the United States' National Institutes of Health, in the 1950s. He had worked closely with Nobel laureate Arthur Kornberg, who had since referred to him (with justification) as "the doyen of biochemistry in Japan" (1989: 101). Mayor Oshima wanted to keep him in the Osaka area. Hayaishi's personal relationships with him and the succeeding mayor were elements that helped sustain OBI's financial well-being, since over 80 per cent of the Institute's operating costs have been borne by the city budget. (Said one informant in 1991, "We're safe for now; the new mayor is a high school classmate of Dr. Hayaishi.")

The 1987 celebration of Osaka's hundredth year as an incorporated city also helped bring plans for a research institute to fruition. OBI was commissioned as a commemorative project. The city provided a building, and the centennial also lent momentum for fund raising. Brochures written to enlist contributions from the business community linked basic bioscience research with biotechnology, which in turn promised product development in the food, pharmaceutical, and chemical industries for a revitalized economy. A well-known journalistic commentator, Taichi Sakaiya, joined in the effort with an appeal to the "Osaka business spirit" of risk taking. Collective efforts yielded an endowment of ¥1 billion (about US$ 6.5 million at the time) for the Osaka Bioscience Institute Foundation, 80 per cent raised from corporate contributions and the remainder provided by the City of Osaka.

Uncertain stakeholders

OBI's local industrial support was tenuous at the outset. Keizo Saji, Board Chairman of Suntory, chaired the foundation for the Institute, but fund-raising among Osaka-based corporations proved no easy matter. Of 150 companies approached in the original fund-raising drive, only 63 contributed. A senior administrator from the City who had been heavily involved said that prospective donor companies made very aggressive demands for concrete returns on their money such as access to the laboratories, and participating companies demanded that solicitations for OBI take place once only. Corporate representatives argued that they "already paid taxes" – i.e., provided money that went to basic science education and research. One of the planners of OBI had seen companies responding positively to the basic research mandate when OBI was proposed, but one vice-head said that industry was concerned mainly with getting some training in recombinant DNA technique.

Once OBI had opened its doors, some of the region's biotechnology-related firms sent representatives to the annual reviews and assigned members of their R&D staff to collaborating researcher positions at OBI. (Five companies were represented when I was there.) In OBI's first ten years, however, only 20 of the 270 or so collaborative researchers had come from corporations (Osaka Baiosaiensu Kenkyûjo Konwakai 1997: 15) – not unreasonable, considering OBI's emphasis on basic research, but not a wide bridge to the local industrial constituency, either. Support for OBI out of concern for Osaka's "cultural" amenities and its bid to attract industry to the area may have been satisfied by the Institute's attractive edifice itself. Pictures of OBI appeared in glossy promotional brochures, like the English language "Osaka–Dynamism and Hospitality," and "Your Invitation to An International Economic City, Osaka." The latter explicitly compared Osaka favorably with Tokyo as a business location for foreign firms.

The titan factor

Perhaps because Osaka presented a mixed picture of support for basic research, the weighty role that Osamu Hayaishi played in creating and shaping OBI figured in everyone's concerns about its future. "OBI is going to need a big shot (ōmono)," said an Osaka administrator. With the same logic, observers both inside and outside OBI conjectured that Hayaishi's retirement from the directorship would doom OBI to becoming a rather ordinary and bureaucratic facility geared to applied R&D. They pointed to the two other research institutes under the City's management, the Industrial Research Institute and the Osaka City Institute of Public Health and Environmental Sciences. OBI's planning paper called for "organic collaboration and alignment" with them but did not elaborate. OBI was not integrated into an academic web, either. Despite the academic theme struck by the image of the Tekijuku, planning for OBI did not involve the cooperation, much less the active support, of other research establishments in the region. According to an academic who participated in the first phase of OBI's planning, planners' low regard for the research potential at Osaka City University prevented them from locating OBI there.

Servants of the City

The administrative and support staff sent from the City of Osaka to OBI were not high-level policy makers who influenced larger issues of City policy toward research or the choice of research topics at OBI. Nevertheless, their attitudes and behavior provided a hint for OBI's fate if priorities and management style were left up to them in a "titan vacuum" scenario. Osaka representatives at OBI were far more intent on applications than on basic science. One of the mid-level officials announced for me and his office mates a small-horizon view of bioscience research that was diametrically opposed to the researchers' aspirations: "Life science is in the technical stage," he said. "The concepts have been determined. The double helix is known. Now it's a matter of money and machinery." A senior functionary told his acquaintances that OBI specialized in "bioengineering" (*seimei kōgaku*), a term that few of OBI's scientists would use.

The civil servants had a very evident interest in promoting income from patents. The Institute's bylaws stated that intellectual property belonged to the Institute and stipulated very modest royalty portions for inventors. Administrative staff reviewed research reports for their patent potential before publication, using a form that required researchers to provide a 200 character-long summary of journal submissions and extramural announcements, with spaces for the seals of four different administrators (director, secretary general, division chief, and assistant division chief or deputy section chief). City administrators also provided a striking example of their desire to control proprietary information when they denied my request to attend the annual research review, for fear that I would pass along unpublished research results to a pharmaceutical company unrepresented at OBI. (Two senior scientists intervened on my behalf to reverse the decision.)

The stance on proprietary information taken by the City's representatives resulted from the rotation system of institutional assignments. Tours of duty determined by City Hall typically lasted two or three years. The individuals sent to OBI were superior by classical bureaucratic standards; according to one administrator, the entrance examination scores of the first group to enter OBI were clearly higher than average. The rotation structure contained a conflict, however. The agency most directly responsible for assignments to OBI was the Bureau of Environment and Hygiene (Kankyō Eiseikyoku), which was also responsible for administering the City's hospitals and related medical services. Although the civil servants sent to OBI had seen some varied assignments – among them the election board and the City's wholesale market for fruits and fish – their points of origin and eventual return were that bureau. That agency also had organized fund-raising for the OBI Foundation, and selected the Secretary General, who was also assigned on rotation.

The City's yearly grants to OBI for operating costs came from the same budget. Osaka's representatives were acutely aware of what OBI was costing, and must have seen the outflow as a drain on their home agency in the event of a budget crunch. Senior administrators from the City unanimously warned that support from Osaka for OBI would eventually be threatened by costs to the metropolitan government from health care and welfare for the city's rapidly ageing population. Hence the functionaries' very evident interest in promoting income from patents as a means to attaining OBI's fiscal self-sufficiency. Their stance was subtly aided by differences among the heads toward ties to drug companies, which fell on a continuum of university-style pure basic research on one end to active collaboration and deal-making for patents on the other. The head most committed to the former approach told me he had come to OBI expecting it to be run "like a university." The head most oriented to industry ties said that OBI was "like a company."

The option of self-support through the sale of information never had been spelled out in the original plans for OBI; the only written reference appeared in a 1986 promotional brochure which listed "miscellaneous commissioned research" among proposed projects. Nevertheless, one senior City representative portrayed OBI's fiscal dependence on the City as a "preliminary phase" (*shoki dankai*). In any event, the option of selling knowledge had little chance of meeting OBI's funding needs, since the Japanese techno-economy has not created a niche for contract research institutes since the 1930s heyday of RIKEN (Coleman 1990). The one notable postwar attempt to form an independent laboratory had failed (Bloom 1990: 60); Nomura Research Institute's biotechnology research institute was formed in 1983 but folded five years later.

Scientists and functionaries at odds

OBI's scientists and the lay administrators with whom they worked on a daily basis experienced contentions that would be familiar to science policy watchers in any industrialized country, but they were intensified by OBI's administrative recruitment pattern. Administrative staff came from a larger, multifunction agency through a top-down directive which did not select for an interest in science or the skills and knowledge needed for the management of basic research. The yearly volume of transfers throughout the metropolitan government was too great to accommodate special requests from OBI; there were 50,000 City of Osaka employees, of whom 5,000 transferred yearly.

Assignees' expertise lay instead in areas like accounting and personnel regulations. When I asked one mid-level staff member his view of his most important role at OBI, he responded laconically, "To make sure that the rules and regulations of the City of Osaka are enforced." To be sure, scientists must be monitored just as much as any other group of specialists when material resources are involved, given human tendencies to opportunism. A lack of familiarity with or interest in scientists' needs, though, means inability to evaluate scientists' demands effectively. A researcher who had requested a gas chromatograph with specific features met with what he called the "tape recorder argument." "I'll want a certain function [in a piece of equipment] and they'll say, 'but a tape recorder is a tape recorder, isn't it?'" Ultimately, he didn't get either the equipment he wanted or a satisfactory explanation for the decision. Travel funding and regulations also sparked disagreements. Knowledge of the nature and importance of professional travel could have helped the city's administrators work out arrangements for scientists while discerning recreational outings from legitimate trips with more accuracy.

Money was indeed a major point of contention between OBI's scientists and the functionaries sent to work with them. Several city administrators mentioned money conflicts when I asked about their least-favorite aspects of work at the Institute. One said "Human relations," and then explained that "researchers think they can bend the rules a little for their own ends ... You can only use this money in these ways. Researchers want to do it in their own way." Another OBI staffer sent by the City had expressed to me a strong desire to play a supportive role to the scientists. He found, though, that his most unpleasant task at OBI was having to ask for more money from the City when researchers' budgets exceeded allocations. "I didn't want to tell the scientists to dig it up themselves, but when [the municipal government] asked me why we were over budget I had to lower my head." One area of repeated negotiation was pay for support staff. In his attempt to raise one technician's pay, a division chief presented a newspaper article quoting higher daily pay for fish cleaners at Tokyo's Tsukiji Fish Market.

Money disputes may also figure in relationships between scientists and administrators in the United States, but not so familiar – at least to Americans in universities – would be the issue of outside colleagues' access to research facilities. One head recounted his frustration at City representatives' attempts to restrict the use of laboratory equipment to regular staff and impose user fees on outsiders, including those in the collaborator category. The head had argued that exchange was one of the Institute's strengths, and that collaborators with the same goals were an asset; his antagonists from the City asserted that City of Osaka facilities should not be used by "outsiders." "Sometimes," said the division chief, "you just can't operate with such a dwarfish sense of values." The head prevailed in that argument, but OBI did not become an open gateway for the participating visitor; former collaborators recalled surprise at how much paper work they had to fill out to use the laboratories.

Osamu Hayaishi attempted to overcome the problem of City officials' unfamiliarity with basic research administration by sending one of them on a fact-finding visit to four laboratories in the United States. Otherwise, though, education in research administration was left tacit and hands-on. The rotation system meant that on-the-job education would have to be repeated at three-year intervals for new staff members, and whatever constructive deviations from City policy each representative had established would have to be renegotiated with his or her successors. Even the investment in the official whom Osamu Hayaishi sent to the United States delivered little in returns: he was transferred out of OBI less than one year after his return to Japan.

Signs of control

The physical layout of the OBI building and campus also bore signs of administrative control by the City. The administrative and staff offices, located on the first floor of the building, provided a corner window view of the front entrance walk and road leading to the freight dock and research staff entrance. Inside the offices were a bank of color television monitors for three cameras mounted in strategic positions outside the building. Access to the building grounds required magnetic cards issued by the functionaries in order to pass through the main gate. The gate was kept open only during regular work hours, and the electromagnetic system recorded comings and goings by card number. The gate also featured a No Trespassing sign about 6 feet in height. Next to the research staff entrance, opposite shelves full of slippers, was a name board for division chiefs, staff, and those collaborators who came on a frequent basis. The name plates were on pivots: one side, having characters written in black, indicated presence at the Institute; when leaving, researchers would flip their plates to characters written in red to indicate their absence. (The name board greatly assisted my investigation of work hours.)

One justification for the elaborate security system was OBI's location in a densely populated area: OBI had materials worth stealing, a functionary told me, and my informants agreed that there were some "odd types" occasionally strolling through the neighborhood. Also, local inhabitants fearful of biohazards had demonstrated in front of the Institute when it opened. The threat of property damage from subsequent demonstrations was hard to assess, but seemed unlikely. Although the demonstration had left an impression strong enough to become an Institute legend, it was nonviolent and unrepeated. The Protein Engineering Research Institute directly behind OBI had a much less elaborate security system. Although PERI's building also made use of electronic passes and video monitors, its campus gates were always open (except for holidays), the video monitors were modest monochrome affairs handled by the maintenance crew in a small side office, and a sign restricting entrance to those with PERI business was far smaller and less obtrusive than OBI's warning sign.

Life at Osaka Bioscience Institute bore more subtle signs of regimentation also. Chime-like tunes from the building's intercom system marked the beginning and end of the work day and lunch period. (The end-of-day ditty was "Going Home," from Dvorak's New World Symphony.) I may have been particularly sensitive to an orderly atmosphere, having come directly from the relaxed environment at the University of Oregon's Institute for

Molecular Biology, where even locks were few and monitoring equipment nonexistent. A few OBI research staff felt the trespassing sign was a bit too much (ōbā), but none whom I asked casually about the name board felt it particularly onerous. I was not alone, however, in noticing the music that played over the intercom system. "I wish they'd stop that," muttered one Japanese postdoc; "I feel like I'm back in grade school." He asked me to recommend silencing them in my final report.

Separate subcultures

Although the single greatest source of differences between OBI's researchers and officials was the City's system of assignments, the gulf between them was widened by other practices. One was different work schedules. Institute regulations called for "43 hours and 45 minutes" of work weekly, divided up into 8 hours daily on weekdays with the remainder on Saturday. The official day began at 9:15 AM and ended at 5:30 PM on weekdays, and Saturday hours ended at 1:00 PM. Unlike the researchers who worked into later evening hours and night, functionaries came and left rather punctually at appointed times, and the lobby lights went off at 5:40. (Vacation time followed a separate pattern as well. A postdoc recounted Director Hayaishi's words, "Vacations are for office people from the City.") One researcher was irked at an official's question to him of why the scientists worked such hours, a sign to him that "the City people" did not understand the researchers' motivations and stresses.

The building's spatial arrangement also separated researchers and municipal staff. Administrative offices were located on the first floor, adjacent to the lobby. Since the laboratories, division chief offices and research staff desks were all located on the second floor, scientists and assistants referred to the City staff as "the people downstairs." Dress patterns set the two groups apart as well; research staff (women included) wore jeans or slacks with printed shirts open at the collar (covered by sweaters in winter), whereas suits with white shirt and tie for men and dresses and business suits for women were *de rigueur* among City staff. Even OBI's annual bowling meet had a division of labor; City staff took charge of assigning lanes and put up a large scoreboard to rank every participant, with prizes for the highest scores and a booby prize (which, as a trivial note, went to an American social scientist conducting ethnographic research among them).

None of these tendencies is irreversible, and individual researchers and a few city officials have had quite friendly interactions. One of the assignees (quoted above regarding budget problems) told me with artless honesty that his greatest thrill would be to see an OBI researcher get an international award like a Nobel Prize. Without reforms to overcome the organizational rift creators, though, the separate cultures of scientists and city administrators will continue to perplex and mislead the two groups in each other's eyes. A senior

110

city official at OBI viewed term employment for scientists as a kind of disciplining exercise; Japan's scientists with permanent employment had been sitting in "lukewarm water" (*nurumayu*), a term used for environments that protect mediocre work. Scientists, he felt, needed a more "hungry spirit" to become productive.

The research staff were curious about what an assignment to OBI meant for the subsequent careers of the municipal representatives. One conjecture had it that an assignment to OBI was tantamount to "banishment to an island prison colony" (*shimanagashi*), although one returned official reassured me that he had faced no subsequent promotion problems at all. Few researchers offered general opinions about city officials, but the ones I heard contrasted the challenge and creativity of the scientists' life with the perceived humdrum of oiling bureaucratic machinery. A young postdoc commented: "You ever notice those people downstairs, how they actually look older than their real ages? That comes from doing the same old job every day."

That opinion on the effects of routine was patently outlandish, but the postdoc correctly sensed a lack of zest. Most of the City workers had a difficult time answering my interview question about what they enjoyed most in their work at OBI. One would never guess that they were at the scene of research in sleep regulation, cold light from proteins, and cellular death. I believe their lackluster answers resulted more from their being assigned from above than from their office routines *per se*.

National problems in microcosm

Informants reached in 1996 said that disagreements between City representatives and OBI's researchers were neither as frequent nor as serious as in OBI's early days. OBI's scientist–official relations were particularly difficult in the Institute's early years. There were no precedents for the first group of administrators sent from the City or the scientists to whom they were assigned, and spending patterns had yet to stabilize. Perhaps symbolic of smoother edges, the large "No Trespassing" sign in front has been replaced by a far more diminutive sign requesting that those without OBI business refrain from entering the grounds.

Nevertheless, the relationship between OBI's scientists and the City would surely be repeated in any other newly minted regional institute for basic science research. Some inkling of OBI's relevance for other regional initiatives appears in a report from another pioneering attempt. The University of Aizu is a new university of computer science formed with support from Fukushima Prefecture. It features such innovations as term appointments and review for tenure and boasts ample electronic equipment, perhaps the most of any school in Japan. But "the power rests with the bureaucrats from the Fukushima Prefecture Government," according to a foreign faculty member, who said also that the innovative university president's efforts have been "hamstrung by the way things have been done here" (Pollack 1994).

The situation at OBI strongly resembled the problem-laden pattern set by Tokyo's ministries' dealings with scientists: the top-down, short-term assignment of nonspecialists from a multifunctioned agency. In contrast with the United States, where PhD holders administer the distribution of scientific funds, the administration of science in Japan falls overwhelmingly to laypeople. The most striking case is the Ministry of Education, which has not developed in-house expertise in the problems of academic research, either by recruitment or on-the-job training and education. There are no holders of PhD degrees among the Ministry's staff, so administrators who deal with academic researchers have no research experience in those fields. Of course, an advanced degree in the sciences does not guarantee administration that is more effective at serving the needs of competitive research scientists. It does, however, increase the chances that administrators will require less explanation of scientists' needs and problems and will identify with their goals, having experienced the frustrations and exhilaration of research.

Scientists in the United States may take their specialist administrators for granted, and American administrators of my acquaintance approach the issue with modesty; one National Science Foundation program director referred to his PhD in botany as his "union card." The popular science career writer Carl Sindermann, however, laid out American scientists' sentiments succinctly: "Professionals within a research organization do not want funding and management decisions that affect them to be in the hands of accountants or ribbon clerks" (1985: 106). In the Ministry of Education, the degree that best situates an entry-level employee for success is a baccalaureate in law from the University of Tokyo. The typical curriculum in a Japanese university law faculty mixes public administration and political science with the coverage of legal codes and concepts, according to observer Ivan Hall; the experience results in "a more narrowly focused intellectual background, and a greater national-interest-oriented zeal" among Japanese officialdom than in the United States (1998: 22). Entry at the BA level allows the Ministry to place its new members on the first rung of the seniority ladder – indeed, one Japanese specialist in his country's science organization pointed out that a PhD holder would be disadvantaged in the seniority scale.

The Ministry's rotation system further frustrates the cultivation of expertise in administering scientific research. Members of its Bureau of Higher Education (Kōtō Kyōikukyoku) and International Arts and Sciences Bureau (Gakujutsu Kokusaikyoku), the units responsible for university education and research support, are rotated in and out on a regular basis every two years as standard Ministry practice. In one case reminiscent of the OBI administrator sent to the United States to learn about research administration, an MOE administrator of my acquaintance was accepted into the United States' National Science Foundation for a year-long study visit. After returning to Japan from a year of interning in a world center of science policy and research administration, he was rotated into Special Education (a section for primary school children with learning disabilities).

Nor does competence in scientific administration reap any particular career rewards for the MOE functionary. Like the multifaceted government of Osaka City, MOE has many activities and constituents. Its operations reach down to pre-schools for 4 year olds, and its employees are trained to know the organization more than a highly specialized area like administration of basic science. The sprawl is exemplified by the Ministry's Gakkō Kihon Chōsa (basic survey of schools), which covers the gamut of statistics from female university admissions to kindergarten enrollments.

Academic specialists in science policy reassured me that stints in science administration were not career liabilities, as some younger Japanese scientists suspected. (MOE's Gulag was Life-Long Learning.) In terms of money and attention, however, the Ministry of Education's first priority lies in primary and secondary education. In the early 1990s, the Ministry's total research budget represented less than a tenth of its outlay for school lunches (Maddox and Swinbanks 1992: 577). The former NSF intern from MOE was not disturbed by his assignment to Special Education on his return; on the contrary, that and his subsequent moves advanced his career in the most promising of Ministry trajectories. When I met him again several years later he had risen through the ranks, and his biggest concern had become the rate of dropouts among high school students.

Distinguished senior Japanese scientists such as Saburo Nagakura, former president of the Chemical Society of Japan, and Yoshiro Shimura, his fellow member of the Japan Academy and former member of MOE's Science Council, had expressed their own opinion to me that there should be more career scientist expertise in the ministries. Koji Nakanishi (the director of the Suntory Institute for Bioorganic Research introduced in Chapter 2) registered strongly his own concern about the lack of scientific expertise in government science agencies in several articles (1983; 1991). A division chief at OBI echoed Nakanishi's dissatisfaction:

> Often, right off the bat, the new person from the Ministry will say, "I don't know anything about matters involving research, so I beg your understanding." Well, it's honest, but on the other hand we're tempted to ask, "Then why haven't you studied it!?"

The OBI division chief was expressing his frustration that, after educating a government representative, his research group eventually had to deal with a new individual who needed the same explanations.

The Ministry of Education would rebut this kind of criticism by describing its reliance on university faculty as advisors and deliberative council members (*kagakukan* and *shingikaiin*) for the necessary expertise. The rejoinder is less than satisfactory. Advisors do not take part in program execution, so they do not deal with matters ranging from grant application format to budget timetables to travel reimbursement. Also, there is some question of how independent of the Ministry these advisors are. My informants were rather skeptical of the practice as a source of independent academic expertise; they believed that the consulting academics were invariably in the over-50 age group, and were hand-picked to agree with existing Ministry of Education policy. That appraisal echoes a biotechnology policy analyst, who wrote that the ministries have cultivated long-term "advisory" roles in biotechnology policy for older professors from the elite universities, who "may well be ... the ones with a predisposition towards legitimizing a ministry's position" (Brock 1989: 23–4).

My depiction of an inwardly oriented officialdom seconded by compliant senior academics requires some qualification. In one instance recounted by Saburo Nagakura, academic advisors proved more conservative than their government counterparts. In the mid-1980s he floated the proposal for replacing each kōza assistant with two or three postdocs before his fellow members of Monbusho's Science Council. The director general of the Science and International Affairs Bureau responsible for science promotion responded positively, but Nagakura's academic colleagues representing medical and engineering schools roundly rejected the idea, saying that it would discourage talented individuals from seeking university careers.

Signs of bureaucratic management

Perhaps the strongest marks of bureaucratic management in Japanese science appear in the dominant forms of resource allocation: seniority-based salaries and uniform research unit budgets. Those features were in Ken-ichi Arai's mind when he wrote critically that

> The kōza system comes equipped with deeply imbued hallmarks of bureaucracy: within each kōza [is] the vertical society, with permanent employment that lacks mobility, and among kōza an unassailable equality. Under the kōza system, from the professor to research staff, is the public functionary's position classification system to which all are bound as national civil servants. (1996b: 6)

The hierarchy among universities, in which the University of Tokyo stands at the pinnacle and the others fall in order beneath without regard to specific academic specialties, also fits a bureaucratic agenda by greatly simplifying management of the scientific enterprise. The allocation of SRF funds in small amounts to many recipients makes bureaucratic sense as well: the practice generates impressive numbers of cases and offers something to a substantial percentage of the academic community without forcing hard decisions. How unruly by comparison is the dynamic of a robust credit cycle, in which recognized elites and dark horse contenders vie for serious money in peer-reviewed competition.

Science historian Shigeru Nakayama also diagnosed the Ministry of Education's management of Japanese universities as bureaucratic, noting their design and execution of programs with accounting rules uppermost. Yearly SRF allocations, he observed, have followed the governmental budgeting schedule, not the scientist's: funds are not distributed until autumn but must be spent before the fiscal year ends on March 31 of the next year, so the researcher must spend his or her allocation within a few months' time. Some forms of seasonal research, as in agricultural sciences, are "quite impossible" under that regimen (1991: 70). The researchers would evidently agree; a 1997 survey found government and university researchers ranking "flexibility of funding" highest among nine factors for a "desirable research environment" (reported in STA 1998: 99).

My portrayal of universities and the SRF in Chapter 2 posed many opportunities for administrative reform. There are other problems that suggest a bureaucracy out of touch with scientists, at the expense of the credit cycle and efficient spending as well. The Ministry of Education recommended in 1991 that each university conduct self-evaluations. Yasuo Kagawa, biochemist and educator, described the exercise as "harmless and non-committal," using criteria like faculty size – an approach he likened to "an evaluation of a biochemist by his body weight" (1993a: 135). Kagawa blamed the ineffectuality, however, on inexperience and a "gentle" national character (a subject taken up in Chapter 9).

Because they sense that the ministries are not spending money optimally and lack confidence in decisions regarding grant awards, the scientists with whom I have been communicating have had a very anxious reaction to the substantial spending increases that I briefly described in Chapter 1. Koji Nakanishi (introduced in Chapter 2) was distressed at the kind of abundance he has seen in the last few years. In the summer of 1996, Science and Technology Agency representatives visited him on seventeen occasions with questions on how to spend the recent surge in funding. He related plans to inject some one million dollars yearly into each of 70 laboratories for each of five years, resulting in considerable funding to 350 laboratories. He doubted that there were that many laboratories worth supporting at that level.

In 1998, Koji Nakanishi visited six universities, in two cases as a member of an external review committee for their departments of chemistry. He saw "superb" physical equipment, particularly large instruments such as nuclear magnetic resonance equipment. He was not optimistic that the magnificent equipment would take Japan to the forefront in such areas as spectroscopy, however, fearing instead "the illusion that expensive instruments lead directly to break-through research results." The lack of highly trained personnel – operation of the instrumentation is left to graduate students and postdocs –

and proper siting for installation will frustrate the development and application of technique.

Foreign researchers in universities and national laboratories have also criticized spending priorities that shortchange or exclude maintenance budgets for equipment or the necessary wiring. Said an American at a MITI laboratory:

> At my university in the United States we wrote maintenance into our grants, so the centrifuges next to Professor H's office were always humming beautifully. Go to a lab here and you'll see ultracentrifuges with just a few years' vintage out in the hall with a serviceable malfunction. But they can't hire service people, so they buy a new one with a grant for equipment. And they can't throw the old one out because it's got one of those government serial numbers on it and someone might check inventory. So you have a hallway that's a goddam museum of equipment.

Japanese scientists with whom I talked in 1996 wondered aloud at how all of the new equipment purchases would fit into the limited laboratory space. They summed their fears in the expression "science bubble," referring to the overheated "bubble" Japanese economy that receded dramatically in 1990. They worried that all the high-profile shower of money, without discerning spending through an effective evaluation system, would come to naught in five years or so, and the public and politicians would say, "We've poured money into you: where are the Nobel Prizes?" In 1998, with Japan's economy in crisis, they were yet more anxious and yet more distrustful of the ways in which research money has been allocated.

Handling outsiders

Just as OBI's City-based administrators hindered the inflow of "outsider" researchers at the Institute, the national bureaucracy has frustrated attempts to involve foreign researchers in Japanese laboratories. The majority of Japanese scientists themselves do want foreign colleagues in their midst. The 1990 Japan Science Council survey found nearly three fourths of the academicians in the natural sciences agreeing that foreigners should be hired as instructors or researchers (JSC 1991: 35). Scientists have also taken to domestic public fora to call for more foreigners in the laboratory (Hashizume and Kamiya 1997; Kamiya 1996; Kagawa n.d.; Yanagida 1996a). These are discussions among Japanese and not image building for foreign observers.

Why Japanese scientists would want to welcome foreign colleagues is just as important as the sentiment itself. One line of thought among Japanese scientists prescribes foreigners as an antidote for indigenous inadequacies like thought monotony and over-regimentation (Anderson 1992b: 569). Another approach, however, identifies the recruitment of foreigners as one aspect of the larger need for open recruitment with talent as the determining criterion – a borderless credit cycle arena. My PERI questionnaire respondents had raised the issue of hiring foreign researchers spontaneously, as a corollary of their assertion that PERI should improve its selection of researchers by hiring with more impersonal, merit-based methods. Although JSC survey respondents put forth the predictable arguments for exchanges of "revitalizing" the universities and "advancing international exchange in research," they also wrote that the issue in academic hiring "should not be hiring 'foreigners,' but individuals with research ability better than Japanese researchers'" (JSC 1991: 137).

The statements of Ken-ichi Arai follow the same vein: for obtaining top talent, recruit without regard to country (or sex, as we will see in the next chapter). The subhead for an editorial in the *Asahi Shimbun* by Tokyo Institute of Technology sociologist Daisaburō Hashizume (1996) argued zestfully: "Break out of the Octopus Trap, Introduce the Principle of Competition, Seek Excellent Talent, Open Research Posts to the World." Hashizume's colleague, RIKEN plant pathologist Yuji Kamiya, conversely observed that the discussion of "openization" (*ōpunka*) of positions for foreigners inevitably led him to see the necessity of recruiting Japanese researchers "fairly, with the principle of competition" (1996).

The actual number of Western foreigners in Japanese laboratories disappoints these aspirations. (Asian countries send more researchers to Japan, among them highly talented individuals, but their organizations have yet to accomplish what the West has in competitive research output.) In 1993 there were 122 Americans in Japanese R&D settings, 102 of them at universities, representing less than 17 per cent of the number of Japanese at work on research in the United States. Including researchers from other industrialized countries in the equation improved the ratio, but it still stood at only one Westerner entering a Japanese laboratory for every three Japanese doing research abroad (Hall 1998: 126).

Perhaps the most fundamental obstacle for attracting foreign researchers from any country to Japan is the nature of the ministries' policy regarding foreign research talent: hire on short term only. Yuji Kamiya recounted attempts to recruit topnotch research talent at international conferences for his plant hormone research team; he was "left at a loss" when asked whether permanent positions were available to foreign researchers (1996). His own home institution, RIKEN (under the aegis of the Science and Technology Agency) had no positions occupied by foreigners to which he could point. Ministry of Education policy effectively excludes foreigners from occupying tenured positions in the nation's universities. Only in 1982 did the law allow universities to provide foreigners with the same terms of employment as Japanese, but unlike the tenure automatically accorded Japanese appointments, foreigners could be hired on short-term contracts.

Ten years later, the Ministry of Education began systematically purging foreign staff in the more senior university ranks as an economizing move (JPRI Staff 1996).

The problem in accommodating foreign researchers that was most frequently cited in the 1990 JSC survey was "difficulty in securing living expenses," with which 72 per cent of respondents agreed. That issue is of course a matter of governmental priorities for allocating resources, as is the second most frequently cited problem, "difficulty in securing housing," chosen by 56 per cent of the respondents. (There were five answers offered as obstacles to accepting foreign researchers and students, in a multiple answer format.) Both of these answers match nicely the problems I had heard over years of discussions with foreign researchers and their hosts. One other survey response, however, qualifies my depiction of scientists at cross purposes with bureaucrats; the majority of the academics surveyed failed to appreciate the problem of secure employment for foreigners. "Difficulty in obtaining secure status" drew acknowledgment from less than a third (31 per cent) of respondents. At least such insensitivity did not signal cultural inflexibility or xenophobia; "differences in viewpoints and customs, including ways of thinking about research" was the least frequently cited problem, garnering less than 18 per cent of respondents' agreement (JSC 1991: 163).

A subtle but nevertheless corrosive element also resides in the different set of motives at the administrative level for greater international scientific cooperation. My impression is that the public relations motive for internationalizing Japan's laboratories grows as one scales the administrative ladder, in inverse proportion to understanding of bench level collegial needs and desires. In contrast to the individual Japanese researcher's wish for stimulating engagement, policy makers and functionaries – where the programs originate and are executed – are stimulated by a pressure for reform that originates outside the country. Indeed, the term "internationalization" (*kokusaika*) came into vogue among policy makers in the mid-1980s as a response to mounting trade friction with the West. Particularly since long-term positions in academia and government laboratories are beyond the reach of foreigners, the resulting program initiatives smack of a century-old Japanese approach to foreign intellectual talent that intimate Japan critic Ivan Hall aptly characterized as "excessively instrumental, while minimally engaged" (1998: 123).

Foreign researchers feel the effects of such motives. When a 1994 survey of foreign scientists asked them why they thought their host institutions had admitted them, 66 of the 114 respondents answered, "to experiment with 'internationalization'" (Japan Techno-Economics Society 1994: 90; it was the most frequently chosen of seven answers, in multiple answer format.) One respondent volunteered: "Scientists should not be invited as 'symbols' of KOKUSAIKA but rather to develop exchanges and enhance the level of activity in Japanese laboratories. The Japanese experience is very stimulating for foreigners and should benefit BOTH sides ..." (Japan Techno-Economics Society 1994: 172; capital letters in original).

There are, of course, other obstacles to realizing a borderless credit cycle besides these administrative shortcomings. Language problems cannot be ignored. They posed a persistent drag on communication at PERI and OBI that required stamina from host and visitor alike. Even rudimentary information like the location of needed reagents and the correct disposal procedure for contaminants typically came to the foreign researchers piecemeal through halting speech from Japanese labmates, to the chagrin of both sides. In the JSC survey, "language differences" ranked third among the seven obstacles, chosen by just under 40 per cent of respondents (1991: 163). Chapter 9 discusses the language problem further.

The tight hierarchy of the Japanese laboratory also stands in the way of more international collegiality. The control of their career fates from above compels Japanese researchers to turn their eyes upward to the "boss" rather than outward to the visitor. Combined with the language obstacle, this tendency could explain the dissatisfaction with collegial dialogue registered by over a third of the 114 foreign researchers in Japan responding to the 1994 survey (Japan Techno-Economics Society 1994: 88). I believe these same factors could explain the disappointment that a former OBI researcher expressed regarding interactions with foreigners at OBI when he complained that "Foreign scholars and Japanese scientists did not mix very well, not only in everyday life but more importantly in science." Both of the suspected causes are susceptible to reform. Administrative initiative could ameliorate the language problem, as Chapter 9 argues, and a viable credit cycle would minimize laboratory hierarchy.

Centralization, privilege, and power

The power of Japan's government officials over scientists aggravates the ill effects of the gap between their career paths and concerns and those of scientists'. Chapter 1 noted that bureaucratic officialdom in Japan wields more power and enjoys more insulation from scrutiny than the bureaucracies of Western nations. The Ministry of Education's administrative prerogatives are no exception. With few exceptions, the Ministry does not make public the names of project evaluators, and there is no appeal process for applicants who believe their SRF proposals were rejected unfairly. Nor is the Ministry required as a government agency to release its documents on request, because the Japanese government does not give its citizens the right to gain access to its records (as in the Freedom of Information Act in the United States and similar laws in Europe).

Funding for basic research in Japan is concentrated in national government hands. Gifts to any of the national universities from industry private or public sources must pass through the "Special Account," so that, in one analyst's words, "fund distribution is uniformly controlled by Monbusho" (Kobayashi 1992: 207). The country's tax code limits deductions for philanthropic gifts far more than does the United States', and tax-exempt status requires passing through the Ministry of Finance's "intricate, red tape-laden approval system" (Wanner 1997: 3). The government's role in controlling research money is not lost on bioscientists: as a prominent immunologist succinctly observed to me, "They'd rather tax gifts and control the money themselves." The national government's approach would not easily accommodate a system of overhead costs in research grants, in which a portion of the local research institution's ongoing administrative and maintenance costs are included in the total budget of each grant awarded the institution. Although the concept has been introduced to the academic policy community (Yamamoto 1992), as of the mid-1990s only one university has adopted the practice (Kinoshita 1996b: 47).

A subordinated private nonprofit sector

Japan has no equivalent of the prestigious and influential Rockefeller Foundation or Howard Hughes Foundation for scientific research – much less Britain's Wellcome Trust, which rivals the Medical Research Council in funding influence (*Science* 1992b). There are some 210 foundations that support research, and the areas of support most favored are science and engineering (and medical research in particular; Kato 1992: 6). Their grand total of awards in those areas, however, amounts to less than 9 per cent of the SRF total (calculated using 1989 figures in Kato 1991: 294). Science and society lore claims that Japan's academic scientists shun money from the private sector as a reaction to university collaboration with industry in Japan's war effort of the 1930s and 1940s. There was no wall of resistance among respondents to the 1990 JSC survey, though; three fourths agreed that universities should welcome contributions for research from the private sector (1991: 157).

Private foundations play a far smaller public service role in Japan than in the United States, with far less societal influence. Estimates of the total number of nonprofit entities vary between 21,000 and 25,000, but very few – by the most liberal estimate, 15 per cent – make grants (London 1991: 31n.16; Deguchi 1994: 6; a simple calculation based on figures in Deguchi 1994 would yield only 4 per cent). In 1989, the twenty largest foundations in Japan granted only about 6 per cent of the funds disbursed in grants by their American counterparts (Jankowski 1993: 15).

This anemic position results from the central government's measures to maintain its centralized authority and control funding. The government will not allow the establishment of any nonprofit foundation or association (including industry research institutes) without its permission, which requires approval from each of the ministries to which the organization's planned activities may relate. Procedures for establishing a foundation vary widely from ministry to ministry (London 1991: 30, 39), and the process requires resources far beyond those of ordinary citizens (Deguchi 1994: 7). OBI was fortunate in this regard; since the Institute was administered by a regional government, it did not need to have supervision under one of the national government's ministries. (OBI also had charters of recognition from the Ministry of Education and the Science and Technology Agency that qualified it to receive research funds from both of them.)

The relationship between government and private foundations is more than close: their functions and personnel merge. Government initiative typically lies behind legislation that creates nonreligious private organizations in Japan, as opposed to private sector initiatives. More than one out of seven nonprofit organizations is established by government agencies directly, and receives both government subsidies and obligatory funds from companies (Deguchi 1994: 7). The required affiliation with a government ministry or agency also provides a doorway for sinecures in the foundations for retired government officials (known as *amakudari*, literally "descended from heaven") from the concerned ministry or ministries. The blur between foundation and government could explain the corporate representatives' argument that they had "already paid taxes" when they were asked to contribute to OBI's cause.

The cost to a viable reward system

Private foundations realize their greatest potential when they support unfashionable or particularly high-risk work by unknown researchers whom large government agencies do not help. An excellent example comes from the John Douglas French Alzheimer's Foundation in the United States. A small foundation that prides itself on supporting areas of research that government agencies tend not to fund, it provided crucial support for Stanley Prusiner's controversial work on infectious particles that won him the Nobel Prize in Medicine in 1997 (French Foundation brochure; Monmaney 1997). The private foundations in Japan do not provide an alternative to the government in this regard, nor do they broaden the pool of deserving players. Their pattern of awards duplicates the SRF: the big winners are researchers at the former imperial universities who have received SRF support (Kato 1992).

Attempts to investigate the research roles of Japan's philanthropic foundations have found these organizations less than forthcoming in relating their activities. Past surveys on grant-making foundations have come up short on such essential information as particulars of the content of awards, methods of recruiting candidates, and criteria for judging applications (Kato 1991: 283). This hole in performance accountability makes Japan's foundation system a drain on the resources needed for a vigorous credit cycle.

The hierarchical dimension in scientist–functionary relations

Japan's scientists are recognizably subordinate to their lay managers. There is an important complaint about power behind Ken-ichi Arai's reference to the "public functionary's position classification" that includes national university faculties as "civil servants." Unlike the teaching staff at state universities in the United States, who are also government employees, national university faculties in Japan find themselves in the lower ranks of a chain of command under the Ministry of Education. Various academic self-governance mechanisms obscure the relationship, but at its core are the Ministry's power of financial decision making and its assignment of administrative staff to each national university.

Sometimes the power dimension of the relationship surfaces in minor but irritating regulations. A newly arrived associate professor at a second-tier national university who needed to move in his research supplies found that he had to file a request to use the elevators in his building. A far more telling illustration of MOE power and its use in university administration surfaced in MOE's 1992 directive to eliminate senior foreign staff at its universities: it was communicated by telephone, giving MOE representatives the opportunity to deny that they had ever issued it (JPRI Staff 1996: 1).

Some scientists expressed the belief that public criticism of MOE would bring them retribution in the form of reduced funding. An associate professor at the Medical College believed that punishment for criticism would be visited on the kôza head: "If a young researcher complains, MOE people would say, 'who's your boss?' we'll make sure he doesn't get any SRF. It's 'mud in the [professor's] face.'" After a mid-career scientist at a major university wrote an article in an international journal critical of SRF and its execution, a colleague told him that he was on a MOE "blacklist." (He shrugged it off, noting that his MOE funding was "excellent.") Conjecture that MOE wields its power of the purse for its own ends has also made its way into the popular magazine *AERA*. In a 1996 article, *AERA* investigated retiring MOE administrators' attempts to occupy university faculty positions at Shizuoka and Hiroshima Universities over the open opposition of academics there. An accompanying cartoon, reproduced in Figure 6.1, likens the move to a World War II air raid; the US bombers are marked with different ministry names, and the klaxon is blaring "Amakudari alert!" The article's author noted that "anyone could imagine back room deals and bargaining" in a scramble for funds, given the ceiling on the government's total university budget and hard fiscal times (Takaya 1996: 69).

Room for resentment

I have encountered various stripes of resentment toward officialdom among both reformers and youthful researchers. Ken-Ichi Arai prescribes "sweeping

Figure 6.1 "Amakudari Alert" (Illustration by Norio Yamanoi, courtesy Asahi
  Shimbunsha *AERA* 23 December 1996)

away the abuse of officials' power," among other measures, to construct new
and better career paths for youthful scientists (1996b: 1). His use of the phrase
"abuse of official power" (*kanson minpi*) strikes an historical chord. It more
literally means "revere the officials, despise the people." The pithy four-
character phrase arose in the Meiji Period, when the government formulated
a generous dose of self-serving authoritarian measures along with widespread
initiatives to catch up with the West. Arai has a lively interest in the history of
his own institute, IMSUT, which had originated in 1892 as a nonprofit
institution, the Institute of Infectious Diseases. In 1914 the Ministry of
Education absorbed it into the University of Tokyo, which prompted the
resignation in protest of its Director, the brilliant toxicologist Shibasaburo
Kitasato. One of Kitasato's objections was prescient: the move would damage

research because the university separated basic and clinical medicine (Bartholomew 1989: 202).

"Abuse of official power" still means something to Japanese scientists. The phrase brings back a particularly visceral memory for Koji Nakanishi from his early days as Director of the Suntory Institute for Bioorganic Research. At the time of its inception in 1946, the institute was named the Institute of Food Science Research (Shokuhin Kagaku Kenkyûjo), reflecting the country's understandable concern with malnutrition. Well before 1979, when Nakanishi became its director, the institute's name had become an anachronism. Changing the name of the institute required MOE approval, however (recall the ministerial supervision requirement for all nonprofits). Nakanishi, accompanied by a member of the Suntory Board of Directors, called on the designated section chief at MOE.

Approval of the new name, said the official, would have to await review by higher-ups because "bioorganic" was a new word that he could not find in his dictionary. Nor did the functionary grace the interaction with perfunctory signs of respect, much less Japanese protocols of business interaction. Throughout the meeting he sat with crossed legs, propped in front of him on his desk. Glancing at Nakanishi's business card, he asked if Nakanishi had tenure – a supremely obtuse question, since the card displayed Nakanishi's named professorship at Columbia, Centennial Professor of Chemistry. The Suntory board member, seeing Nakanishi's face darken, averted a confrontation by tapping frantically on the back of Nakanishi's suit jacket.

I have not systematically studied the attitudes of my own subject researchers toward national government officials, in part because few whom I had sampled were in positions high enough to involve negotiations with ministerial representatives. Several informants revealed a trace of hostility, though, in their ironic view that MOE officials were members of the country's least prestigious Ministry (in their eyes) but were placed over highly educated scientists. If the topic of the ministries' expectations of scientists came up in discussion, my informants were likely to say that either raw numbers of publications or work resembling the latest vogue in the West were officialdom's only criterion of successful research.

The fractionation of government life science programs

Life scientists are probably among the most critical members of Japan's research community regarding government scientific research policy and administration. Biomedical fields there lack a badly needed interdisciplinarity and coordination of resources and regulations, and the recognition of far superior research in the United States only sharpens these feelings of organizational inadequacy. Japan has no funding body that provides comprehensive support of bioscience research like the United States' National

Institutes of Health and National Science Foundation, or the United Kingdom's Medical Research Council. Three government agencies besides the Ministry of Education and the Ministry of Agriculture fund research in the life sciences: the Science and Technology Agency, the Ministry of Health and Welfare, and the Ministry of International Trade and Industry. Unlike the United States, where NIH formulated guidelines in the 1970s for experiments involving recombinant DNA and kept its policy-making structure intact to deal with subsequent issues in gene therapy, each ministry in Japan has formulated its own recombinant DNA guidelines. When gene therapy and associated problems arrived on the scene, MHW created yet another deliberative body to create policy. Such moves have been criticized domestically as a "patchwork" response (IHEP 1996: 31–2).

This fractioning represents a duplication of effort in program development and administration. There may be a stimulating element from competition, as some observers claim, but the prevailing lack of cooperation among ministries (known as "vertical administration," *tatewari gyōsei*) makes it difficult for researchers at one ministry's facilities to accept funding or equipment from another ministry. Also, scientists' affiliations with one ministry discourage them from cooperating with scientists sponsored by another ministry. Hence the diplomatically phrased complaint from the life scientists in the Japan Science Council's natural sciences division that, although the country's various bioscience initiatives have had some effect, "It is hard to say that adequate coordination and cooperation is taking place" among them (1988: 172). The division of authority between ministries that takes the greatest toll on research progress is the split between MOE, which oversees-medical school education, and MHW, which assumes responsibility for clinical practice, deepening the cleft between clinicians and researchers in Japan's medical schools as described in Chapter 2.

Even relations between OBI and PERI may have been affected, in some subtle fashion, by their separate affiliations. (Although OBI was independent of ministry jurisdiction, it was perceived by many as an MOE affiliate.) Aside from individual or adventitious arrangements (like Hiroyuki Toh's initiative, or OBI's agreement to handle laboratory animals for PERI), there were no systematic efforts to get the two institutes' researchers to communicate with each other. Granted, many interinstitutional collegial arrangements in the United States have far less substance in day-to-day collaboration than promotional descriptions would have us believe. Nevertheless, these two institutes were separated spatially by no more than a few hundred meters of back yard.

An organizational remedy

In my hypothetical world for OBI, I would heal the rift between the two cultures of scientist and government representative by populating the downstairs office with people who sought out their jobs to satisfy their fascination with basic science and its practitioners, and to gratify their sense that they were seconding a very worthwhile effort. If future organizational attempts like OBI and the University of Aizu could devise a way to fill their administrative ranks with people who better understood and appreciated the scientific enterprise, the organization would be taking a sizeable step in the direction of genuine regional reform of research organization. Such an attempt in Osaka, however, would run into the same stumbling block seen among the national level ministries: science administration is one cog in a larger apparatus with other priorities.

Behind my prescription here is an ideal of placing people in slots requiring specialized knowledge and interest for which they have prepared enthusiastically. Those are aspects of the credit cycle. It is not hard to imagine credentials that reflect expertise and accomplishment in the management of science, either. In the past the national ministries have produced interesting pockets of protected expertise like the Population Problems Research Institute (Jinkō Mondai Kenkyūjo) in MHW. (Its research staff were not rotated out, and several of its directors have held doctorates, the most recent in sociology from the University of Michigan.) Engineers had fought for and won posts with authority in the Ministry of Construction in the 1910s (Nakayama 1991: 87–8). Chapter 8 conjectures on the chances that such a development may reoccur for basic science researchers.

OBI lives on

OBI celebrated its tenth anniversary in October of 1997. In mid-1998 it was hosting forty-two regular and part-time research staff (excluding assistants) and eighty-three research collaborators. It preserved its four-department structure also. (The Department of "Enzymes and Metabolism" was renamed "Molecular Behavioral Biology," and the "Cell Biology" department was renamed "Molecular Medical Science.") OBI's creators have given it another ten-year lease on life, and as the century ends there are no signs that it will be pushed into applied research. In its written statement, the prestigious seven-member committee (introduced in the last chapter) endorsed the Institute's commitment to basic research in biomedical science, and encouraged invitations to outside researchers.

OBI's reliance on the City of Osaka for much of its operating costs has changed little over the years, representing 84 per cent of the Institute's income in the 1997 budget. Perhaps OBI's accomplishments and its ten-year-old tradition of dependence have solidified its bid for City resources. The City of Osaka had reportedly wanted for OBI's next Director someone who, like Osamu Hayaishi, had a high international profile. They succeeded. Hidesaburo Hanafusa was a chaired professor at Rockefeller University who had attained a very high level of recognition and acclaim worldwide for his research in viral oncology. (Among his honors was a prestigious Lasker Award, which he received in 1982.)

The national university pedigrees of OBI's new director and division chiefs may be sufficient reason to expect continued support from the City and expanded funding from national government sources, particularly if the latter's pool of research money grows as expected. The special seven-member panel authorized to chart the Institute's future termed the support the "base" revenue source, but warned that increasing research costs would have to be borne from other sources.

Shortly before his retirement from the directorship in 1998, Osamu Hayaishi offered a retrospective.

> When I started, the mayor gave me a completely free hand. Whatever I needed money for, he said he'd provide it, and leave the rest up to me. I had a lot of good people giving me advice, too. My closest friends, though, told me I was too idealistic. I was "Don Quixote." I've said before that this is the biggest experiment of my life. I've had times when there were troubles and I worried a lot about what I was doing. I've had to repeatedly explain and justify OBI to government people and the subsequent mayor. But, anything I would have done differently? No, I have no regrets.

If the national government were to provide a professional niche for science administrators and decentralize the resources related to research funding, Hidesaburo Hanafusa could spend less time explaining and justifying OBI to government people, and OBI could play an even more dynamic role in creating talented scientists.

7

GENDER

A laboratory produces its best results when its researchers are recruited and rewarded purely on the basis of their ability and performance. The assertion sounds rhetorical, but it ensues simply as a logical corollary of the credit cycle concept that has guided our study of Japanese science. The political economics of every industrial society skews its scientific community's recruitment and reward process away from pure credit cycle dynamics to some degree, resulting in various drains on talent. Sex discrimination may well be the most costly drain worldwide. The case of Japan's life science community lends particular weight to that suspicion, since women participate in large numbers but encounter severe obstacles to career formation. As organizational experiments in mobility, OBI and PERI have hosted women researchers whose competence and tenaciousness challenge the commonly held perception that Japanese women are passive and expendable commodities in the professional workplace.

Women's participation in the life sciences

Japanese society is perceived abroad as quite sexist, and much of the reputation is well earned. What concerns us first, however, are two more specific issues: the woman life scientist's experience, and the prospects for a decrease in sex bias. Japanese bioscience does not exclude women from its everyday life; it would be hard to find a life science laboratory in Japan completely devoid of them. A third of the members of the Food Research Institute's Division of Food Physics and Chemistry were women. (The Medical College's biochemistry department had the lowest proportion of women, who comprised only two out of nineteen staff members.) Some 20 per cent of the 15,000-member Japanese Biochemical Society membership is female, also. Almost half of the total staff at OBI and PERI were women, but their OBI and PERI members perceived that as an unusually large proportion.

Women in Japanese science gravitate toward the life sciences. PERI's researchers represented a range of scientific specialties, among them physics and computer science, but the women researchers, like the technicians, were recruited into the bioscience area of research. This pattern also resembled the nationwide proportion of women among researchers in these specialties. As of the early 1990s, about 14 per cent of Japan's life science researchers and 13 per cent of medical and dental researchers were female, but mathematics and the physical and chemical sciences claimed less than half that percentage (Endo et al. 1993: 21). Similar biases exist in the West, though not so acutely. The appeal of the life sciences to Japanese women would look familiar to Westerners; a survey among Japanese high school science majors, for example, found girls expressing more concern than boys in "living things" (*seibutsu*) and "human life" (*jinsei*), and less inclination toward investigating theoretical principles (Endo et al. 1993: 15). (Among my interviewees with PhD degrees, however, there were no discernible differences between men's and women's accounts of how they first became interested in science.)

Much of the work of women in bioscience lies in the manipulation of materials – the "wet" end of the process, as Westerners call it – in contrast to the pencil-and-paper theorizing in mathematics and theoretical physics on the other end of the brain–hand continuum. Monthly meetings at PERI made visual testimony to the arrangement: the women invariably wore white lab coats – practical attire for working at the bench – and they sat in the rear of the lecture hall or near the entrance so they could leave the room to tend to timed bench processes and reenter without disturbing other audience members.

The women technicians in all of the laboratories I visited also handled messages from outside, and were best at knowing where anyone was at any time. They also provided some smooth edges for the rigid atmosphere of experimental work, by drawing amusing artistic embellishments on bulletin boards or laying out snacks of regional delicacies brought back by lab members who had traveled out of town. The role of coffee and tea server – that flashpoint in the redefinition of women's work roles in the United States – fell to them as well, although at PERI men also took turns at stocking and tidying the coffee tray.

The biggest problem of gender in Japanese bioscience is the underrepresentation or total absence of women among senior researchers and administrators, and overrepresentation in the lower ranks of technical assistance staff. At the time of my field work, women accounted for less than 2 per cent of the professoriate in the natural sciences in Japan's universities (Endo et al. 1993: 28), and women scientists in administrative positions were a rarity. In this regard, PERI and OBI did not depart from the status quo. With one exception (at OBI), all of the technical support staff at every one of my research sites were female. The ratio of females dropped steeply as status rose. Out of twelve (native Japanese) OBI postdoctoral fellows three were female; among the nine regular researchers, only one was female, and none of the six department chiefs and their assistant chiefs was a woman. Women were absent from PERI's administrative ranks as well. There was only one woman each among the industry and academic researchers at PERI. Few women enjoy promotion in the larger society also; in 1995, women accounted for 41 per cent of all employees in Japan but less than 3 per cent of chief clerks (*kakarichō*, the first step to section chief; Takahashi 1998: 7).

Female = temporary

Among those assembled at PERI and OBI, the technicians held the most tenuous positions. The technicians at OBI were limited to two-year contracts, without renewal, and PERI's technicians were hired on one-year renewable contracts via a company that acted as a subcontracting agency for their labor. (The arrangement was known as "talent dispatch," *jinzai haken*.) This short-term dimension was not just a function of nonprofessional work content: it was a feature of female labor. As one PERI administrator explained, the arrangement was meant for hiring women, due to PERI's "uncertain future." He had simply assumed that women were appropriate for positions having this unattractive dimension.

Japan's labor market systematically allocates its most stable and remunerative positions to well-educated men while limiting women to temporary and part-time positions. Women's labor force participation varies considerably with age. Graphs of women's labor force participation which place their rate of participation on the vertical axis and age on the horizontal axis reveal a marked "M"-shaped curve. In the mid-1990s the first peak of the "M" represented roughly three fourths of the country's women in their early 20s, but the percentage dropped sharply to a little over half of all women in their early 30s and then rose more gradually to another peak around 70 per cent for women in their late 40s; Ministry of Labor 1998: 3). The dip reflects women's dropping out of the labor market to become full-time housewives and mothers.

This "M" pattern – a staple of writing on Japanese women's status and labor force participation – contrasts with the industrialized countries of the West, where the participation rate for women 30 to 34 years of age edges downward a few percentage points to around 70 per cent (OPM 1994: 62). Japan's high turnover rate in positions occupied by women (along with older workers) makes it easier for employers to eliminate their jobs during economic downturns, creating an economic shock absorber that allows organizations to keep their permanently employed male staff.

So pervasive is this pattern of "permanent equals male, temporary equals female" that it exaggerated OBI members' perceptions of their institute's gender ratio. Women were clearly in the minority among postdoctoral fellows and regular researchers, and only two of the thirty or so collaborative researchers were female. Nevertheless, OBI was a place with "a lot of women." Some of the male researchers at OBI told me that "so many women" was an ominous sign of instability and dead-end career prospects. As one (male) former researcher put it, "There are a lot here because there's no guarantee of what happens next." A woman postdoc explained the presence of more women by saying that "men want permanent posts more than you'd imagine – for one thing, they've got wives and children, and they worry about where they'll be in ten or twenty years."

The name handicap

Japanese law poses a qualitatively distinct problem for the professional woman who marries; she must use her husband's surname in official transactions. Article 750 of the Civil Code requires married couples to use only one surname, either the husband's or the wife's. The latter provision may seem egalitarian, but it was devised to accommodate a variation on patriarchy, the adoptive husband marriage (*muko yoshi*) for propertied families without sons; the son-in-law becomes a surrogate son who can inherit the family's productive property. The law represents quintessential bureaucracy: it preserves hierarchy and deflects individual variation that would subject the bureaucratic machinery to various irritations and extra effort resulting from separate spouse names. At the time of my field work, however, the arrangement was generally accepted by a slight majority of the general public (OPM 1991: 13). The media have introduced the surname problem for professional women now and then since the late 1980s, with coverage that describes unusual solutions such as couples choosing to divorce while living together and maintaining their relationship, or registering some of the couple's children under the wife's original name (making them illegitimate).

The surname change for a woman scientist can range in severity from mildly vexing to disastrous, depending on the extent of credit and name recognition she has earned under her original name. Thus, women who only begin making scientific contributions after marriage feel the least inconvenience. The worst rub comes when the woman researcher is married and affiliated with a laboratory financed by the government – as in any public university – because the law requires her institution to use only her legal (i.e., married) name. Affection and gratitude to her parents have posed a name problem for PhD biophysicist Noriko Mochizuki-Oda. When she was 12 years old Noriko Mochizuki was inspired by Marie Curie's biography to study science. Her parents took her desire seriously then, and they had supported her professional aspirations ever since. As one of two sisters who both married, Mochizuki-Oda wanted to use the family name lest it disappear. "It's a matter of gratitude to the people who most supported me in finding the path I wanted to take," she explained.

Women scientists attempt to cope by using their married surnames in daily life but hyphenating both names on publications, or by steadfastly using the original name wherever possible. The married women bioscientists in my sample took the former approach; I had known them by their husbands' surnames, and only when I saw copies of their publications did I learn their former names. Noriko Mochizuki-Oda has yet to find a satisfactory solution; she had been publishing domestic papers in Japanese under her married name and papers in English under Mochizuki-Oda, but the increase in international conferences held in Japan (among other consequences of internationalization) has complicated that approach. For example, colleagues have to match an abstract in English written by Mochizuki with a paper in Japanese authored by someone named Oda.

The pharmacy science bridge to research

The proportion of Japan's female researchers is particularly high in pharmacology, where a little under a fourth of all researchers are women (Endo et al. 1993: 21). Of the nine PhD holders in pharmacology in my own interview sample, four were women, and over half of the technicians had a bachelor's or master's degree in pharmacology. Pharmacology claims a relatively large percentage of female researchers because it provides women a bridge to research from pharmacy, a female sex-linked occupation in Japan. Pharmacies have long been small, family-operated businesses in a shop front connected directly to the pharmacist's home, allowing women to manage a business while tending to domestic responsibilities. (The proportion of female research personnel is twice as high in public health, which is connected to the female-typed occupation of nursing, but public health is also a field science whose members rarely enter the laboratory.)

The Japanese pharmacist's calling does not afford the income or status from dispensing a high volume of prescription drugs, as it does in the West; Japan's physicians control the lion's share of prescription drug sales by selling them from their own hospital dispensaries. This division of labor lessens women pharmacists' head-on economic competition with men. Nevertheless, the sex-linked occupation has evolved into a range of job opportunities in industry as well as the hospital dispensaries and apothecary shops that my interviewees had said they originally considered when choosing pharmacology. One industry survey from 1994 found that food processing, pharmaceutical, and toiletry producers have been hiring about 15 per cent of their R&D work force among women, some three times the proportion found among major Japanese firms in general. The leader was Tanabe Pharmaceuticals, at 22 per cent, and most recruits were master's degree holders (*Nikkan Kōgyō Shinbun* 1994a).

The combination of sex-linked occupation and a range of employment opportunities helps explain the two thirds female proportion of undergraduate pharmacy science majors (Endo et al. 1993: 13). Some of the pharmacy degree holders whom I interviewed said they believed that as women they would experience a more fair treatment than they would get in other technical or scientific fields. A few of my interviewees also said that they had entered a graduate program in pharmacology because they couldn't get into one in the life sciences, but ease of entry is a function of the status of the target university as well as the discipline: it is far easier to gain admission to a pharmacy science program at a small private college in the hinterlands than, say, at the University of Osaka.

Credentials

Pharmacy-related occupations in Japan require a license (the *yakuzaishi menkyo*), which the Ministry of Health and Welfare confers through an examination taken by graduates in pharmacy sciences. My interviewees with pharmacology degrees said that the license was one attraction of the major. In their words, the degree and the license offered "security." A few were apologetic about putting mundane job opportunities first; "Not a very pure reason," said a PERI technician, influenced, no doubt, by the rarified atmosphere there. Nevertheless, her motivation fitted with the special attraction of degrees and other credentials shared by other science-oriented Japanese women. The tendency is evident even at the high-school level; in one survey of high-school students wanting a science track in college, 84 per cent of the females indicated that getting credentials (or "qualifications" – *shikaku*) was a major consideration in their choice of a science major. The males' percentage was 58, resulting in the survey question's biggest contrast in priorities between the sexes (Endo et al. 1993: 15.)

This appeal of credentials has adaptive significance for women who seek self-sufficiency. Degrees and licenses may differ in the proportion of each sex that obtains them, but the degrees themselves are gender blind – i.e., there are no separate pharmacy licenses, one marked for men and the other for women, even in Japan. Individual credentials are also quintessentially portable, which makes them particularly valuable in the term employment labor market that women face. The portability value isn't lost on Japanese men, however. An industry researcher in automotive engineering (a male bastion in Japan) summed the position nicely for a popular science publication: "'Section chief' is no more than a title. If I leave the company, or if it no longer exists, [the title] is meaningless, but a 'PhD' has value even if the university I got it from disappears" (Hidaka 1991: 119). The thesis degree seekers among PERI's male industry researchers may not have been as irrational as they appeared.

OBI and PERI technicians: blurring job and career

The technicians at OBI and PERI offer a view of the aspirations of women on the border of the science profession. (All of the 20 technicians in my interview sample came from OBI or PERI; there were very few people at the other locations who held technical support staff positions.) Technical support workers in the West are usually regarded as a clearly defined group subordinate to researchers. (Germany may offer the most clear-cut distinction, given the distinct educational track for technicians there.) Their pay is their sole reward, with no credit cycle dynamic. (As phrased in Latour and Woolgar's *Laboratory Life*, technicians' salaries are not "capital which can be invested"; 1986: 218.) In short, technicians have jobs, not careers.

This was certainly not the case among the technicians at OBI and PERI, however. Both institutions offered technicians the chance to conduct research and garner professional credit, depending on their ability and sophistication. The chance to leave the confines of rudimentary tasks and paperwork and take part in experiments attracted most of the assistants to PERI, particularly those in their early twenties, and older technicians were attracted to research subjects that fitted with their past work. The youngest women compared their situation favorably with the industry jobs taken by classmates, which were far more routine and involved much more clerical work. Remuneration, on the other hand, was not a motive for either of these places. Technicians' pay at OBI and PERI was considerably lower than industry levels, and a clear majority of the technician interviewees at both locations expressed very explicit dissatisfaction with their salaries.

The possibility of earning a thesis PhD (as described in the chapter on PERI) also made the technician's job more attractive. The chance to earn a PhD in the course of working at PERI was an explicit part of the initial job offer to some of the technician recruits. Over a fourth (five) of the PERI technicians were either taking steps to obtain a thesis PhD or were seriously considering the possibility. (Another three said they had also considered the possibility, but did not think circumstances or their ability would get them a degree.) At OBI, four of the seven female technicians I interviewed were in various phases of obtaining a thesis PhD. When the technicians recalled their initial expectations on entering their institutions, the answers reflected all of these professional attractions: the chance to learn, to be allowed to conduct experiments, work toward a PhD, and, in a few cases, to work on specific research goals.

Technicians with advanced degrees could, on occasion, become co-authors of publications; nine of the seventy-three articles published by PERI researchers between February, 1990 and March, 1991 included technician co-authors, in two cases as first author. Of fifty-six OBI publications in 1990, five technicians appeared as co-authors, one as first author. Technicians at PERI also made presentations at seminars and colloquia. (OBI's technician jobs demanded much more paperwork, and the "research assistant" category included four women who did desk work exclusively.)

One might wonder how the most mundane and repetitive tasks were accomplished if the technicians were aspiring to researcher status. Evidently the dishes did get washed, and more. Although I did not ask everyone systematically for their evaluations of technicians' performance, when I did ask I received almost all favorable responses, including some impressive ones. An industry researcher with experience in the United States (himself an excellent performer) praised the PERI technicians' perseverance in solving technical problems, and two foreign postdoctoral fellows from Western Europe said that PERI's technicians were better than the assistants in their home countries.

A clear majority of both the OBI and PERI technicians felt they had received what they had initially expected from their jobs, though most also qualified their statements. There were two PERI technicians who did not feel that their original expectations were met, and in both cases they described frustration of their hopes for professional development. Dealing with younger researchers from industry generated some tension between career aspirations and the technician role. According to the technicians, the industry researchers needed guidance in technique and additional help to finish their projects by the end of their terms at PERI. In the questionnaire survey described in the chapter on PERI, technicians were more likely than academic researchers to disagree with the suggestion that PERI be evaluated in terms of an educational function for corporate participants. Their written questionnaire responses also elicited very critical views of the ways in which research topics were chosen, reflecting disappointed expectations for a more participatory selection process.

Partial overlap with researcher roles made the position of technician an uncertain rung on the career ladder. At the time of my field research, one of the women at PERI had originally entered as a postdoctoral fellow but then became a technician. (She was later named a researcher as part of a larger organizational change.) "I get the feeling that the kind of qualifications needed for researcher at PERI aren't clear," complained one of the PERI technicians, herself a higher degree holder. "If it's just [among] master of science holders, isn't the only distinction that the women are assistants and the men are researchers?" OBI had moved at least two women PhD holders into technician slots after their postdoctoral terms had expired.

The will to do research

There were other signs of motivation among the women I studied besides their eagerness to pursue professional opportunities at PERI and OBI. Of thirteen women with PhDs, four were living apart from their spouses in order to maintain their careers, as was one of the thesis PhD hopefuls. Three of these women had young children. Although Japanese men have been separated from their families on a systematic basis for job assignments (*tanshin funin*), separation for the sake of the wife's career is rare in the larger society and, in the cases I saw, the arrangement represented considerable personal sacrifice for both partners.

The women in my study did not intend to accommodate the Japanese female work pattern of dropping out of the work force for marriage and childbearing in their late twenties and early thirties. My modal female interviewee was a youthful 25 years old. (The average age of all of the women was 30.) When I asked thirty-two of the thirty-three women interviewees what they would like to be doing ten years hence, however, only two stated that they wanted to be housewife mothers (one with an ironic laugh at that), and one other mentioned that she would like to be married in addition to doing basic research. There were five other women who had difficulty coming up with an answer because, they said, they faced so many uncertainties, but most answered in the ways that the men did, discussing their research themes and hopes for the freedom to choose their own topics for investigation. The women who had PhDs or were pursuing them were just as animated as the men in their discussion of their careers. They talked about their careers as much as the men, too; a check of their average interview time found them the same length as the average for my sessions with men. (I controlled statistically for age.)

Midori Nomura

Soon after I had settled in at OBI, the ranks of the technicians in my laboratory grew by one with a rather remarkable entrant. Midori Nomura neither looked nor sounded remarkable (see Figure 7.1). She was so withdrawn that I was ready to resign myself to a rejection when I asked her for an interview. I first learned what was remarkable about her from Fred Tsuji, the laboratory chief. Midori Nomura was a biochemist interested in doing nucleic acids research at OBI – so interested, in fact, that she had left a secure job which she had held for some eleven years at the Suntory Biomedical Institute, with three times the salary of her temporary OBI position.

At work in the laboratory she showed another side, deft and purposeful. The bench was her altar, and it suffused her with an assertiveness and self-confidence that approached serenity. Nomura said she had always had a fascination with life as a phenomenon. She took an interest in genes during her junior high school years, under the influence of her older brother, a junior high school science teacher. In 1979, in her third year at the University of Osaka as a major in biology, she gained her first laboratory experience and chose a kōza where she could learn more about genetics. "I thought it would be wonderful to understand life through study at the genetic level, though my interest was kind of vague at the time."

The times were on Nomura's side in science but working against her socially. Interest in the genetic bases of life processes had just taken hold in Japan, and she was among the first to learn recombinant DNA technique. The prospect of graduate school appeared perilous for her future employment potential, however; what did a woman do with an advanced degree? Her

Figure 7.1 Midori Nomura, 1998

parents, worried about her job prospects, suggested she become a teacher.
Nomura, ambivalent to the end, scheduled herself to take examinations both
for teaching certification and for entrance to graduate school. A purely
coincidental scheduling conflict for the graduate school entrance examination
and an oral examination required for teaching certification dimmed both
prospects, but by that point a third option had emerged: Suntory's

Biomedical Research Institute. Midori Nomura had visited some pharmaceutical companies only to find that they were not hiring women into research jobs, but Suntory was different. Suntory would allow women to do research. A student from her university division who had graduated the year before was working there, and their discussions gave her valuable information.

Midori Nomura's familiarity with DNA technique made her an attractive job candidate; Suntory had joined the quest for new drugs through recombinant DNA technology, and was assembling the talent to do it. In her subsequent ten years at Suntory she had published several articles as first author. Work there, though, "had a somewhat narrow frame" for her interests. When she saw an ad for postdoctoral positions at OBI that Tsuji had placed in a Japanese professional journal she inquired, half-knowing that her bachelor's degree in biochemistry – albeit from the University of Osaka – would probably not qualify her. But she had hoped for some kind of arrangement that would let her do research that interested her.

The only option available at OBI was a technician's position, which Tsuji offered her reluctantly after discussing the painful financial consequences of such a move. Nevertheless, the job would mean a chance to explore a topic that interested her and pursue a thesis degree, so she accepted.

Midori Nomura's first impression of OBI was "a world outside of Japan," particularly since she had entered a research group with several foreigners (and their own foreign social scientist). The place at first seemed "free and easy" in contrast with the more structured corporate research environment she had left behind, but the impression of relaxation was deceptive. Building her research career demanded her spending week nights and Saturdays at OBI – a palpable adjustment, but she willingly invested her time as she savored her new self-determination. Midori Nomura was single. (I didn't ask her about any marriage plans.) Living with her parents took care of her personal household needs, but her daily commute of three hours was twice the average for my sample.

While at OBI, Nomura's work with her new research team on photoprotein mutants earned her first authorship in an international journal article. Some four or so months after Nomura had accepted the position at OBI, Fred Tsuji was ready to raise her status to research associate and help her attain a doctoral degree. At that point, however, her undergraduate professor contacted her to introduce her to a position with a fellowship at Osaka University's Research Institute for Microbial Diseases. She did not take the decision to leave OBI lightly, given the arrangements Fred Tsuji was making for her. He himself counseled her to consider the offer seriously, however, noting that his own role in her career would be limited by the fact that he was a foreigner, unaffiliated with a Japanese university.

Midori Nomura did decide to relocate to the Research Institute for Microbial Diseases, and while there she completed the research that earned her a doctorate in medicine in 1994. At that point she became a "research associate" – the Institute's English translation of the title joshu – but with the understanding that her employment would be limited to three and a half years. Near the end of her term she quietly married an anatomy researcher employed in the Tohoku region. After she relocated there with him, her search for a research job there that would allow them to be together turned up nothing. Just as it became clear that Tohoku job prospects were nil, word came from a senior faculty member at the Research Institute for Microbial Diseases that the Osaka Medical Center for Cancer and Cardiovascular Diseases was looking for a researcher. The research area was immunology, but the project's director reassured Nomura that she had enough relevant background, and told her that her grounding in molecular biology would be particularly helpful.

The decision to return alone to Osaka was not easy for either Midori Nomura or her husband, but he agreed. Nomura's current position does not achieve her earlier goal of studying phenomena subsumed in developmental biology such as development and differentiation, and that has dealt her some anguish with which she must still cope. Her greater love of biology has sustained her in her decision, though: "This is unlocking the world of immunity at the molecular level, and I'm using the same techniques as before to do it. Immunology is also an important domain of life phenomena, so in the big picture maybe it's not such a big transition." Her work situation has rewarded her decision as well; she feels "blessed" to be in the company of a group that is intense and persistent yet so mutually supportive that "the whole lab feels a lot like a family." Her current contract as a "Visiting Ministry of Health and Welfare Researcher" has a five-year limit.

There is no absolute scale for assessing the overall talent of a bioscience researcher, particularly one undergoing the transformations that Midori Nomura has been experiencing. For some indication, though, Fred Tsuji, himself a professor at Scripps Institution of Oceanography, offered a concise assessment of Midori Nomura when she left OBI: "She is a capable young lady who deserves to be an assistant professor at a university."

Holding it all together versus willing to let go

Naoko Negishi and Mayumi Kitamura (both pseudonyms) were technicians whose motivation contrasted sharply, but both illustrated the problems for women in bioscience when I asked them about their hopes for the future. After receiving a master's degree in pharmacology, Negishi worked at a government research institute in Tokyo, but she quit when she married a researcher at one of Japan's major pharmaceutical companies because it meant moving to Osaka. She was 32 years old when I interviewed her, and working toward a PhD. Since she was childless she did not have to concern herself with child care, but housework fell to her and, as the person responsible for meals, she was bothered by having to leave the laboratory before the stores closed. (Her 40 liter refrigerator – lilliputian by Western standards – was no help, and there were no all-night supermarkets in the area, either.)

> Ten years from now? I hadn't thought of it. To tackle my work and get the most out of it for the future . . . But I don't know how much I can think about that because I also have family problems. [Coordinating with your husband?] Yes, and children. We really have to think about that but we've both been so busy. If I really could have whatever wish, he and I would be roommates. Yes, I mean it, roommates. It feels like that a lot anyway – he doesn't get home before 10 at night. Saturdays and Sundays he's on the job, too. We ought to take more time together, but if we want that we have to plan it three months in advance! If we were roommates everything – housework too – would be fifty-fifty, but we aren't. That's the way it is in Japan. If I would just stay at home – that's the old system. The wife as "dependent." I don't want to be supported. And there are still families that look at the wife as their property. There were two months when I wasn't working – yes, just two months, and I really started feeling ill. I lost seven kilos of weight in one month. I went to a hospital three times for gastritis from stress. After I started working I felt much better again! I gained my weight back, too.

Mayumi Kitamura had a bachelor's degree in agricultural science, specializing in bacteriology. When she married a businessman she quit her assistant position at a private medical college. After moving to Osaka for her husband's transfer, however, she responded to a newspaper advertisement for a temporary technician position because she found her "laid back" life boring. She was 29 years old and childless when I met her.

> Ten years from now . . . I probably can't continue my job. When I got married I thought about working but there were various circumstances so I had to give up. Now I'm glad I can continue, though the subject area is different. For me, putting on a lab coat and entering the lab every day is a blessing. But I have no big hopes. Once you're married there are lots of considerations – husband's transfers, children. So after ten years I probably will have quit. If I could have my way I'd have some kind of job, though.

My sample did not include women who had dropped out of research careers, but informants' accounts concerning their acquaintances suggested a syndrome: married with unsympathetic families, particularly husbands who needed their household and parenting services, and supervised by laboratory heads who parceled out work for a project in top-down fashion rather than cooperatively hand-crafting tasks for researchers in response to their individual interests and circumstances.

Mass media accounts of women researchers' problems have also highlighted the problem of child care responsibilities. The availability of child care facilities is indeed limited, as is husbands' domestic task sharing. According to international time use studies, Japanese husbands provide by far the least household labor among husbands in industrialized countries, despite a substantial increase since the 1970s (EPA 1995: 116, 118). Nor is the situation better for Japanese women who work; they have not enjoyed appreciably more help from husbands than have full-time housewives (OPM 1994: 20).

The attitudes of male bioscientists

Japanese men in bioscience are not necessarily biased against their female colleagues. Rather, they hold a wide range of opinions which I would summarize as cautiously and pragmatically favorable. Some well-known Japanese bioscientists have made public statements in support of career equality for women. Mitsuhiro Yanagida called for opening positions in Japanese universities "to all, regardless of the nationality, sex and age of the applicant" (1996b: 3). Ken-Ichi Arai advocated organizational reform "where excellent people can move freely regardless of nationality, age and sex" (1994: 2), and identified the "low profile of female researchers" as one of five major problems in Japan's "traditional research structure" (1996a: 10). My field work experience was dotted with spontaneous comments from male bioscientists who benefitted in one way or another from working with talented women. When I visited him in 1998, for example, Akikazu Ando noted that almost three fourths of his undergraduate students in recent years have been women, and they have been outshining his male students in eagerness and wits.

In my more methodically gathered data as well as casual discussions, the majority of my male interviewees did not express the belief that men and women differed in their ability to do basic science research. When I phrased the possibility as an opinion question to sixty-one of the men I interviewed, thirty-five of them said that there was no difference, and another two responded that women were *better* than men. (Among the thirty-five, two mildly upbraided me for asking the question, telling me I should know better than to think there were any differences.) Only five stated that women were not as good. These were not just responses to placate an inquisitive American. Only three of my interviewees said they had no opinion, and most of the interviewees elaborated thoughtfully on the subject, even though the question came near the end of a full hour of interviewing.

Since the question sought an open-ended response regarding the issue of ability, respondents could (and did) logically state that there was no difference in ability and then describe differences in performance and their causes. The men who discussed reasons for differences in performance typically cited women's "handicaps," chief among them household and child-raising responsibilities. From a 30-year-old industry-based biochemist at PERI:

> Women are the same if it's on the same footing. If someone were to look after the kids, they'd be better than men. They stick to it. But women have a lot of shackles – kids, house, and they can't return home too late. Men don't worry like that – drink, go back home and go to sleep. Women can't do that. If they had that kind of back-up [from housewives] they'd be excellent.

Less frequent but notable responses were mention of lower expectations conveyed to women by their families and educational experience, or management policy in Japan that confines women to simpler jobs and presses them to quit or go part-time when they marry.

The remaining sixteen male interviewee responses essentially claimed differences in approach to basic research between men and women, along with denials that neither women's nor men's approaches were qualitatively inferior – just "different." This group also included several men who said there was no difference in ability but whose subsequent description of women's approaches clearly questioned women's competence. Running through almost all of the accompanying descriptions of differences was a theme of women's more conservative performance: cautious, meticulous, and persevering. The negative dimension lay in an accompanying lack of boldness, intuition, or inspired overview. (If there were a popular expression for "big picture" in Japanese, these respondents would have used it.) "They all listen to their superiors so their ability to perform experiments is extremely high," according to a PERI biochemist male. "But when it comes to ideas and planning ability, well, I don't know, you see."

The men's responses showed no correlation between the respondents' ages and their opinions about women researchers, which is very unusual for a Japanese sample. Public opinion in Japan regarding women's equality in the workplace typically falls out in a very clear linear relationship: the older the individual (male or female), the greater the preference for confining women to domestic roles. I believe this exception resulted from the professional competition to which the men were exposed, especially at OBI and PERI; they were particularly pragmatic about women because they sensed that talent allied to theirs was more important than gender lines.

The men's discussions often had an empirical element as well; those who had worked with very competent women cited their experience when claiming that women were equally capable in science, and those who had few or no women colleagues offered that fact as a qualification, whatever their answer. The performance-first attitude struck me when I asked a researcher from academia to evaluate a technician in his group. Parenthetically I noted that she had a Korean last name, a spontaneous probe of his attitude toward minorities. He dismissed the observation with an irritated furrowing of his brow. "All I know is she's *very* good at what she does."

Women discussing women's ability

Like their male counterparts, the majority of my female interviewees did not believe that there was a difference in the ability of men and women to do basic science research. Of the twenty-six women to whom I posed the question of basic science ability, fourteen said there was no difference in ability. The range of assessment was somewhat less positive than the men's, though; four replied that women had less ability, and none ventured the opinion that women were better. The remainder of six (leaving one respondent who had no opinion) described differences in style that resembled the men's descriptions.

The women's discussions of contrasts in ability or performance resembled the men's – remarkably so, in fact. When it came to explanations, by far first in frequency came the tension between family responsibilities and careers. Their descriptions of the restraints, like Naoko Negishi's, were vivid. Those women who had had postdoctoral fellowships abroad, particularly in the United States, had seen a life style among men and women that gave them plenty of food for thought. One biochemist saw a resemblance between the extended absences from their families among "top level" men in the United States and what she saw at OBI. Her own laboratory "boss" in Colorado, though, had told her "this isn't Japan," and encouraged her to spend evenings with her children, who had accompanied her to the US. "If Japanese men and women in bioscience could balance leisure and work," she said, it would cancel out the "terrific differences between them that we see now . . . When women are asked to do everything in the household, and men just do research, everyone is going to be only half a person."

One type of minority opinion and explanation hinted at a broader undercurrent of male resentment. A handful of the men and women said that women were not sufficiently professional in their attitudes. A few men (and one woman) also complained that women affected a coy helplessness. (The Japanese term *amaeru* captures the strategy nicely.) Several men aired the suspicion that the women's alternative of dropping out and becoming full-time housewives sapped their motivation; they had a less professional attitude – or "hobby" approach – because they weren't sufficiently "hungry." A related men's theme was the perception that women had more freedom than they did in determining their careers because they had material support (from parents or husbands) unavailable to men. "They don't have to earn all their own income so they can do a light part-time job," said a 38-year-old male collaborating researcher at OBI from a pharmaceutical company. "Men basically have to get the income. That's unfair." A male medical student said that it was easier for women to enter basic research because men "have to make money instead."

Explaining perceived differences

The generalizations about women's approaches as thorough but timid may have some validity. One woman familiar with the diagnosis is Yoshie Souma, the chief researcher in the Synthetic Chemistry Section at MITI's Osaka Industrial Research Institute. A lack of "planning ability," she said, resulted from a syndrome of low positions with repetitive work assignments, along with the need to leave the laboratory at "5 or 6 PM, instead of 8 or 10 PM" because of child care and domestic work demands. The perseverance and meticulousness, she said, are essentially signs that the researcher is making the best of a difficult situation.

That some women lack dedication is plausible, given the obstacles to career development. Nor are cases of coy manipulation inconceivable, given human opportunism. If there is a more relaxed approach among some women, however, there is also evidence for a more relaxed approach *toward* women, in lower standards and expectations. A woman with a PhD in biophysical engineering said that men's questions to women research presenters were "somehow, subtly, a little kinder and softer. It's a kind of subtle condescension. There's tremendous attrition among the women, so the sense is that they'll be leaving anyway and won't be relevant to the future."

Chapter 2 argued that Japanese graduate education in the life sciences does not cultivate initiative in the selection of research topics. My interviewees' recollections indicated that women get even less experience in independent thinking than do the men. In fifty-three accounts (thirty-eight male and fifteen female) of how their masters thesis research topic was decided, three fourths of the women described a passive role in the process (in which they were either assigned the topic outright or had it offered by the kōza professor). A little under half of the men reported the same experience. Among the twelve interviewees who had clearly taken initiative in topic choice only one was a woman. In PhD research topic choice (forty-seven accounts, thirty-nine male and eight female) more of the women had the topic assigned to them than did the men (one half and one third, respectively). As in the case of master's degrees, only one out of twelve who clearly took initiative was female.

A PERI technician who had recently graduated from a first-tier national university in pharmacy science provided this contrastive snapshot of women students' treatment:

> My undergraduate advisor was a woman, an associate professor, so it was really awesome (*sugoi*). She was about 20 or 30 years older than we, and for a woman in her generation to become an associate

professor must have been really hard. And she was really severe, too. The usual male professors' treatment of fourth year female students was, well, in the worst cases they wouldn't require a graduation report or attendance at seminars, if the student wasn't going on to graduate work. As you'd guess, the pharmacology division has that kind of professor. So with that kind of person around her, my professor would say that every student should work hard, and every student should have the will to do work she could call her own ... Now when I think of it, it's been a real plus, but at the time it was hard. My parents were thinking I shouldn't be doing research!

The softer set of standards for women fits with the paternalism young women have experienced as job candidates as well. When hiring single women, pharmaceutical companies in the Osaka area preferred hiring those who lived with their families. (Four of my seven unmarried technician interviewees at PERI lived with their parents as well.) "I guess it's because if a single girl has problems, even though they're hers, her parents and family press the company to take responsibility," said one of the unmarried technicians living alone. "That's why a lot of women choose foreign companies if they can."

Tairyoku

Discussions of men's and women's abilities uncovered another theme; several of the male and female bioscientists tended to assess research ability through the lens of "stamina," sometimes in combination with qualities like perseverance and diligence. (The term they used most often was *tairyoku*, literally "body strength.") There was no consensus among either men or women about which sex had more stamina, but the issue attracted my attention because my American informants had never brought it up. Surveys of men and women college students in the Tokyo area also found that science majors of both sexes were far more likely than humanities majors to believe that "stamina" was important for studying in their fields (Muramatsu 1996: 21). The concern probably resulted from cram-style studying for entrance examinations. I suspect another source among bioscientists as well, aptly identified by a microbiologist at the Food Research Institute: "Well, there are fewer support staffers in Japan, and that may have something to do with [the importance of tairyoku]. If it were a university there are students [to do the work], but at a place like this it naturally comes down to stamina."

The prospects for change in women's status

Fundamental trends in Japanese society will result in more professional opportunity for women. The crux of the female disadvantage in career trajectories lies in marriage and childbirth, but fewer Japanese women are committing themselves to those options, or are devoting a smaller proportion of their lives to them. As Japan entered the 1990s, the percentage of women between the ages of 25 and 29 who had never married had climbed to an unprecedented 40 per cent (twice the 1975 proportion), and birth rates had fallen to unprecedented lows. By 1996 the projected lifetime fertility per woman had fallen to 1.43 births – still higher than Germany's, but lower than England's, France's or the United States' (MOL 1998: 35).

These developments originated in Japan's shift to a more service-centered, low-growth economy, which has discouraged marriage and childbirth in several ways. Over the past two decades or so, Japanese men's earning power has fallen, requiring them to postpone marriage and a family having a full-time housewife. (The decline in actual earnings has been particularly evident in residential purchasing power – getting a place to raise a family.) Since men can no longer anticipate increased earning power with age, marriage offers less economic security for women than it had in the past.

At the same time, the proportion of jobs in the service sector and the number of jobs requiring more education have both increased, with terrific ramifications for women's status. The trend has twin depressing effects on fertility: service sector jobs have recruited women, so the time away from work to bear children has become more of an opportunity cost to a woman who could be working instead; children have become more expensive to raise because their educations are more important (and lengthy). The results can be seen in upward shifts over the years in the "M" pattern of women's labor participation rates by age that was described at the beginning of this chapter: the whole curve is rising (indicating increasing percentages of women in the work force at all ages). The greatest change has occurred among women between the ages of 25 and 29; over two thirds of these women were in the labor force in 1996, up from a little over half in 1986; the proportion exceeds 80 per cent if unemployed women wanting to work are included (MOL 1998: 3, 44; the latter figure comes from 1995 statistics). The change in employment patterns has also made marriage a less stable institution; divorce has been on the rise since the mid-1970s as well. (Crude divorce rates are currently in the range of France's and Germany's.)

Public opinion polls reflect the changes. Only one out of five women in their 20s and 30s would agree unconditionally with the statement that "A woman finds her happiness in marriage," half the proportion of their mothers' cohort (OPM 1993a: 26). The proportion of respondents agreeing unconditionally with the statement "The husband goes to work and the wife maintains the household" fell from 32 per cent in 1979 to 21 per cent in 1997 (OPM 1998: 20). Public opinion also provides a trenchant explanation. The response by far most frequently offered in a 1991 public opinion poll concerning the reasons for delaying marriage was, "The number of women having jobs has increased and their personal economic power has improved" (OPM 1992: 6).

This trend does not validate the "having their cake and eating it, too" depiction of women's careers that the more critical male bioscientists painted. Young Japanese women realize that, unlike their mothers and grandmothers, their standard of living will depend more on their own resources and less on those of the men they marry. They have responded by seeking four-year degrees in unprecedented numbers, to fill the recently created jobs requiring more education. In the mid-1970s, a four-year college education for a woman looked like an exercise in masochism, with employment rates at graduation some 20 percentage points or more below men's. By the late 1980s, however, an extraordinary closing of the gap with men's employment rates at that level of education had appeared. The recessionary 1990s introduced a gap again, which the mass media have touted as the "ice age" for female college graduates. In this case, though, the newspapers overlooked the fact that this time the pain of unemployment has been distributed far more equally between men and women (in 1997, fewer than 3 percentage points in favor of men; MOL 1998: appendix p. 49). A perceptive commentator, noting that there was no such media hand-wringing over unemployed women college graduates in the starker 1970s, suggested that the fuss resulted from expectations based on women's greater participation in the work place today (Murata 1996).

The surname bellwether

A 1998 judicial decision signals an accommodation, albeit incomplete, of Japanese professional women's credit needs. Reiko Sekiguchi, a woman faculty member at Toshokan Joho University, brought suit against the government and her university in 1989 for the burden imposed on her by the name law (Chira 1989). In 1993 the Tokyo District Court ruled against her, but five years later the Tokyo High Court prescribed a three-part "reconciliation": Sekiguchi (by then aged 61) could use her original name in public research and teaching activity; she would "line together" her original name and married name for the Ministry of Education personnel directory; and, for "personnel-related materials" she would use her married name (*Asahi Shimbun* 1998). A compromise over surnames had also taken place at OBI. In 1993, the Institute's office staff insisted that a woman postdoc use her married name on the nameplate in front of her office and she complied. (Her labmates continued to address her by her original name, however.) In 1995, however, another woman postdoc was allowed to place her original name on her nameplate in parentheses after her married name.

Will Japanese science accommodate women?

In the coming years, demographics could stimulate demand in the R&D labor force to the benefit of women scientists. The proportion of Japan's population in the productive age groups is shrinking rapidly relative to its elderly, threatening a labor shortage that includes the technically and scientifically trained. One government-sponsored estimate claims that fewer than half the needed R&D workers will be available by the year 2010. The Japan Science Council took the prediction seriously enough to propose "reverse discrimination" measures such as scholarships and research funds earmarked for women (*Nikkan Kōgyō Shinbun* 1994b).

The participation of Japanese women as equals in the research enterprise will also depend on larger reforms for the credit cycle as discussed in Chapter 8. Women in the life sciences believe that open recruitment practices would give them a better chance at employment. In its 1979 report of a survey of hiring practices for university assistants, the Young Biochemists' Association argued that open recruitment would require an interview and consideration of the candidate's past work, whereas the decision in hire-from-within and introductions would be ruled more by "emotional ties among the researchers and the teacher–student relationship" (Sehara 1979: 1469) – interpersonal dynamics labeled "male bonding" in the West. Women also feel more need for impartial judgment than do their male peers. A 1996 nationwide survey that drew responses from 1,868 researchers, 5.8 per cent of them female, solicited two answers for an eight-option closed answer question of what would facilitate the work environment for female researchers. Men and women alike offered "the understanding and support of family and community" as their most frequently chosen answer, but men and women diverged noticeably when it came to "thorough evaluation of ability without regard to sex"; over 40 per cent of the women cited that factor, leading the men by some 14 percentage points (STA 1997a: 10).

Although women's pay levels in the sciences and engineering in Japan are not as high as men's, the difference is less severe than among regularly employed workers in the country as a whole. Yearly pay for women graduates of science and engineering programs at the major national universities in Japan averaged 78 per cent of men's earnings in 1992 (calculated from a sample of cohorts that graduated between 1965 and 1986 in IFT 1993: 15), compared to a society-wide figure of 62 (MOL 1995: appendix p. 58). Education is a powerful gender equalizer in salaries, and seniority a gender discriminator. Women and men in the higher educational levels start off on an equal salary footing, but women lose out from dropping out from work and returning.

OBI and PERI offer a vision of potential for women bioscientists in several respects. Neither women's level of motivation nor male scientists' attitudes pose a profound attitudinal barrier. OBI and PERI show us evolutionary changes in institutions like pharmacy science and the technician's role that can work to women's advantage, particularly in combination with the thesis PhD for women who have already entered the work force. But neither OBI nor PERI has eliminated discrimination, or taken programmatic steps to alleviate the stress that comes from working women's persistent competition with the domestic performance standards of full-time stay-at-home housewives. A 1992 public opinion survey found over 80 per cent of women in their twenties agreeing with the statement that "It's fine for a woman to have a job, but she should also do housework and child raising scrupulously" (OPM 1993a: 37). Among the women who feel this way are many who are opting out of the marriage option entirely, precisely because their desire for a career and the current domestic division of labor prevents them from meeting those standards.

8

THE OBSTACLES TO CHANGE

I believe that if the organizational problems that I have identified persist, Japan will always be the "odd man out," the least distinguished in science among the world's wealthiest countries. The obstacles to change, however, are truly formidable. As Chapter 1 observed, the needed changes will not come easily because they necessitate sensitive trade-offs involving power, authority, and security. This chapter lays them out. Ultimate prediction of whether the reforms will ever occur involves some considerations that I adumbrate at the end of this chapter.

Dissatisfaction among scientists

If younger scientists' attitudes were to dictate developments, fundamental reform would fast be on its way. My sample of informants and discussants is probably biased toward the discontented because it is relatively young and heavily populated with fugitives from the kōza. Members of mainstream academic society have also been expressing dissatisfaction with the status quo, however. The Japan Science Council's 1990 questionnaire survey, aptly entitled "The Academic Research Environment," offers a valuable source of information that I have cited extensively. It tapped the intensity of researchers' concerns about organizational problems, eliciting a response rate of 91.7 per cent, with 1,869 valid responses from 2,038 researchers between the ages of 30 and 50 (88 per cent of whom were employed by universities; calculated from figures in JSC 1991: 175). Over 90 per cent of the respondents in turn used the space provided in the survey form for write-in comments, which also attested to researchers' organizational concerns. This level of cooperation did not result from a more general Japanese spirit of compliance; at the time of the JSC survey, only about one out of six publicly conducted surveys in Japan could boast a response rate of 90 per cent or better, and response rates of less than 50 per cent were more common (calculated from statistics in OPM 1993b: 9).

Fewer than 10 per cent of the JSC survey respondents favored maintaining the kōza as the unit of research organization. Over half of the respondents disagreed (with or without qualification) with the statement that the current statuses of assistant through professor should be maintained as is. Also striking were responses to a question concerning permanent employment: given five alternatives, ranging from the current arrangement of permanent employment for all teaching staff to term employment for *all* ranks with mandatory review for renewal, only 14 per cent of respondents chose the status quo and 40 per cent opted for the latter system (JSC 1991: 154, 156), which is more rigorous than the tenure system for associate and full professors in American universities. I believe this response pattern reflects a view of the upper strata as marginally productive; recall the lack of felt need among OBI's younger researchers for a senior stratum of colleagues.

Over 80 per cent of the JSC survey respondents agreed with the statement that open recruitment (kōbo) should be a principle of hiring (half of all respondents agreeing without qualification), and half of all respondents also agreed that the hiring process should include the judgment of participants from other organizations (JSC 1991: 155; results from respondents in the natural sciences did not differ from those in other sections; JSC 1991: 87). Public recruitment was the preferred method of assembling applicants in another survey as well. A 1989 poll of some 1,350 researchers concerning private nonprofit research funding found over 80 per cent of respondents preferring public announcement over recommendation of candidates by academic societies; the percentage rose to well over 90 per cent among researchers under 50 years of age (Imada and Yamaoka 1990: 5).

JSC committee members also criticized the status quo. Almost four out of five members (78.5 per cent of 791 respondents) from the Natural Science Division of the Japan Science Council's Research Liaison Committee, polled in 1986, believed there were "weaknesses and faults" in the organization of academic research in their country. Life scientists in the Natural Sciences Section recommended a "reevaluation of the kōza and graduate education systems" (JSC 1988: 173). The Medical Research Section was more direct: in its words, reorganizing the kōza was essential to progress in research (JSC 1988: 353). Well-established professors invited by the STA to lecture on basic research in Japanese universities also criticized the kōza and university research. A summary of their presentations by STA staff observed: "A distinctive feature of Japanese universities is their pedigree ideology, or what is known as inbreeding, which makes the introduction of an evaluation system very difficult" (Itoh, Shimoda and Hirano 1993: 42).

Officialese wording tends to soften the statements in reports by agencies within or close to the government, like the STA or JSC, but the expressions of frustration with the obstacles to the credit cycle are there. The term that appears almost universally in these materials is "rigidity" or inflexibility (*kōchoku*, a word also used in the term for rigor mortis). More explicit are scientists' statements that have appeared in the domestic newsletters and conference proceedings of professional societies. The professional journal *Kagaku* (*Chemistry*, 1991) provided a point-by-point description of "kōza

Table 8.1 A Japanese researcher's contrast of Japanese and American academic research units

	Japan	*USA*
Structure	Hierarchical	Horizontal
Employment	Permanent	Term
Evaluation	No	Yes
Young researchers	Dependent pattern	Independent pattern
Driving research team	Graduate students	Postdoctoral fellows
Support system	No	Yes

Note
Based on Arai 1996a: 16.

evils" written by Koji Nakanishi, who hammered on the prevailing secrecy in academic hiring and promotions, immobility of young researchers, and improper attribution of credit (1990). Nakanishi's academic colleagues had asked him to write on the subject, he said, because they were aware of those problems and wanted a crystallized statement of the problem. In the Japan Polymer Society's forum on internationalization of basic research, Akio Yamamoto proclaimed that academic research in Japan was "wretched" (1991: 85). Recall also from Chapter 6 biochemist Yasuo Kagawa's criticism of university self-studies ("like evaluating biochemists on their ambitions and body weights"); it appeared in Japanese in *Seikagaku* (*Biochemistry*, 1993b: 126) as well as the English language *Biochemical Education*. The terseness of Ken-ichi Arai's comparison of research units in Japan and the United States, taken from a presentation slide (Table 8.1) says volumes in frustration.

International scientific journals have occasionally picked up and transmitted signals of aggravation and distress from Japan's scientific researchers. In 1990 *Nature* carried an article by Mitsuhiro Yanagida criticizing SRF, and the year before that same publication related, with some irony, that "more than a few" of the *successful* applicants for the largest of MOE's competitive grants had criticized the selection process (Swinbanks 1989). Academic scientists who have taken their case to the domestic popular media have been just as straightforward, and at times more provocative. An article in the weekly magazine *Shūkan Asahi* owed its title, "And the dregs stayed behind," to an assertion by University of Tokyo Associate Professor of Geophysics Takafumi Matsui: Japan's better talent went into industry and government during the country's postwar period of rapid economic growth, leaving posts in higher education to inferiors. He argued that talented people would replace them when allocation of rewards and prestige go to universities based on comparisons of their field-by-field performance in research and education (rather than the difficulty of their undergraduate entrance examinations, a point to which we will return), and when recruitment and promotion operate through an open, merit-based process (Nakamura 1992).

Figure 8.1 The researcher as cormorant (Illustration by Isao Ando, from *Bessatsu Takarajima*, "Oisyasama", p. 65 Takarajimasha, Inc.)

Dissident physicians found a forum for criticizing medical school education and research in a volume of the *Bessatsu Takarajima* series (Ueda 1993). Some of the criticism was humorous and colorful. One account of the junior-level researcher's life contained an illustration, reproduced in Figure 8.1, depicting the scientist with a "research paper" in her mouth while her professor, dressed as a cormorant fisher, held a rope attached to her neck (Tanaka 1993: 65; a tight ring around the fishing bird's neck prevents it from swallowing what it catches, which is delivered up to the cormorant fisher instead). In the same volume, Nobusuke Asahi, an internal medicine specialist, recounted his dashed hopes for intellectual autonomy and accomplishment in a medical school PhD program. He likened the PhD in medicine to the proverbial naked emperor's clothing, with one exception:

the emperor thought he was clothed, but "we [PhD recipients] know we're really naked" (1993: 163).

Popular sentiment

Although the mass entertainment media in Japan (or any other country) rarely use scientists as fictional characters, Japan's animated cartoon media offer us one portrayal of resentment over unjust allocation of publication credit, and a dark one at that. Konan the Great Detective, a popular television cartoon and serial comic book character, solves grudge murders on a regular basis. When a prominent professor of surgery at the "University of Toto" School of Medicine becomes a stabbing homicide victim, the perpetrator turns out to be one of his own assistants, a 30-year-old woman. After her father had died of colon cancer she had become a medical researcher to find a cure, but the professor appropriated her six years of hard effort by insisting that her paper on "gene therapy for colon cancer" be published under his name. No one would believe her, he argued, while his name would assure attention – adding, with a callously hearty laugh, "Your dead father would be happier that way." The published paper was (of course) highly acclaimed (Aoyama 1996a, b).

Dissatisfied scientists are not alone in Japanese society when it comes to honoring merit over privilege. There are words in general parlance for favoritism (*jōjitsu*) as well as the more extreme collusion (*nareai*) and bribery (*wairo*), and each term has all of the negative freight of its English language equivalent. Nor is even seniority sacrosanct. Two thirds of employed respondents in a 1995 nationwide survey favored basing wages primarily on ability rather than seniority (OPM 1996: 14). Advocates of ability over ascribed status have figured importantly in Japan's history as well. In the latter half of the Tokugawa Period (1600–1868) in particular, influential thinkers advocated filling important government posts on the basis of merit, as opposed to the more usual reliance on social rank, lineage, and primogeniture. Their conviction, intensified by economic upheavals and the threat of foreign domination, fueled the overthrow of the quasi-feudal Tokugawa regime (Smith 1988b).

The possibility of cumulative gradualism

Perhaps the needed revolution in the organization of Japanese science could result from synergy among modest increments. International competition has made its way into Japan's laboratories, as administrators look more to international publications for measuring researchers' performance. As the century ends there appear many small steps forward to which the government can point. In 1996, *Science* magazine reported that MOE had begun requiring reviewers in one of their grant programs to provide explanations of their decisions to applicants (Kinoshita 1996b). MOE has also loosened restrictions on funding of university research by other government agencies (the first to make substantial headway was a MITI program; Barker 1995), and the proportion of university research money allocated through regular, non-competitive institutional budgets (as opposed to competitively earned outside grants and project contracts) has steadily decreased from about three fourths in the mid-1970s to less than half in 1993 (Kobayashi 1993: 236; latter figure based on statistics in NSB 1996: 156). In 1993, RIKEN (the Institute of Physical and Chemical Research, under the aegis of the Science and Technology Agency) underwent its first review by an international visiting committee (Swinbanks 1993).

A perceptible shift in attitude toward the Ministry of Education has pervaded discussions of problems among scientists. The Dean of Nagoya University's School of Science observed for *Science* in 1996 that complaints about MOE among his faculty have dissolved into feelings that the ministry "is doing its best to support academic research" (Kinoshita 1996b: 48), and my own discussion partners have been suggesting that relations with MOE have improved since the turn of the decade. As early as 1991, inveterate critic Koji Nakanishi declared that his "very negative" image of science in Japan had become outdated because of rapid change (1991: 31).

With the exception of diversification of funding sources, however, all of these shifts are relative. The MOE reform requiring reviewers' justifications of their decisions, as *Science* noted, applies only to two classes of large grants having some 300 applicants; still unaffected are the 90,00 applicants to its standard grants program (Kinoshita 1996b: 48). As of this writing, none of Japan's universities is committed to an outside review like RIKEN's on a regular basis.

The change in scientists' perceptions of government efforts is notable but relative, also. MOE may well be more sensitive to scientists' needs in response to the intense criticism fielded in the media in the early 1990s. Nevertheless, the 1990s have also witnessed funding increases that please a larger pool of participants, sidestepping the direct confrontations that accompany allocation of scarce funds using objective evaluation. Even the most optimistic of Japan's scientists do not anticipate an organizational revolution. "And how long before Japanese originality flowers?" asked *Science*. "Let me have 30 years," replied physicist Akito Arima, then the "feisty and optimistic" University of Tokyo president (Anderson 1992b: 569). Many of my bioscientist informants have been downright pessimistic when it comes to the future; they still expressed their fears of a "science bubble" in 1998, along with their skepticism and dismay about the ways in which research funds were allocated. A scant 3 per cent of responses from biochemists (polled in the 1997 Japanese Biochemical Society survey described in Chapter 2) agreed with the statement that the budgets for different ministries' recent large-scale projects were awarded fairly (JBS 1997: 1311). A very successful academic biochemist in his early forties confided to me in 1998, "I like to think my work is excellent, and perhaps every scientist does. But I've really had to work the social connections with the powerful to get my funding."

Increased labor mobility

One other recent change has much more significance: the rapid increase in term employment among Japanese researchers. As of 1996, the Ministry of Education (as reported in the *Asahi Shimbun*) could state that nearly 18 per cent of the country's universities were already hiring teaching staff for limited periods, by informal mutual agreement (1996b: 1). The percentage of term researchers at national research facilities increased five-fold between 1988 and 1996 (calculated using figures in STA 1998: 103). Regular posts accounted for only 40 per cent of the staffing at RIKEN as of 1997; nearly a third (32 per cent) were postdocs, and the remainder (27 per cent) were other term researchers, the latter participating in programs of limited duration such as the Frontier Research Program (STA 1998: 104).

The trend is actually modest. Compared to RIKEN's 40 per cent permanent staff proportion, only 23 per cent of NIH personnel had tenure in 1993, and the figure was lower for permanent staff at Germany's Max Planck Institute for 1997. For all of Japan's national research facilities, regular employees accounted for 90 per cent of staffing in 1996 (STA 1998: 102–3). There are two developments, however, that give the term employment trend particular significance. First, the Japanese government is dismantling legal barriers to term employment, particularly in universities. In 1996 opponents of tenure in universities launched a major proposal for term employment through a subcommittee of the University Council (Daigaku Shingikai), which advises MOE on administrative policy for universities (Swinbanks 1996). The initiative resulted in a law allowing term appointments for entry level faculty that went into effect in 1997. Another law passed in 1997 defined two types of term employee researchers at national research facilities, the "invitation category" and the "youth education category" (STA 1998: 218–19).

Another reason to take this increased mobility seriously is the weakening of permanent employment in the larger Japanese labor market. Permanent employment in Japan can be understood in terms of cross-culturally understandable dynamics (Reed 1993). Neither labor nor management in any country is intrinsically attracted to practices that bind an employee to a workplace. During times of economic downturn and accompanying labor surplus, employees want security but employers benefit from the power to terminate them; when the economy is growing and opportunities proliferate, employees find that leaving (or threatening to leave) improves their lot, but employers (particularly those needing skilled workers) lose from the turnover and competition with other employers.

Enter the government as both sides push politically for laws and administrative practices that will favor them. Pre-World War II Japan did not feature permanent employment, but the early years of the American Occupation presented a powerful configuration for establishing governmental support of job security: in the midst of a devastated economy and its massive insecurity the Occupation encouraged union activity. The subsequent decades witnessed defeats and compromises for both sides, but there remains a legacy of keen union sensitivity to layoffs and an accumulation of legal rulings that restrict management's ability to fire.

Analysts have been surprised by the resilience of permanent employment in Japan during the postwar period in the face of economic downturns, including the oil crises of the 1970s. Nevertheless, current conditions strongly suggest that well-educated Japanese men are going to lose their position on the far end of the international employment stability continuum. In the last years of the twentieth century, Japan's labor force is experiencing its highest unemployment rate since the government began monitoring it in 1953 (Ostrom 1998: 1). Membership in unions has also been declining in Japan, from about 35 per cent in the early 1970s to 24 per cent in the mid-1990s (Japan Institute of Labour 1996: 48).

The well-documented erosion of seniority benefits also augurs a shift away from permanent employment. (As Chapter 1 noted, seniority practices suppress mobility because workers cannot transfer their number of years with one company or government organization to another workplace.) The upward curve by age for white-collar males' salaries peaked in 1972, and has been flattening consistently since then. Promotions are occurring more slowly as well, with average ages for section chiefs and division chiefs rising visibly (EPA 1995: 62, 65).

There are several sources for the trend, among them the demographics of a baby-boom era cohort too large to fit into available promotions, a mature, slow-growth economy, and the effects of international competition. Corporate personnel representatives polled in a 1997 survey identified the growing payroll burden of an ageing organization as the biggest problem of permanent employment, and fewer than half of the respondents indicated that their companies were committed to continuing permanent employment (JPC 1998: 6). The declining membership in unions (which, as discussed in Chapter 3, defend seniority practices because they ensure uniform treatment for members) also contributes to the decline of seniority benefits. These developments are unlikely to bring American levels of mobility, but they should put the Japanese statistically in the midst of their European counterparts.

Mobility, period?

The increased interinstitutional mobility of researchers is only one component, albeit a critical one, for attaining a dynamic credit cycle. Chapter 1 warned against regarding increased mobility as some kind of random movement among researchers beneficial in and of itself. To effect the full benefits of the credit cycle, mobility must be accompanied by mechanisms that promote genuine career development and optimal fit of interest and ability between individual and research group. This requires open recruitment and promotion through a transparent, impersonal selection process, along with impartial peer review for all publication and award decisions. These ingredients are particularly important for Japanese science because hierarchy and elitism figure so strongly in the allocation of rewards. Increased term employment in Japan as a stand-alone reform would result in a two-tiered system of elite, immobile researchers and a gypsy caste. The latter would be populated by the young, the female, and graduates from universities other than the top national universities.

Conditions for acceptance of mobility reform

The success of term employment reforms requires the enthusiastic support of the science community. Despite a palpable dissatisfaction with the status quo, Japan's scientists are not ready to accept the new mobility unconditionally. As Shigeru Nakayama pointed out (1996), the community is losing a privilege that it has always known. Since tenure begins at hiring, a larger proportion of the instructional work force has more to lose at the outset than in countries like the United States, where entry-level faculty are hired on successive multiyear contracts as a probation period. Resistance to term employment schemes comes from the lack of a reliable, generally accepted system of evaluation for judging who enters, who stays, and who leaves. Write-in comments in the JSC survey made clear that support for term employment would require a fair review process for hiring and promotion decisions, conducted with openness (JSC 1991: 132). The problems of how to conduct reviews of candidates for renewal and the arbitrariness of criteria loom large in current arguments against term appointments, reflecting the lack of procedures for evaluating research and teaching. In that regard, the proposal by the University Council literally left each university to its own devices (*Asahi Shimbun* 1996b: 13). A sweeping editorial criticism of the term employment proposal in the journal *Kagaku* (Science) asserted that personnel stagnation had resulted from the lack of fair review and not permanent employment, and further argued that reform would necessitate outside reviewers, thoroughly open recruitment, and universally acceptable criteria for evaluation (Yahara 1997: 429).

The term employment reform movement has already been compromised by age hierarchy, and perhaps by university hierarchy as well. The 1996 University Council initiative called for limited term employment for all faculty levels at all universities; resistance from professors (including council members), however, necessitated revising the recommendations so that term positions would apply only to entry level faculty, and individual universities could apply the recommendations at their discretion (Swinbanks 1996). My discussion partners felt that the reform would be more fair and practicable if all universities were to adopt term employment at once. One noted that the burden of reform was placed on the shoulders of the youngest, also. That the older members of the profession have more political clout is not unique to Japan, but the potential for intergenerational antagonism is particularly strong. Recall also the indifference (or sense of relief) among the OBI researchers at not having a senior mentor in their midst.

Widespread acceptance of term employment would also require providing rewards commensurate with those received by well-trained professionals outside of academia. Seniority benefits may be flattening out in the Japanese labor market, but the benefits of permanent employment are by no means gone. The statements of the OBI postdoc who discussed his classmates' salaries in industry are revealing. He enjoyed a measure of freedom and creativity denied them, but he was well aware of the difference between his material well-being and theirs. Respondents to the JSC survey observed that unless "all of society" became more mobile, term academic careers could prove ruinous to those who accept them. "Term appointments," they wrote, "would have to be part of a larger system in which moving would prove more advantageous to careers than staying in one place for a long time." Improved compensation would be needed. As one respondent noted, "It's certain that the number of aspirants to university teaching careers would decline sharply with pay left as is and no guarantee of lifetime employment" (JSC 1991: 133). The observation highlights a trade-off between higher salaries and job security that is seen in the United States as well, where eliminating tenure would require raising salaries substantially in order to attract and keep sufficient talent. As the JSC report recognized, "Academic ranks and term employment appear to be a problem involving the total social system" (133).

Punitive overtones and the potential for backlash

If revisions focus only on term employment and promote it under the banner of imposing discipline rather than rechanneling resources to reward excellence, Japanese scientists' sentiments could shift radically against attempted change. Reformers' descriptions of term employment as "drastic medicine" and a "whip to activate the universities" (*Asahi Shimbun* 1996c) have an undeniably punitive bite. They resemble the City of Osaka officials' condemnations of the scientists' "lukewarm bath" environment. The Japanese universities' notoriously low rates of interinstitutional mobility and extensive intellectual "inbreeding" appear to beg for reform through term employment – hence the University Council subcommittee's proposal that faculty remain at their universities under renewed terms of employment only in exceptional circumstances and after stringent evaluation (Swinbanks 1996). Nevertheless, the recommendation smacks of a forced march.

The kōza status quo lacks ardent defenders, but even critics have pointed to desirable features. Some of my informants familiar with the heavy reliance on outside research grants in the American system and its uncertainties pointed to the kōza's stability and the predictable allocation of research funds. After experiencing life as a postdoctoral fellow at the Harvard School of Medicine in an intensely competitive laboratory with a high turnover of members, a molecular biologist (then in his mid-thirties) returned to Kyoto University with an appreciation of the "continuity" afforded by the kōza. Both he and Akio Yamamoto (the critic I quoted earlier) credited the kōza for allowing its members to "settle into their research." "It's comfortable," said one academic biochemist in his late thirties who had also gone to the United States as a postdoctoral fellow. "You aren't working for the sake of a grant, but to realize your own ideas. It can be a good system – that is, for people who stick to it." Indeed, the pressure to produce manuscripts in the United States, combined with the job insecurity, were among his reasons for returning to Japan.

The lack of a widely accepted, reliable system of evaluation for allocating rewards could also help explain university researchers' acceptance of equal allocations of funds and laboratory space. The practice has been buttressed by an ideology of an "equity principle" (*byōdoo gensoku*) or "fairness principle" (*kōhei no gensoku*) that might strike the outside observer as a misplaced and dysfunctional attempt at democracy, or an odd expression of "communism" (as its detractors in Japanese academia label it). To the recipients, however, those resources represent a better deal than "competition" stacked in the favor of elites who already benefit from biases in both the Science Research Fund and the private sector foundations. In the 1997 JBS survey, well over half of respondents called for modest increases in kōza research budgets instead of the various ministries' large-scale research budgets, which they viewed as unfairly awarded (JBS 1997: 1311).

The union factor

University faculty and government laboratory workers belong to unions in Japan. (Chapter 3 discussed the influence of union activity among the latter.) The All-Japan Union of University Higher Education and Higher Special School Teachers (Zendaikyō), claiming some 39,000 members, and the Federation of Private University Teachers (Shidai Kyōren), with a membership of 20,000, responded jointly within days of the University Council's formal announcement of its proposal with a declaration of opposition and plans for a signature petition to the Minister of Education (*Asahi Shimbun* 1996d).

Even R&D staff in Japan's industrial sector have shown a high rate of unionization; a multinational survey, conducted between 1988 and 1990, found 60.5 per cent of Japan's technical specialists in the private sector reporting union membership, a rate almost three times higher than that of

R&D workers in England, four times that of Germany, and some seventy-five times the minuscule (0.8 per cent) rate among survey respondents in the United States sample (calculated from figures in JPC 1990c: 119; JPC 1990b: 133; JPC 1990a: 119). In the past, Japanese researchers have resorted to organizational tactics when pressed with highly unfavorable conditions. In 1951 scientists at RIKEN (at the time reorganized as the Science Research Institute) went on strike for two weeks over a salary supplement (Coleman 1990: 249). According to lore among Japanese students of science policy, the Earthquake Research Institute at the University of Tokyo has several times been the scene of a very pertinent dispute: part-time research assistants successfully petitioning, with union help, for permanent employment status.

Raw militancy at the university may be the stuff of history books, but my discussions with medical school graduate students made me wish I had a meter for measuring accurately their resentment. On the one hand, long hours of work are part of the initiation to physicianhood in the United States as well as Japan, and inspire many complaints in the process. The metaphor of PhD in medicine as grain of cooked rice on the sole of the foot may have been whimsical. On the other hand, not so whimsical was the historical reference I heard among the complaining students: the ferocious University of Tokyo riots of 1968, they correctly noted, began among medical school students (*Sekai Dai Hyakka Jiten* 1981: 25), and they attributed the rebellion to oppressive working conditions. Although my student interviewees were toddlers when it happened, they felt it relevant to their own situation.

The lab support impasse

University and government laboratory researchers feel the need for more support staff acutely (STA 1998: 99), and never fail to list it highly among the handicaps they face in international competition. Chapters 1 and 2 described the very sparse ratio of support staff per researcher in Japanese laboratories – hence Ken-ichi Arai's succinct summary, "Support system: no" in Table 8.1. The problem has actually worsened over the last two decades. In the mid-1970s, the ratio of support staff per researcher was over 0.8 – hardly luxurious, but it approached respectable European levels. A rising investment in science since then brought an increase in the number of researchers, but the absolute number of support staff actually decreased, and the staff to researcher ratio of the mid-1990s had shrunk to half that of the mid-1970s. Research support staff in universities had declined to 0.2 staff per researcher in 1997, the lowest point in over twenty years (STA 1998: 158).

The biggest source of this productivity bottleneck is the government's reluctance to hire more regular employees. The mid-1990s have been a time of cutbacks in hiring as austerity measures for a troubled national budget, but the operative words here are "regular employees," because the permanent–temporary divide – that is, the legal-political dimension of guaranteed employment – greatly exacerbates the problem of hiring technical and clerical support staff. The Ministry of Education forbids using SRF grant money for personnel expenses (*jinkenhi*). The 1996 instruction booklet expressly lists spending its grant money on "any compensation that could give rise to an employment relationship such as monthly salary, severance pay, or bonuses" (MOE 1996b: 13).

The shadow of the labor union in Japanese science could help explain this reluctance to allow an "employment relationship." The Ministry of Education has a financial reason to resist changing the regulations: it would bring demands for money to pay for services that are already being provided by unpaid graduate students. The more intractable problem, however, is the dilemma for the government posed by a Trojan Horse full of temporary government-paid employees wheeling into the midst of the securely employed; after several years, the temporaries might successfully mount a legal campaign to gain permanent jobs with the support of labor unions. The government could approach the problem by formulating legal initiatives for laboratory assistants resembling the law for term employment in universities. Meanwhile, the ministries are creating job categories for technical support staff, including MOE's "research assistant" (*risāchi ashisutanto*) for advanced doctoral students (STA 1998: 216), and the JBS has reported that 1997 changes in labor law enabled hiring from "talent dispatch centers" (subcontractors like those providing PERI's technicians) with SRF funds (JBS 1997: 1309).

Sources of resistance to open recruitment

Open recruitment may have increased somewhat in Japanese laboratories through the 1980s. A 1979 survey found only 16 per cent of the 142 biochemistry laboratory heads surveyed (of them 103 university professors) stating that they selected their assistants "mainly through open recruitment" (Sehara 1979: 77), less than half the percentage of natural scientist respondents in the 1990 JSC survey for whom open recruitment was "entirely or almost entirely" the mode for hiring their fellow academic officers (JSC 1991: 89). If there is such a trend, however, it cannot be credited to Japan's science policy makers; they have yet to launch an assault on introductions and hire-from-within with the zest they have devoted to promoting term employment.

Open recruitment unravels the intricate channels of reciprocity and empire-building that introductions provide. At their best, introductions offer the employing organization a steady supply of known commodities. Introductions also provide a measure of reassurance that the hiring group's interpersonal relations with the proffered candidate will not sour, given the guarantor's own responsibility in the matchmaking. This dimension of introductions is particularly important in Japan, where permanent employment means having to live with hiring decisions for a long time.

At their worst, as in the case of the medical school ikyoku, introductions form the fulcrum of power, piping in political favors and money to senior faculty in exchange for placements. Several knowledgeable observers believed that OBI was not more enthusiastic about open recruitment because, in the words of one medical researcher, "they were worried that some big shot would get on the phone to offer his own student, and then get very angry if he were turned down." The role of academic advisor as patron and advocate also benefits chosen students in a world of tight labor markets and insecurity. An OBI researcher acknowledged the allure of such protection. "Obviously I myself didn't go that way, but ..." he added pensively, "It's sweet. It can be very sweet."

The case of Kochi Institute of Technology's reliance on the Tokyo Institute of Technology for the majority of its staffing, as described in Chapter 2, can be understood in terms of these and other advantages of introductions and institutional conduits. Relying on a key university of higher status serves, in the words of several knowledgeable Japanese observers, as a means for "securing talent" (*jinzai kakuho*) when establishing new universities or academic divisions. The prestige of the genitor institution promises high quality faculty. The "boss" dynamic operates here as well, as higher education specialist Shin'ichi Kobayashi explained:

> In order to gather together talent expeditiously, getting an influential VIP researcher to become the center of recruitment is first and foremost. Then the natural turn of events will be for him to call on researchers with whom he has had some kind of connection, beginning with his own students. (Kobayashi 1991: 166)

MOE procedure contributes to the preference for institutional conduits as well. An MOE-appointed committee must evaluate the qualifications of the proposed new faculty members for MOE approval; as Kobayashi noted, a "boss" can expedite committee acceptance, and deal with committee members' own introductions of individual candidates. Kobayashi's exposition also mentioned accepting candidates proposed by committee members as another "expeditious" way to fill positions (1991: 166).

What would thorough reform look like?

A scorecard for judging reform should include open recruitment and a transparent peer review process. Any checklist of diagnostics should begin, however, with two fundamental issues. One is the ways in which funds for basic research are channeled on the national level. Chapter 4 illustrated the organizational problems of relying on the for-profit sector in basic research. (See Sakakibara 1991 for a comprehensive argument against relying on industry for basic research.) Chapter 6 described the problems stemming from

Japan's extremely high degree of central government control of funds for basic science. Decentralization of funding through revision of tax laws, the creation of indirect cost features in grants, and the nurturing of genuinely independent, tax-exempt nonprofit foundations would encourage the creation of more OBIs, with healthy competition among them.

The scorecard should also feature the extent to which the administration of the scientists is conducted by the scientists and for the scientists. Chapters 3 and 6 have described the setbacks to research careers when articulated with organizations having multiple priorities, or researchers who must work with administrators and their assistants who do not understand science. The issues that surround the introduction of term employment and individualized reward systems among Japanese researchers are a political minefield. The ultimate success of such organizational reforms requires execution by administrators who are familiar with scientists' career building needs and sensitive to their aspirations.

These core criteria for reform are important to bear in mind because many complicated, high-level administrative changes with uncertain consequences have been taking place in Japan throughout the late 1990s under the banner of "administrative reform" (*gyōsei kaikaku*; the transformation of the Food Research Institute into a more competition-oriented "agency" is just one example). Rather than dissect each official announcement of structural change, we should ask if funding control will be decentralized, and if Japanese scientists will work with administrators who have science backgrounds and are dedicated to meeting scientists' professional needs. Japanese scientists have long wanted their own institutions dedicated to funding and administering basic research. In the course of my research, innumerable scientist discussion partners wished out loud for a United States-style National Science Foundation or National Institutes of Health, independent of any one Ministry. As the twentieth century ends, however, the government's reorganizational prescription for science is to fold the STA into the already mammoth MOE.

A resistant and resilient bureaucracy

Chapter 1's observation that reform means relinquishing power is particularly pertinent regarding the national bureaucracy. The cost to them in decentralizing funding sources is obvious. The recruitment of scientists into the bureaucracy's midst would require it to share its authority and base its rewards on new criteria alien to those that have served to buttress its organizational integrity. The modification of administrators' career paths to accommodate more expertise in science management would challenge seniority-based status and promotion, and would compete with the carefully nurtured alignment (with its attendant loyalties) to the organization that is reinforced by rotations.

Transparency in decisions affecting scientific awards would also pose a sore sacrifice to the bureaucracy. Chapter 1 observed that Japan has no legal provisions for making available information on its activities to its citizens. In early 1998 the Diet was considering a freedom of information law, but the bureaucracy has taken many imaginative steps to limit its powers (Choy 1998b).

The government's *modus operandi* is surely one source of Japanese scientists' pessimism about the future. This is no ordinary bureaucracy. Although it ostensibly claims its powers by virtue of legislative mandate, the bureaucracy initiates and crafts the great majority of laws relating to its operation (including the recent freedom of information law). Its former members (the amakudari mentioned in Chapter 6) staff not only nonprofit organizations but the managerial ranks of Japan's top firms (Johnson 1995; Orr 1996). Western scientists in the postwar Occupation were skeptical of government-affiliated institutions for science (Coleman 1990: 237–8), and they recommended filling policy-related administrative positions in science with individuals trained in science rather than specialists in law and economics (NRS/SCAP 1948; Bartholomew 1989: 125), but to no avail. The Occupation scientists' own leaders, in one of the cosmic ironies of modern history, were instead preserving the bureaucracy and amplifying its power by relying on it to execute reforms intended to create a more open, democratic society.

Who wants better science?

Rather than ask if substantial reform is coming to the bureaucracy (for which there are no clear signs in any event), we could pin our prediction for reform of science organization on the question of whether Japanese society really needs and wants better basic science. Calls for more indigenous research ability are nothing new; prominent figures in Japan have argued for more domestic research capability since the turn of the twentieth century. Japanese industrialists felt the need particularly keenly at times when geopolitical developments restricted their access to foreign laboratories (Bartholomew 1989). Scientific achievement may reap international prestige, but the chronically low presence of Japanese science in arenas like the Nobel Prizes has not prompted Japanese policy makers to act effectively, even when Susumu Tonegawa pointedly criticized them as he accepted the 1987 award for Physiology or Medicine.

Japanese industry has long been the adept borrower and improver (a subject to which Chapter 9 returns in its discussion of science and global geography). The lack of preferential treatment for basic science PhD holders in government and industry described in Chapters 3 and 4, and the ubiquitous PhD in medicine among clinicians analyzed in Chapter 2, may simply reflect the absence of need for indigenous basic research capability. The degree means little because the skills it is supposed to represent mean little.

Universities reflect priorities

The anemic state of the kōza's credit cycle for researchers reflects what the MOE, Japanese industry, and the Japanese public demand most from universities, and it is not scientific journal articles or a sophisticated synergy between research and teaching. Rather, these groups look to the universities to evaluate students as grist for prospective employers. This personnel screening function is hardly unique to Japan's universities: universities in every country provide the same service via their admission standards and their evaluations of students' course performance (in grade point averages and faculty letters of recommendation). The Japanese version, however, concentrates on admission standards; employers in Japan select first and foremost on the basis of the names of their candidates' universities and the perceived difficulty of entering them, as opposed to how the candidates had performed academically during their university student years.

University admissions in Japan, in turn, are based on entrance examinations – some of them grueling – which select for diligence, command of factual knowledge (chiefly from memorizing large amounts of information), and the ability to solve problems in well-established areas as opposed to ingenuity and creative problem-solving. These emphases best serve large-scale private and government employers who provide their own subsequent training to impart the knowledge and problem-solving skills particular to their organizations. Japanese critics and reformers are well aware of this obstacle to more lively basic research activity. Jun-ichi Nishizawa, a highly regarded solid state physicist, railed against the industry attitude of "Hand over your science students fast – we'll have them do research after they've joined our company, so they don't need to do it at the university" (Nishizawa 1986: 51). The "thesis PhD" described in Chapter 4 owes its widespread adoption to this training configuration.

Research prowess does not figure highly in the status of Japanese universities. (The Ministry of Education does not designate which universities are research institutions.) Rather, the most influential criterion is the difficulty of its entrance examination, as measured in widely available statistics on standardized scores for success–failure ratios (known as *hensachi*, deviation values). The prestige is accorded to Japan's universities in a very explicit hierarchy, and the annual examination season is a high-profile contest that spotlights the most prestigious national universities and a handful of elite private universities (Rohlen 1983). The evaluation of universities according to the difficulty of their entrance examinations preempts their differentiation by areas of research strength. Hence the "department store" quality to the spectrum of specialties at the larger universities and another reason for equal funding among kōza, as opposed to more dynamic "specialty stores" or "centers of excellence" in which competitive science thrives (Nakamura 1992).

166

Rising stakes

Several important indicators suggest that the need for high-quality domestic basic scientific research is growing. Studies by Francis Narin and colleagues (Narin and Frame 1989; Narin, Hamilton and Olivastro 1997) capture quantitatively the changing relationship between science and industrial technology in Japan and the other major industrial nations. Creativity *per se* (about which Chapter 9 says more) is not the issue. One of the Narin and Frame databases, all United States patents issued between 1975 and 1985, documented a growing share of patents issued to Japanese inventors, with a corresponding decline to their American counterparts. In the watershed year of 1984, the number of patents to Japanese inventors exceeded the combined total for the United Kingdom, France and West Germany (1989: 246). Narin and Frame's analysis of scientific productivity, however, further substantiates Chapter 1's view of Japan's scientific effort as – in the authors' words – "fairly modest"; in stark contrast to Japan's towering position in US patents over its combined European competitors of the UK, France, and West Germany, those three countries' output of scientific papers totaled more than two and a half times the number published by Japanese scientists in the period under study (1989: 603).

The Narin studies portray the growing importance of science to technology by looking at another quantitative measure afforded by US patent records, a section of each patent titled "References Cited – Other Publications" (as opposed to citations of relevant patents, which also appear in patent records). Since most of the citations are to scientific literature, the study counted examiner citations to nonpatent literature to examine the extent to which patented technology builds on science. In 1975, each of the five countries under investigation had roughly the same average number of citations per patent (about 0.2), but the next decade witnessed an upsurge in nonpatent literature among inventors from all the countries under study, and a measurable shortening in the time span between the dates of the scientific publications and the patent to which they were linked (Narin and Frame 1989: 602, 605). Between 1985 and 1995 the trend continued (Narin, Hamilton and Olivastro 1997: 320).

These statistics are particularly satisfying because they argue quantitatively what observers have been saying with case studies and anecdotal evidence since the early 1980s: basic research, particularly creative research conducted in universities, now fuels the creation of new products more than ever before. In the United States, the list of illustrious companies that originated in academic circles includes Chiron, Cisco, Genentech, Hewlett-Packard, Netscape, and Sun Microsystems (Schrage 1997). These trends suggest that Japan's weak scientific capabilities will exact a greater price in international economic competition, and the Narin and Frame study supports this suspicion by noting a dramatic divergence: by 1985, Japan had grown the least in nonpatent citation frequency among the five countries, and the US had grown the most. The science linkage for US-invented patents had come to double Japan's (Narin and Frame 1989: 602). As of 1995, Japanese patents were still lowest in science linkage among the five major nations' patents (Narin, Hamilton and Olivastro 1997: 320).

Japan's weak basic research in the life sciences compromises its efforts in biotechnology. As Chapter 1 mentioned, the life sciences have a particularly close connection to applications. Industrial innovations in biotechnology, pharmaceuticals and medical instrumentation rely particularly heavily on advances in basic science. Some quantitative corroboration comes from the analysis of science citations in US patents: drug and medicine patents are the most highly science-linked. Among such patents filed in 1995 the average number of references to scientific papers per patent was an impressive 8.66 for all countries studied (Narin, Hamilton and Olivastro 1997: 321). Biotechnology-related industries, as analyst Steven Collins put it, advance through "risky and painstaking 'trial and error' research, whose impetus is knowledge creation based on revolutionary learning," in contrast with the "linear, incremental advance" driven by "evolutionary learning rooted in production experience." The latter brought success to such industries in Japan as consumer electronics and machine tools, but the former represents a basic research orientation that thrives in good universities (1992: 19).

Japan's pharmaceutical industry is displaying the signs of weakness in such basic research. Another careful observer found that Japan's major pharmaceutical companies have not increased export shares since the early 1990s, and the country's pharmaceutical industry as a whole has been spending a larger proportion on technology imports in the years between 1984 and 1994. Given the industry's sore need for "innovative basic R&D," Japan appears doomed to an inferior position in the life sciences "well into the twenty-first century" (Oberländer 1998: 180; 182–3; 191).

Global nicheing vs. borrowing vs. commitment to science

The prediction of a country's industrial trajectory is a remarkably complex undertaking, but for our interests I will limit the possibilities to three. In one scenario, Japan – through policy priority or default – ends up specializing in industrial areas in which it is already strongest, competing through improvement and refinement on core technologies. Areas like automobiles, machine tools, and robotics would be strong, but biotechnology would be allowed to wane. This would lessen the country's technoeconomic handicap from weaknesses in its university research system, and also greatly lessen the probability of the kinds of reforms this chapter has been discussing.

The second possibility is that Japan will nourish its more science-linked industries by tapping knowledge from abroad, sidestepping weaknesses in indigenous basic research capability. The Japanese scientist's stint abroad has been part of the classical formula for supplementing domestic deficiencies. Globalization of capital and advances in communication technologies have facilitated this strategy, and since the mid-1980s corporations around the world have entered into thousands of international research partnerships. Japanese corporate R&D facilities in the United States in the mid-1990s outnumbered by far those of other countries (NSB 1998: 4-4, 4-51). One survey reported in 1997 that Japanese firms hired foreigners more often than Japanese university faculty for mid-career recruitment of research talent (12.5 per cent for foreigners versus 11.7 per cent for all faculty ranks totaled; calculated using figures in STA 1998: 50).

The third possibility is that the government will respond to industries that rely heavily on scientific advances by strengthening domestic basic research capabilities – the option that requires organizational reform in basic science research. There are some good reasons for favoring this strategy over a heavy reliance on information from abroad, and signs that the government will take this direction. There is a definite tendency for technical innovators to prefer the basic science generated in their home countries: inventors participating in the US patent system cite their own country's papers some two to four times more often than unity across countries, and the same strong national ties between scientists and inventors appear in citations from papers to papers and patents to patents (Narin, Hamilton and Olivastro 1997: 321–2). In addition, indigenous basic science ability is like self-sufficiency in food production: if geopolitical instability or confrontation limit access to foreign sources, ability to grow at home averts critical shortages. Also, even if the government were to commit itself to relying heavily on scientific information from foreign sources, the information has become so sophisticated that commensurate research ability is needed at home for sufficient absorptive capacity – the ability to evaluate and assimilate information and technology from outside sources.

In 1992, the Japanese Federation of Economic Organizations (Keidanren) issued a document that called on the government to double the budget for science and engineering in the nation's universities (Kobayashi 1993). The government's budgetary response certainly looks serious; as Chapter 1 described, the government has been pouring more money into basic research, and signaling its intention to commit more. The desire for more domestic basic research capability explains the origins of the Protein Engineering Research Institute and much of OBI's support as well. If the third scenario does prevail, I invite readers to wager on the chances that genuine change will occur in the career trajectories and reward systems for Japanese scientists.

9

THE UNIQUE AND THE
PARTICULAR

I have been arguing that a career system in Japan for scientists with a stronger credit cycle would yield more excellent scientific research. But what if there were, in fact, a pervasive, deeply rooted feature of the Japanese psyche that makes it inhospitable soil for science? The suspicion arises perennially among both foreign and Japanese observers, prompting some to claim that the whole culture militates against creativity. Such national character and "cultural" explanations do not withstand important facts and tests of logic, but there *are* some special obstacles to international scientific competition and cooperation bequeathed by Japan's history and geography. Although these obstacles may seem far afield of a discussion of careers, overcoming them requires professional tools critical to success in global fora.

Group consciousness, politeness and passivity

National character explanations of Japan's disappointing performance in basic research revolve around the assertion that creative thought cannot bloom because individual Japanese would rather suppress their own interests and inclinations in deference to the group to which they belong. Japanese national character, goes the argument, cannot support the skepticism, irreverence, and occasional confrontation that feed dynamic scientific inquiry. Japanese individuals are predisposed to dislike fielding renegade ideas that go against the grain of received knowledge, or criticizing the work of a fellow Japanese in the peer review process.

Two components of the argument are valid: first, scientific inquiry does thrive on lively communication and debate that criticizes and compares research methods and conclusions. Convictions that are not expressed with self confidence and even forcefulness may not get the forum they deserve. "You have to be forceful, you have to be aggressive, you have to be pushy ... I don't know any scientists who don't push, and some push harder than others," said Nobel laureate Stanley Prusiner (Monmaney 1997: A18). Second, Japanese scientists do not engage in this kind of discussion and criticism with the frequency and vigor of their Western counterparts. Science journalists John Maddox and David Swinbanks called on Japanese scientists to shed their "habitual politeness . . . and the tendency not to criticise in public others in the 'same village' of research" (1992: 582). Japanese commentators like geneticist Katsumi Isono have also noted a reluctance to criticize, observing that Japanese scientists' reticence "makes it exceedingly difficult to have a peer review system" (1991: 35). Maddox and Swinbanks also noted that peer review would benefit from more critical public discussion.

The question and answer portions following presentations that I attended in Japan were somber affairs compared to presentations and symposia at my home university in the United States. The latter featured lively give and take among speakers and audience, and dissolved into spontaneous, post-event knots of participants who enthusiastically "cartooned" concepts on the nearest available blackboard as they argued their ideas. American and European researchers at my fieldwork sites observed the same contrast with their home institutions, as have other Westerners, like the German researcher who told *Science* magazine that "it's hard to find a hot discussion here" (Sun 1989: 1546).

Separating causes and effects

Japanese scientists' passive interaction style reinforces foreigners' impressions that their Japanese counterparts prefer deferring to the group. The crucial term for a national character explanation here is *prefer*, and it is unwarranted. First, Japanese bioscientists do not universally prefer polite passivity and reluctance to criticize, and some have roundly denounced those tendencies to their fellow countrymen in print (e.g. biochemist Tasuku Honjo 1992). Japanese researchers who have attended meetings and symposia in the United States express envy of the American discussion style. Recall also the dissatisfaction among researchers at PERI with the extent and quality of intramural discussion, discussed in Chapter 4. Two Japanese neuroscientists in their mid-thirties offered me an exception to Japanese passivity in formal gatherings. They insisted, proudly, that meetings of the Japan Developmental Biology Society (Nihon Hasseigaku Gakkai) were just as lively and critical as any in the West.

Japanese society offers many examples of individuals as independent, eccentric, or rebellious as any Westerner. Personalities who have carved out unique paths for themselves have been very popular figures in postwar Japan (Mouer and Sugimoto 1986). An experiment in social psychology conducted among Japanese college students in 1966 exacted *less* conformity than did the same procedure among Americans. In these "Asch-type" experiments, the subject must state his or her perception of the relative lengths of two lines, but only after a group of fellow subjects who are actually confederates has given theirs; confederates' responses sometimes clearly contradict the actual lengths of the lines being compared. The point of the experiment is to see if an individual will ignore or defy his or her own perceptions in order to show agreement with the group. Not only was the average conformity score in Japan lower than that for American subjects: over a third of the Japanese subjects disagreed with the confederates even when the confederates' comparisons of the two lines were factually correct! This "anticonformity" had never been observed before in such group studies (Frager 1970).

What, then, causes the oft-observed reticence among scientists? When the discussions are conducted in English or other foreign languages, Japanese scientists may have real difficulty for linguistic reasons, but my observations (and others') are also based on meetings conducted in Japanese. Research group members who have neither an active interest in the research topic nor the same level of ability as their fellow group members dampen discussion, their presence a result of permanent employment or top-down assignments to research groups, as discussed in Chapters 2 and 3.

First and foremost, however, we should not underestimate the thoroughness and subtlety with which hierarchical power can permeate styles of personal expression. My informants were most likely to explain the absence of debate at scientific meetings in terms of fear of retaliation for criticisms and perceived slights. "If I were in the position of the person getting the question I'd feel uncomfortable," said a government lab biochemist in his mid-forties. But when I then asked if audience members' feelings of sympathy for the speaker were behind their reluctance to pose questions he replied, "No, it's self-preservation (*jiko hozon*). When you ask a question you're challenging the professor's invisible authority in front of others. The older the professor the worse the attitude, too." The young neuroscientists who delighted in telling me about the lively exchanges at the Japan Developmental Biology Society explained that theirs was a relatively new organization, and their meetings were blessed by an absence of medical school faculty who, they said, dominated the subdued biochemistry society meetings with their "vertical" style.

Informants also noted that long-term professional association in the same organization (thanks to permanent employment) could mean repercussions from perceived affronts for years on end. Some perceptive observations about the interpersonal effects of permanent employment came from Thomas Rohlen's study of a Japanese bank: long-term employment fosters "caution, compliance, a highly developed sensitivity to relationships and emotional states, a smothering sense of no escape . . ." (Rohlen 1974: 89).

Humorless labs

There is another indicator that hierarchy and not innate preference is at work suppressing individuality among Japanese scientists: visual humor in the lab. Humor was a stock item of laboratory wall decoration in laboratories in the Anglophone countries I have visited. Americans may be the most adept at this pursuit, and perhaps the most outrageous. Cartoons and humorous signs are laboratory fixtures, and even formal presentations are not immune from some raillery. A doctoral student treated his dissertation defense audience at the University of Oregon's Institute for Molecular Biology to an extra projection slide that followed the usual graphs, charts, and final list of acknowledgments: a photograph of the candidate's advisor, pants down, seated on a camp toilet stool. (The audience roared with laughter and, yes, he did pass his defense.)

Some channels of humorous expression among scientists in the United States are even institutionalized, the most famous the *Journal of Irreproducible Results*, and the tradition of pranks and parody at MIT (chronicled in Leibowitz 1990). Jibes among Western bioscientists can be downright rhetorical. An Australian biochemist told me how he had once passed out paper glasses with pink plastic lenses to the audience for a competitor's presentation, explaining to all that "You'll need these rose colored glasses to interpret my colleague's data the way he intends."

In all of the laboratories in Japan that I have visited over the years, however, there was only one that offered passers-by a visual joke. It was a stylized silhouette of a defecating bull, encircled and slashed with a "not permitted" symbol. It was hanging on one of the doorways in an agricultural chemistry laboratory at a second-tier national university, its owner a postdoc who had brought it back with him from a two-year stint at a university laboratory in Texas. The problem is not a society-wide dourness. The Japanese can certainly enjoy humor, including humor about science; *That's Kanningu* (That's Cheating), a 1996 movie reminiscent of *Animal House*, lampooned college students' ingenious and outrageous cribbing methods at a science and engineering university, and the attempts of authoritarian faculty to squelch them.

The issue may seem frivolous, but cartoons and humorous signs and notes taped on doors and hallway bulletin boards serve several psychic functions, among them release of nervous tension, a declaration that occasional bouts of silliness are permitted, and – last but not least – pokes at authority. There is a subtle but real dampening effect on creativity underneath this nearly inconsequential iceberg tip of submission in Japan: to be creative one must risk looking silly or irritating to an authority. A glimpse at the cause of this solemnity came from an assistant in agricultural chemistry at a Tokyo area second-tier national university. He had once had a cartoon tacked on his office door, he said, but his professor had ordered him to remove it because "we're supposed to look serious." Japanese responses to a vignette from the United States were also instructive. I had several times told Japanese researchers about an American organic chemist and his colleagues at a major industrial laboratory (also in the United States) who responded to continuous visits and detailed inquiries from managers by putting up a large sign that read, "If We Knew What We Were Doing It Wouldn't Be Research." The Japanese researchers would invariably say, after polite laughs, that if they ever did something like that they would be punished for it.

The appeal of national character explanations

Japanese scientists themselves have several explanations for the passivity/politeness syndrome, among them national character or circumstances unique to Japan, but these attempts at social explanation do not have the rigor that these same specialists would demand in their own fields. The geneticist Katsumi Isono (1991: 35) suggested that the avoidance of conflict is a way of adapting to high population density. (By that logic, Koreans and Bangladeshis should be even more demure.) Medical researcher Kyoko Imamura attributed medical school students' passive acceptance of low-quality education to Japan's "traditionally agricultural society" and Confucianism (1993: 280), but less than 6 per cent of Japan's labor force is involved in agriculture, and since 1970 over half of the population has been living in cities of 100,000 or more (almost twice the proportion found in the United States). Confucianism was swept from the school curriculum fifty years ago.

In any event, a thorough and vigorous demonstration of the flaws of national character or "cultural" explanations would probably not eradicate them. They offer a convenient apology for the stubborn problem of collegial acquiescence, thus making it a bit easier to live with. This type of explanation also has ideological value for proponents of the status quo. Noboru Makino, Director of the Mitsubishi Research Institute, vigorously defended Japan's strengths in applied research and opposed more government funding for basic research by asserting that Japan's "natural national milieu," in which "individuals are held back from high profiles, and collaborative projects receive priority" makes Japan (inevitably) superior in development research rather than basic research (1992: 4).

There is a ready-made body of thought with an extensive literature known as "*Nihonjinron*" (commentary on the Japanese) that lends intellectual credibility to Japanese national character arguments. The literature's most influential explanation of hierarchical groupism springboarded from the writings in the mid-1970s of a Japanese psychiatrist, Takeo Doi, who asserted that dependence on a hierarchical group leader is a universal trait of the adult Japanese personality (resulting from certain child raising practices). Nihonjinron also has a conservative ideological appeal, since it ignores or rejects outright the effects of inequality. That favorite hoary bromide of the Nihonjinron school, "The nail that sticks out gets hammered down," does not tell us who is doing the hammering. None of the Nihonjinron proponents has been able to account for the myriad instances of nonhierarchical behavior that historians and social scientists have documented, nor has anyone demonstrated convincingly that instances of Japanese reticence and passivity come from a sense of wanting to be the same, rather than from a fear of punishment for bucking established power. Until the current system of hierarchical controls is weakened, we cannot assume that Japanese scientists avoid open disagreement because their personalities demand it, even at the price of excellence in research.

Philosophical apologists

Another attempt to explain Japan's disappointing scientific output in terms of unique thought processes enlists Japan's metaphysical traditions. The argument, in a nutshell, holds that Western religion created an intellectual predisposition for Western-style scientific inquiry that Japanese religion lacks. Japan's religious traditions are relativistic and mystical: in Shinto there are "eight million gods" (and, technically speaking, new gods can still arise); Buddhism, the other major traditional religion of Japan, abjures any distinction between self and object, including human and nature. The effect on scientific writing is lengthy description that does not boil down to a few powerful rules, presented in a sequence connected by a loose imagery rather than a clear logic (Motokawa 1989). In Western religions, by contrast, the universal one God of Western religions inspires the pursuit of a small number of all-powerful rules based on the premise of knowable uniformities in nature, replete with objectification and strict logic.

The "different religions" argument surfaces occasionally in international discussions of Japanese research performance. A Japanese participant from the Tokyo Institute of Technology suggested to conferees at a US–Japan conference on the international dimensions of high technology that progress in basic research is more difficult in Japan because, due to Japanese polytheism, "the way of thinking in which one believes in only one truth is not strong" (Okamura 1986: 11). A Japan Research and Development Corporation officer posed the argument to a group of foreign researchers in 1990, perhaps to stimulate a larger discussion of differences and similarities.

The argument's assumption that religion provided the intellectual birthplace for science in the West ignores a history of bitter antagonism between science and Christianity, from heliocentric theories of the solar system to biological evolution. Philosophical apologists for Japanese uniqueness might be better off arguing the reverse, that basic science in Japan has weak philosophical roots because its advocates never had to sharpen their arguments in fights with theologians, as in the West. Indeed, science historian James Bartholomew found a Japanese physicist who expressed precisely those misgivings in writing (1989: 3). Then, however, the philosophical apologists would have to overlook the antagonism between Japan's early advocates of scientific rationalism and Buddhist mystics. Genpaku Sugita, Baien Miura and Hoashi Banri, all major figures in the introduction of Dutch medical science and Western astronomy in the late eighteenth and early nineteenth centuries, were direct disciples of anti-religious rationalists who openly – and frequently – articulated their hostility to Buddhism (Furukawa 1963).

Thinking and communicating science in the Japanese language

One other argument of unique thought processes points to features of the Japanese language itself. Cultural commentators on both sides of the Pacific have described Japanese as ambiguous and imprecise, requiring high-context situations loaded with nonverbal cues to compensate for its inherent vagueness. The language, so the argument goes, is both product and perpetuator of homogeneity and groupthink. It is true that Japanese does not share certain features with Western languages. There is no plural inflection for verbs and nouns; for example, "Samurai going" in Japanese could be one or twenty knights, depending on context. Sentences do not require grammatical subjects, either; "Going" is grammatically sufficient in Japanese, in contrast to subject-ridden English, where even the verb for falling rain requires a subject ("It's raining"). Nor does Japanese make use of definite and indefinite articles.

The consequences for scientific communication ought to be debilitating. None of these features hampers either spoken or written scientific communication, however, for several reasons. (The following is based on linguist Christina Honde's 1996 paper.) First, every language – Japanese included – has many varieties (or "registers," the term used by linguists) that speakers use in different contexts for different sets of tasks. The popular stereotype of Japanese as imprecise is based on one type of situation, the face-to-face interpersonal communication which in every culture relies on emotion-sharing and attention to subtle social cues. When Japanese people take part in goal-directed activities requiring impersonal, objective information, they can communicate it precisely. No plural inflection in Japanese, for example, simply means using other strategies, like straightforward counting ("ten cultures," "five cells," etc.), plural deictics like "these" and "those" (*korera*, *sorera*), and several other devices to denote plurals with no ambiguity. Similarly, even though Japanese sentences do not require a subject, neither is one prohibited, and speakers and writers do indeed respond to the need for clarity by signaling topics or subjects with nouns, noun phrases, and demonstrative pronouns.

Written scientific and technical (WST) prose must provide more precision than social conversation in any language. Informational prose of this order cannot, of course, involve real-time negotiation of meanings during discussion; it relies on a body of well-established laws and practices. The Japanese language demonstrates the same capabilities in WST as Western languages, and may even possess some slight advantages. English WST style relies on passive constructions, like "E. coli carrying only YEp13 *was mixed* with yeast," in order to center attention on substances, phenomena or arguments rather than on agents. Japanese grammar allows its writers to focus on the same points while using the more common active voice, "[we/no subject] mix E. coli carrying only YEp13 with yeast." Also, precise WST prose requires the coining of new terms for items and processes newly generated at home and abroad. The written Japanese language has, in addition to symbols for transliteration of foreign terms (*katakana*), Chinese characters that allow compact and efficient creation of terms whose meaning can be understood at a glance. The characters, introduced to Japan some fifteen centuries ago, could accommodate terms and concepts during the late nineteenth century assimilation of information and technology from the West, and still find use today. The term "cell fusion," for example, has been translated directly into the four-character term *saibō yūgō*,

細胞
cell (characters for "small" and "sac")

融合
fusion (characters for "melt" and "join").

What about the work ethic?

One more supposed psychic uniqueness also has special significance for scientific effort, this time in the opposite direction from hindrance: the fabled Japanese work ethic. The Japanese as a nation do log more hours on the job than do their Western counterparts, earning a reputation that extends to scientists as well. Natalie Angier's depiction of life at a Cold Spring Harbor oncogenetics laboratory introduced the Japanese as "the hardest-working scientists in the world." When two "imported biologists" lived up to their reputation an American colleague marveled, "I work hard, but you can't compare me with the Japanese. They're not even Earthlings" (Angier 1988: 277).

The distinction is more apparent than real. Chapter 5's comparison of work hours at OBI and other research institutions showed that not all of Japan's researchers were putting in uniformly long hours. The nationwide study used for that comparison had yielded a spread of 56 hours a month among categories of R&D workers, with researchers in the laboratories of mid-size private companies logging the fewest hours (IFT 1990: 46). Nor has Japan been in the forefront of the diligent throughout its modern history. Western observers in the late nineteenth century were singularly unimpressed. Among many examples were the 1889 *Japan Weekly Mail* editorial decrying "anti-work" attitudes in the Japanese national character (Smith 1989: 26–7), and German missionaries' accounts that criticized the lack of "steady, systematic work" (Linhart 1988: 271).

Coming closer to the present, hours of work in Japan were indeed high but falling steadily in the post-World War II period with greater affluence. They stalled in the mid-1970s, though, reflecting the economy's bruising from yen reevaluation and two international oil embargoes. Permanent employment practices then, as in every downturn since, have inclined employers to restrain hiring and respond to upturns in demand by allocating more overtime to existing staff. Inflation, meanwhile, began gnawing at workers' earning power, making shorter work hours at lower pay levels less attractive and overtime pay more attractive.

The economic stage was thus set for a society of workaholics, but the inadequacy of Japan's recreational facilities has played a part as well in failing to offer alternatives to work. There are few public recreational facilities, from swimming pools to campgrounds in national parks, and privately operated facilities are much more expensive than overseas. Japan's generally high cost of living has taken its own toll on access to leisure pursuits, and even recreational shopping is costly. Thus, average daily expenditures by Japanese families for vacations and traveling in the mid-1980s were four times those of France and six times the figure for Germany (Takahashi 1990: 9). In urban areas, cramped housing space has also discouraged recreational activity at home. Listening to music with headphones is one option, but such pursuits as carpentry, mechanical tinkering or gardening are out. The rush-hour strain on transportation flows also keeps Japanese in large cities at their work places longer, to avoid dealing with crushes of fellow commuters.

As a result, the typical laboratory in Japan has resembled other work places in serving as a setting for leisurely activities such as reading newspapers and comic books, watching baseball games on television, and snacking with beer. Many are the mystified Euro-American co-workers, whose visceral response is, "If you aren't working, why don't you go home?" The American scientists in Angier's study were simply dealing with a rather selective sample, in a setting removed from the factors that shape work time in Japan. Younger life scientists in my study were genuinely concerned that laboratories in the United States would accept them as postdocs expecting constant hard work rather than inventive thought. "I don't want to be cheap Asian labor," said one.

More problematic than the mixing of work and pleasure is the subtle but ever-present problem of substituting physical effort for creative thought. Few are the great scientific breakthroughs achieved without prodigious effort, but in the business of new insights hard work alone does not bring scientific progress. Chapter 2 described the kōza's tendency to reward graduate students for relatively menial tasks, and argued that it encourages working harder at the expense of working smarter. A 34-year-old OBI biochemist (the one who had mused that Japan would be the world leader in science if the only criterion were time spent in the laboratory) was struck by Kary Mullis' story of how he first conceptualized the famous polymerase chain reaction while driving through the redwoods of northern California in 1983. "I think I need time to stop the job and think now and then like that," said the OBI researcher.

Historical perspectives

Historical fact has fueled the suspicion that the Japanese are intrinsically uncreative: throughout its modern history, Japan has systematically absorbed technical and scientific information from abroad. During over two hundred years of state-imposed insulation from Christianity and European subversion (from the 1630s to the 1850s) the country's elites gathered scientific and technical information methodically via Dutch sources. A wave of European and American intrusions in Northeast Asia beginning in the mid-nineteenth century prompted Japan's rulers to seek more information from the West, with an urgent focus on military and engineering applications.

In the last decades of the nineteenth century, the Meiji Period saw rapid industrialization, modernization, and accommodation of Western organizational practices. These developments spurred the Japanese state's formation of a university system. The emphasis in the organization of higher education, however, fell decidedly on assimilating foreign information and technology transfer, particularly in areas like engineering that afforded immediate applications. The overall pattern of take-from-abroad persisted for some decades after the end of World War II, as evidenced in extensive patent licensing and reverse engineering (dismantling and examining a competitor's successful product). Even post-war foreign language education, with its cultivation of reading ability at the expense of productive skills, reflected the country's information-gathering stance.

This history of a century plus several decades of absorbing from abroad has encouraged both American observers and Japanese scientists themselves to perceive the Japanese as copiers. With predictable regularity, my informants began their discussions of Japan's science by referring to the "hundred years of borrowing," a legacy that had yet to be overcome. Students of the late biochemist Shosaku Numa said he often stated that "We have only had science for one hundred years." These references to history typically concerned outdated but entrenched organizational forms. "The big problem," observed Kyoto University neurologist Shigetada Nakanishi (introduced in Chapter 2), "is how to change a system that has been so successful at borrowing from abroad for a hundred years."

There is also an element of self-doubt in these open musings, a genuine expression of the fear that science is truly an exogenous creation, alien to Japanese culture and ultimately incomprehensible. In the early post-World War II period, Japanese scientists summarized that misgiving with the poignant metaphor of Western science as "cut flowers" (Kikuchi 1950): beautiful, but lacking Japanese roots. Nearly half a century later, some knowledgeable Japanese scientists are still haunted by the possibility that their country's history as borrower has deprived them of some kind of scientific comprehension. Hiroyuki Toh, whom I introduced in the chapter on PERI, felt that the understanding of science in Japan was "surface" only, but he also believed that courses in the history of science would deepen understanding. Mitsuhiro Yanagida, Kyoto University biophysicist, smarted under an American colleague's offer to teach "what is science" in Japan, but didn't refute it. Japanese scientists, he suspected, could stand to learn more about "how science develops." Somehow, Yanagida suspected, Meiji leaders had not let the spirit of science into the country along with its products (Yanagida 1996b). A PERI biophysicist also suspected that science was a shallowly rooted import. He echoed the assumptions of Mitsubishi's Makino, but with misgivings: "Technology, especially the way it's done in Japan, is a group enterprise. But science, really basic science, isn't something you do as a group. The most creative things come from individuals. So how do we nurture that in people?"

The borrow-versus-create dynamic

These lingering doubts are best dispelled with some perspectives on Japan's career as borrower. In looking at Japan it is too easy to forget that the great majority of *every* culture's repertory, from decorative styles to technologies, has come from some place else. Some sixty years ago an astute anthropologist described just some of the inventions in the United States that had originated elsewhere – among them, cotton domesticated in India, soap invented by ancient Gauls, and cigarettes invented in Mexico. The typical American man, unaware of these origins, would nevertheless "thank a Hebrew god in an Indo-European language that he is 100 per cent American" (Linton 1936: 327). This forgotten staple of comparative social science needs repeating when Europeans and Americans look at Japanese borrowing, because Japan's figurative and literal location outside the Euroamerican cultural sphere – and as an island nation at that – has made its borrowing from the West look conspicuous. Far less apparent to most observers is the terrific volume of mutual borrowing and information transfer among Western countries in modern history, as when excellent European scientists poured into American laboratories and classrooms in the 1930s.

Another forgotten staple of anthropological wisdom also provides some needed perspective. Effective transfer of scientific and technical knowledge – at which Japanese manufacturers have repeatedly succeeded – requires a degree of technoeconomic sophistication that stands just one evolutionary step from independent, home-grown innovation. Japan might well have industrialized on its own without Euro-American contact. The Tokugawa Period was by no means a "Dark Age" of technoeconomic equilibrium. One indicator of agricultural sophistication is varieties of rice: by one estimate, they proliferated during the period from about 175 to over 2,000 (Hane 1986: 56). Reliance on inanimate power energy was growing; by the time Japan entered the nineteenth century, its coal mining industry was as sophisticated as any other in the world of its time (Samuels 1987: 68).

Urbanization had progressed beyond European levels; by the mid-eighteenth century, Japan's city of Edo had over a million inhabitants, larger than any city in Europe, and by mid-nineteenth century, literacy rates were comparable to contemporary England's (Hall 1970: 219).

Nevertheless, Japan's geographical separation from Europe left it outside the sphere of international competition and cooperation that accelerated scientific and technoeconomic development in the West. At the time of increased contact in mid-nineteenth century, Japan lagged behind its European counterparts in certain critical areas, most notably metallurgy and its application in cannons and steam engines. Japan, after all, was emerging from some two and a half centuries of peace, unlike its European counterparts whose military-industrial development had been spurred by trade and incessant warfare among themselves. Japan's reward for eventually mastering those technologies was to escape from Euroamerican domination, and Japan – unlike its hapless neighbors – survived intact in large part because a base of indigenous knowledge and skills enabled technology transfer from abroad. Cannon casting, for example, was ultimately enabled by indigenous abilities despite a disastrous wholesale transplant-from-abroad approach to iron making by industrial policy makers (Nakaoka 1980).

The price of distance from Europe

By the early twentieth century Europe had become the undisputed center of scientific activity. Japan's geographical separation from that center exacted a toll on Japan's own scientific progress. One striking example comes from the case of the talented physicist Torahiko Terada in the diffraction of X-rays by crystals. (This account is based on Shimao 1989.) Inspired by research conducted in Germany in 1912, Terada devised a technique that greatly sped up the photography process used for data gathering. Terada's reporting of results, however, lagged some months behind Britain's W.H. Bragg and W.L. Bragg. The geography of science in those days gave the Braggs a lead of two months over Japan in obtaining the report of the German research, and an additional month when submitting their own results to *Nature*, the premier forum for reporting research. (Papers mailed from Japan took a month or more to arrive by steamship.) By the time Terada reported his research results in Tokyo in May of 1913 he was aware that W.L. Bragg had reported on the same phenomena in November of the year before.

Not all of the Braggs' lead could be attributed to communication lags, but the disadvantage of distance was palpable. Terada's pride led him to drop X-ray diffraction studies, and he did not encourage any of his students to pursue them, either. This incident represented a setback for future research in Japan's life sciences as well. X-ray crystallography in the Bragg laboratory provided the concepts and techniques for the atomic arrangements of proteins and DNA essential to the work of Rosalind Franklin in the early 1950s, which in turn provided the information that unlocked DNA's double helix structure (Watson 1968). The Braggs won a Nobel Prize in 1915 for their work. Is it too hypothetical to picture what a Nobel Prize for Terada would have done to stimulate support in Japan for research in X-ray crystallography?

Retreating geographical barriers

Innovations in transportation and communication have reduced dramatically the problem of Japan's sheer distance from the United States and Europe, a point so obvious that it is regularly ignored. Between the mid-1970s and mid-1980s, the proportion of Japanese articles having foreign co-authors more than doubled, in a trend also seen in the United States and the United Kingdom (Okubo and Miquel 1991: 263; Hicks and Katz 199: 395). Between 1981 and 1986, Japan's rate of increase in internationally co-authored scientific articles was the highest among twelve industrialized countries, including the United States (Okubo and Miquel 1991: 264). The remarkable increase in international publications by Japanese bioscientists in recent years that was described in Chapter 1 also suggests that geographical barriers are less formidable than in the past.

The incidence of "scooping" reflects international activity. American scientists use the term (from journalism) when someone has published a report of successful research outcomes in advance of one's competitors investigating the same subject. I asked Japanese researchers if there were a term in Japanese for a situation in which "another researcher announces your research subject before you do." (Two thirds of the sixty-four researchers whom I asked came up with one or more expressions.) When I then asked about experiencing a scoop, I found both losers and winners in international competition. Of the sixty-three researchers for whom I have responses, seventeen specifically mentioned getting scooped by Americans or Europeans. (Another three had cooperated with colleagues who lost out to Americans.) Unlike the adage that "a miss is as good as a mile," these incidents indicate participation in international competition.

There were also five researchers who knew they had published ahead of specific competitors in the West. In one exciting case, PERI researchers studying a specific protein's structure found themselves in direct competition with a National Institutes of Health senior researcher with whom one of the PERI team had had a long-standing cooperative relationship. The NIH-sponsored effort was led by researchers at Columbia University. According to one of the researchers on the PERI side, the PERI group proposed cooperative research or information exchange and simultaneous publication, but the principal investigator at Columbia decided on head-on competition. What could have been a bruising experience resulted in the happiest of endings: the PERI group published in *Nature*, the Columbia group in *Science* simultaneously (Katayanagi et al. 1990; Yang et al. 1990).

My inquiry about "scoops" had several sources of imprecision, of course. First, research projects can overlap rather than compete head-on. Even when two different research groups study one protein's structure using X-ray crystallography, biophysicists may not regard their output as direct competition, arguing that structural analysis is part of a larger goal, such as functional studies, with results open to interpretation of varying quality. Also, important scientific contributions do not always depend on direct competition, and individual scientists – excellent ones among them – may wish to avoid it. Wrote Arthur Kornberg:

> I am . . . uncomfortable with the emphasis on competition in science. It is no fun for me to strive to do something that is likely to be done just as decisively by someone else at about the same time. Unless it is urgent to clear away an obstruction in the path to a major objective, I would rather work on one of the many problems around the core of my interest and competence. (1989: 236)

Nor did my scoop question pin down the extent of lost effort by defeated interviewees, which is a matter of degree. On one end of the continuum in such competition is a set of ideas in one's head, and at the other, a paper painstakingly prepared and ready to be submitted. A few of my bested interviewees specifically mentioned papers in the final stages of preparation, and the rest whom I counted as "scooped" spoke with enough chagrin for me to include them as well. Those who had been scooped as graduate students preparing research to submit for publication felt the most pain of all: the situation could slow completion of PhD requirements by a year or even completely derail getting the degree. (I did not include those who talked only about ideas anticipated by Westerners, and they did not consider themselves seriously scooped, either.)

Identifying bested competitors in the West involved yet more uncertainty, since getting such information depended on a network of potential foreign competitors, or self-identification by the hypothetical dropouts – not unknown, but not that frequent an event, either. Nevertheless, despite all the indications that "scoop" information is more suggestive than definitive, my interviewees gave me one more indication that they were very much part of a global scientific dialogue.

Language as barrier

That hoariest artifact of geographical isolation, the Japanese language, remains Japan's most formidable barrier to international cooperation and competition in science. There is nothing intrinsically more complicated about Japanese than any other language, of course; the problem is the vast difference between Japanese, on one side, and the Indo-European languages, including

English, on the other. The closest linguistic relative to Japanese is Korean; the two split off from a parent language some six thousand years ago, making Korean the least difficult foreign language for Japanese speakers to learn (and vice versa for Koreans).

Writing is an important skill for posing an argument in the life sciences, and it poses a lot of problems for Japanese researchers attempting to publish in foreign languages. The precision of science does make for a more straightforward, mechanical form than other prose, but freedom from qualification, nuance and dictates of style is a matter of degree. Little writing skill is needed for biochemists' reports of the amino acid sequence of the gene for a particular protein, but these tasks are at the least verbal end of the writing continuum. For other articles, the ability to use language for accurate, clear communication and argument is essential.

Japanese bioscientists acutely feel the need for foreign language skills for persuasive writing. Respected biologists in Japan have observed that "half of a biologist's academic ability is linguistic" (Yanagida 1996a). The eminent geneticist Tomoko Ohta commented that writing articles in English with enough appeal to attract readers was her "most difficult of tasks." Being a native speaker of Japanese had posed far more of a handicap to the international evaluation of her accomplishments than being a woman (though she also suspected that her foreign readership assumed she was a man; Ohta 1990).

During my field work I learned first hand the numerous pitfalls in translation with which Japanese scientists must deal when I provided my informants English editing and translation assistance. The use of articles (*a*, *an*, and *the*, collectively known as *kanshi* in Japanese) poses a constant problem, as do prepositions, verb–subject number agreement, and placement of modifiers. The limited flexibility and power of vocabulary compared to a native speakers' repertory take a toll in communication also. For example, the conservative estimate generated by a computer program was described by a Japanese author as an "underestimate," leading the reader to believe the program had erred.

Writing skills are also important in communicating with the editors of foreign journals, particularly when negotiating revisions: ineffective defenses and poorly executed bids for compromise add months to the realization of a published product. I suspect also a psychological bargaining disadvantage to letters that begin with, "We are very grateful you have accepted our manuscript." My informants guesstimated one to four months of additional time for writing articles in English over the time needed to write identical articles in Japanese, and an estimate reported by Shigeru Nakayama put time needs for writing articles in English at four times the amount of time needed for those in Japanese (1991: 83n.21).

The language problem hampers Japanese scientists in discussions with foreign colleagues at the most informal level as well. At least a third of my researcher interviewees who were otherwise inclined to use the telephone to secure helpful information abroad have been held back by language difficulties. I asked eighty of my researcher interviewees if they had ever made "cold calls" – spontaneous self-introductions on the telephone – to ask another researcher outside one's network specific questions concerning laboratory technique. Although I hadn't specified foreign or domestic calls in my question, twelve of the thirty interviewees who had made such calls said they confined them to Japan. Expense may have been a factor, but these interviewees specifically mentioned the problem of understanding and being understood in an overseas phone call. In other discussions about contacting foreign researchers, my suggestion of an overseas call often rewarded me with a nervous laugh. Talking on a telephone is much more difficult than face-to-face discussion, which affords the opportunity for visual cues and more generosity toward groping and pauses ("dead air" in a telephone exchange).

In light of these obstacles, the foreign language publication record of Japanese bioscientists must represent a heroic effort. The ultimate source of Japanese scientists' foreign language torment lies in the fact that English is taught in Japanese schools more for purposes of reading comprehension than for communication, and rather ineffectively at that. In tests of English as a foreign language (TOEFL) for foreign exchange student candidates in the 1995–6 academic year, mean scores for Japanese test takers ranked 85th among 107 comparable scores. Even if we generously consider some skewing downward by test takers wanting to study abroad precisely to improve their English ability, the figure reflects poor preparation for using English.

One might argue that the bioscientists' language difficulties reflect their original choice of science in preference to specialties requiring the manipulation of words and foreign language study. (Some informants recalled half jokingly that they settled on a science emphasis for college because its foreign language requirement was lighter than the humanities'.) Many of my informants, however, were eager to learn principles for future use, as opposed to fixing a problem document just enough to push it out the door and into a journal. An informal poll of mine among PERI researchers found them very favorably inclined to the idea of classes and workshops on scientific writing and editing.

The need for structured language instruction is widespread. Academic scientists and engineers responding to the 1991 JSC survey (introduced in Chapter 2) reported publishing research results in foreign languages more often than in Japanese (agricultural science was an exception), and assistants were actually writing more in foreign languages than were their seniors (JSC 1991: 34). The spread of e-mail fuels the need for these skills also. There is not much help available, however. Book stores offer a steady stream of volumes on the subject of English for Japanese speakers, but even the ones specifically designed as self-help texts cannot address the individual problems that face-to-face instruction and editing assistance can. Hiroko Kataoka, a Japanese language pedagogy specialist, said she and her colleagues liken the use of such texts to learning to play piano by looking at sheet music.

Despite the need there are no foreign language writing or editing programs to aid Japan's scientists. (Not even the elite, innovative OBI or PERI have such programs. Research reports at the OBI annual review that I attended were conducted in English, but the question and answer sessions were in Japanese.) The absence of such intervention reflects another yawning gap in understanding between scientists and the government agencies who fund and regulate them. Perhaps because the need can be filled by a rather mundane-looking service it would be more difficult to get funded than would a highly visible, state-of-the-art piece of experimental machinery that looks impressive to a layperson.

Resentments

The problem of English language skills combines with Japan's second-place position in international bioscience to fertilize the soil for insecurity and distrust toward the Western scientific community. The worst of the fears circulating among my informants focussed on the vulnerable period between the submission of an international article and its acceptance for publication. One PERI biophysicist told me he was scooped twice by Western competitors: "While you're arguing with a referee the same kind of work gets announced [by a European or American]. I don't know what actually happens, but I'll bet the referee leaks it." He didn't see much recourse, either.

> Since the US and Europe are the center, their researchers are familiar with each other, and have face-to-face contact. We don't know their names, either. They wouldn't do that to someone they knew ... I'm sure the Americans and Europeans do it to one another, but they can take steps and complain. If you [a Japanese] send a letter it has no compelling power.

The "them–us" sense is subtly reinforced in Japanese by Chinese characters (*kanji*) that compress "the United States and Europe" into the convenient term *Ōbei*.

Mitsuhiro Yanagida wrote this striking statement:

> Many Japanese researchers think that their submitted papers are often treated unfairly by their foreign reviewers. Some dare to say that they have to produce twice as much data to convince their Western peers, whose papers are quickly published ... a well-known Japanese biochemist, whom I respect very much, told me that he failed to get credit for 90 per cent of his major studies because his

submitted papers were delayed in publication by unreasonable referees. (1996b: 2)

The most famous case of suspected discrimination in postwar Japanese bioscience lore concerns Akira Arimura, an expatriate endocrinologist on the team of A.V. Schally at Tulane University. Schally won the Nobel Prize in Medicine or Physiology in 1977 for elucidating the structure of an important releasing factor. As the *Asahi Shimbun* put it, "It is said that Akira Arima's superlative ability and research skills stood in the shadow of that glory" (1981). Ichizo Kobayashi, an associate professor at the University of Tokyo's Institute of Medical Science, put it to me impatiently: "You don't think it [exploitation] happens to Japanese? It's in the book by Wade on the race between Schally and Guillemin." He tore a piece of paper from his notebook, tersely scribbled the names "Wade Guillemin Schally" on it, and passed it to me. Indeed, the account made clear that a team of Japanese researchers had handed Schally his victory (Wade 1981).

Even the staid *Asahi Shimbun* complained, albeit in multiple negatives: "We cannot say that there is no tendency among US and European scholars consciously to ignore excellent research by Japanese" (1981). A few of my interviewees said that their work was overlooked in favor of Westerners in subsequent citations. One private medical school biochemist had reported his research on a synthesized enzyme in the *Journal of Biological Chemistry* ahead of a European biochemist, but found that the European (whose paper had appeared in *Biochemical and Biophysical Research Communications* a week later than the Japanese announcement) was subsequently cited more often for the same work. The Japanese biochemist's explanation: "I'm Japanese." His competitor, he also noted, was a distinguished figure, and had written influential review articles that drew more attention to his own work.

The extent and depth of these feelings is hard to measure. There are no systematic, large-scale studies that have explored the extent of these suspicions in Japan and other countries, much less the frequency of actual abuses. One mass media portrayal of the problem provides an appealing hint of how young Japanese competitors would *like* to see the problem resolved, however. *Dōbutsu no Oishasan* (The Animals' Doctor) is a rather whimsical but widely read young adult comic series by artist Noriko Sasaki (1990) that depicts the life and tribulations of Seiko Hishinuma, a woman PhD veterinary science student at "H" University in Hokkaido. In one episode, Hishinuma has to produce three journal articles in English by the end of the year for her degree requirement. Her experiments have been progressing well, but writing in English has been a slow and painful process – "The wall of English composition," reproduced in Figure 9.1. "Don't you think it's unfair?" she ponders. "I'll write it in English if I'm told to, but the English speakers ought to write in Japanese, too!" In the midst of this struggle some disastrous "top secret" news hits by word-of-mouth: an American has

Note
The text reads: Hishinuma's papers have hit some rough sailing ... The experiments have been progressing well enough, but the writing has been slogging along without getting anywhere ...

The reason is that the text is in English ...

Figure 9.1 "The wall of English composition" (Sasaki 1990) *Dobutsu no Oishasan* © 1989
      Noriko Sasaki/HAKUSENSHA, Inc.

scooped her. Hishinuma considers starting another project but the time constraints are too great. Demoralized, she envisions her rival "spending money like water" in a sparkling, state-of-the art laboratory. Pushed by her advisor to call the American researcher and ask about the content and progress of research there, Hishinuma finds that her adversary (also a woman) has not conducted the same experiments (for lack of funds, not interest), has been learning Japanese (enough to communicate on the telephone), and suggests further correspondence. Readers who find this denouement too candy-sweet improbable will be consoled by the last frame, in which Hishinuma finds herself back at the "Wall of English composition."

One other complication

The preeminent status of Western bioscience poses a quandary for Japanese researchers. Accomplishments in the United States and Europe provide standards of excellence and bench marks for competition. The international science community also offers a forum beyond clique politics for evaluating research in areas that are sparsely populated with fellow researchers. Ken-ichi Fukui, 1981 Nobel laureate in Chemistry, encouraged young scientists to venture off of heavily beaten research paths and announce their research to international academic societies: "There's sure to be someone there who can evaluate your work fairly. A just evaluation of a piece of work requires the same degree of judgmental ability that the person who did the work has" (1984).

At the same time, however, the pervasive assumption that the West produces the best diminishes regard for indigenous creativity, and aggravates the tendencies toward fashion and faddism that dismay good scientists in every country. Akinori Kidera, a PERI biophysicist (now at Kyoto University), was amused by the juxtaposition of his work with that of a famous researcher in England:

> Last year my paper came out in the same month as one by D., in another journal. The content was about the same but it was clear that the approaches were different. (I liked mine better, by the way.) I wasn't particularly anxious, but the problem was my name value in comparison with *his* name value. He's really big. So in Japan, what sort of evaluation do my colleagues give my work? I reported my research at the same time as D's, so I'm someone in Japan doing the same work as D. "Wow!" they say.

Other interviewees were less amused about seeing the West used as standard for comparison. A biochemist at a second-tier national university expressed his dissatisfaction:

> Everyone's looking at America ... There are extremely few [Japanese scientists] who rely on their own originality. There are those who are real good at looking at what the fashion is and then getting money. If someone is doing original work, hard and steady for years, they can't get a grant from the Monbusho system. It's fashion. Pure fashion.

Shigetada Nakanishi saw dramatic shifts in research topics in response to major advances abroad, especially in the United States, exacting a price in creativity and progress. "The foreign countries greatly influence the direction," as in the study of cancer genes and neuroscience. He acknowledged the impasse of cultivating originality without an independent domestic base from which to judge it.

Grant application forms for certain categories of the Ministry of Education's SRF competition (discussed in Chapter 2) and several other programs such as the Ministry of Agriculture's Life Sciences Specified Industrial Technology Research Promotion Project specifically ask for information on the status of the proposed research subject abroad. My interviewees said that their chances of funding would be compromised if they couldn't demonstrate that Americans and Europeans were working on the same subject. Morio Ikehara identified and criticized the originality-killing suspicion behind the question: "If no one elsewhere is doing it, does it really have any value?" (1995). Other Japanese scientists have expressed similar concerns on paper. Hitoshi Nozaki, Emeritus Professor of Organic Chemistry at the University of Kyoto, complained to his colleagues of the persistent tendency to "accept rehashed Western research with a sense of reassurance" (1990), and Jun-ichi Nishizawa (introduced in the last chapter) wrote, "A deep-seated defect in Japanese society is to not appreciate a fellow countryman's contributions" (1991: 33).

The direction of the resentments – and their resolution

Japanese scientists' nation-conscious statements about scientific competition are part of a larger discussion of ways to attain better basic research, and are not some kind of resentment-driven, techno-national chauvinism. Nozaki's criticisms appear in an article entitled, "Why are there so few Chemistry Nobel Prizes?," and Nozaki uses a perceptive rationale when he urges colleagues to cite Japanese accomplishments: "when Japanese scorn the work of fellow countrymen, it's only natural for foreigners to depreciate their evaluations [of Japanese research] as well. Circles of colleagues who praise each other flourish; groups whose members hold each other back are ignored" (1990). Nishizawa's criticism appears in an article in English explaining the weaknesses of basic research in Japanese universities.

Foreigners who fear that the Japanese will mobilize basic research "like war," in an aggressive, juggernaut fashion, will find little in Japanese scientists' domestic discussions to justify their misgivings. There is more military rhetoric in the West, where a metaphor-driven philosophy of science and technology asserts that war and science display compelling similarities (Latour 1987: 172). My own investigation of the literature and discussions of scientific strategies and priorities, written in Japanese by and for Japanese, found only one reference to war: chemist Akio Yamamoto vented his exasperation over anemic budgets for university laboratories by writing that "it's hard to win in a modern war with bamboo spears" (1991: 13).

When Japan's critics of the science status quo discuss what should be done to compete more effectively internationally, the similes and metaphors they use most often come from sports, and baseball in particular. The sport's contract system illustrates the benefits of career mobility by invoking illustrious teams having a reward system for individual talent. Covering OBI's 1993 fifth-year celebration ceremonies, newspaper articles likened OBI's term employment system of one-year contracts to baseball players'. As a gesture in the same spirit, OBI instituted a yearly "MVP" award, for "most valuable postdoc." Genya Chiba's repeated call for "home runs" expresses the need for exciting, internationally recognized research.

Benign metaphors aside, the various barriers to full participation in the global scientific community, and the ways in which Japanese scientists have tried to cope with superior foreign accomplishments, should temper any assumption that the Japanese are always deft and supple absorbers of foreign knowledge and methods. Their sense of unfairness and vulnerability in the international arena is perhaps the most ambiguous and difficult of problems to solve directly. One powerful antidote to feelings of mistreatment comes from the research and writings of bioscience information specialist Shigeaki Yamazaki. His 1996 book, a guide for submitting life science papers to international journals (1996a), elucidates all of the rules of submission to major international journals, including ethical considerations. Within a year of publication it sold a brisk 2,300 copies. One chapter describes the referee processes for twenty-nine international journals, based on a survey that Yamazaki himself conducted among the editors of the thirty-seven international bioscience journals having the highest frequency of contributions from Japanese researchers. (Yamazaki identified them by surveying Medline citations from the first half of 1993.) Yamazaki also solicited advice for Japanese contributors from the editors, and distilled it for his readers. He summarized their responses: "As in the comments of the chief editor of *Nucleic Acids Research*, the most important point for a scientific paper is not English ability but above all critical inquiry. It is gratifying to hear such a just argument" (1996a: 71–2).

If international editors maintain their standards of fairness and if Japanese scientists get the training to overcome the language barrier, "unique cultural obstacles" should become quaint artifacts of a past age. And if Japanese scientists gain independence and respect in their relations with their own country's officials, they will have the self-confidence to assert themselves when they are harmed by infractions of the rules abroad.

APPENDIX I

BRIEF DESCRIPTION OF RESEARCH METHODS AND CONDITIONS

Chapter 1 and my 1996 article in *Human Organization* discuss the ways in which I gained access to my research sites. When I arrived at OBI in early September of 1990 I was provided a desk in the writing area of the biochemistry and metabolism laboratory. I talked with researchers, technicians, and administrators to identify the most important organizational issues in their eyes and the terms they used to communicate them. Meanwhile, I attended meetings and social functions, and I kept a diary for incidents, thoughts, and impressions. I became a "participating observer" by editing papers and correspondence in English for the researchers and administrators. It afforded me chances to reciprocate for the cooperation I received, and opened a window on one part of the work of producing knowledge.

My discussions with laboratory members began as casual lunchtime and hallway chats, and evolved into one-on-one interviews that took on more structure as I developed a sense of the most productive issues to follow. Having a daily presence at a predictable location (my desk) greatly facilitated interviewing; I was "on tap" for discussions and interviews at the convenience of the Institute's members. Structured interviews averaged just under one hour in length. Of the 110 subjects whom I approached for interviews at all locations in the course of a year, two declined; participation rates and refusals are discussed in Coleman 1996.

Within two months I had developed a question schedule for interviews. I went to the Protein Engineering Research Institute (PERI) in mid-January of 1991 for the second phase of my research. The PERI administration permitted me to join their Third Department, which specialized in mutant protein synthesis, and they too had provided me with a desk. By the time of my move to PERI I had developed a set of thirty-three questions that I used for interviews at my subsequent locales. The format was open-ended, however, favoring depth of response over point-for-point completion of the question schedule; as at OBI, I did not interrupt interviewees who talked at length about an important issue in order to ensure an answer for every question in the schedule. As a result, some questions had fewer responses than others, but my interviewees' involvement in our discussions yielded a very high degree of validity in their responses.

My logistical arrangements at the Medical College, the third of my originally proposed field work sites, were less favorable. I was given a desk in a building separated by several minutes' walk from the university's main laboratories, which reduced my interview turnover substantially. The arrangements at the Food Research Institute's Carbohydrate Laboratory during my ten-day period of observation, however, resembled conditions at OBI and PERI. My final data set containing 110 structured interviews for numerical analysis contained, in addition to the 38 OBI and 50 PERI scientist and technician interviews, 10 interviews at the Medical College, 9 at FRI, 2 at second-tier national universities, and 1 at a national institute for biomedical research. That data set was composed of seventy-seven men and thirty-three women; average age for the entire group was 34.7 years (36.5 for men and 30.4 for women). This was a relatively elite group; all but a few were PhD and master's degree holders, and about three fourths of these degrees were awarded by first-tier (former imperial) national universities and the Tokyo Institute of Technology.

The 1991 self-administered questionnaire survey at PERI (conducted in late June) consisted of a form having six Likert-type five-point opinion questions and four follow-up (elaboration) questions soliciting both yes/no responses and open-ended comments. Each form had a code identifying its respondent to me but guaranteed confidentiality of reporting. After pretesting it among four researchers, I distributed forty-eight forms to staff research personnel, yielding forty-six useable responses. Of the forty-six respondents, forty-three wrote comments elaborating on their answers. The 1991 self-administered questionnaire survey conducted at OBI (in August), discussed in Chapter 5, also guaranteed confidentiality of reporting but was not anonymous. After pretesting it serially with the cooperation of two OBI researchers, I distributed it to thirty-six subjects, thirty-one of whom returned completed forms. Since the second pretest form was identical to the final instrument, I included its responses in the analysis for an N of 32.

Japanese friends and colleagues have helped me supplement and update my 1990–1 data sets while I was outside Japan. During trips to Japan in 1992, 1994, 1996 and 1998 I briefly revisited my major research sites for some updating. In 1996 I enjoyed a three-month stint as a visiting researcher at the National Institute of Science and Technology Policy; it proved particularly helpful for gathering aggregate figures on different aspects of Japanese bioscience and getting answers for some persistent questions.

Although all of my data sources have proved essential to the composition of this book, the group of people who allowed me in-depth interviews has provided the most important foundation for my understanding and subsequent writing. I have attempted to maintain contact with them since the days of my first field work, and a few have become friends with whom I correspond.

APPENDIX II

PERI DEPARTMENTAL STRUCTURE, AND LIST OF CORPORATE PARTICIPANTS IN PERI, 1986–96, AND BERI, 1996–

Organization of research departments at PERI

Department number	Activity/specialties represented

One	Structural analysis of proteins (x-ray diffraction, nuclear magnetic resonance, electron cryomicroscopy):
	     biochemistry, chemistry, physical chemistry
	     physics, materials engineering

Two	Structure–function studies of natural proteins
	   artificial protein design:
	     biophysics, pharmacology/pharmacy science,
	     agricultural chemistry, polymer chemistry,
	     physics, applied physics, food science

Three	Mutant protein synthesis:
	     biochemistry, biology, medicine, pharmacology,
	     agricultural chemistry, chemical engineering

Four	Characterization and modification of proteins (isolation, purification, preparation in quantity, and analysis):
	     pharmacology/pharmacy science, chemistry,
	     fermentation engineering

Five	Computer database analysis: mathematical biology, physics, applied physics

Note
Based on the January, 1992 PERI brochure, *Protein Engineering*, and interviewees' advanced degree specialties (MS or PhD)

194

List of corporate participants in PERI, 1986–96, and BERI, 1996–

PERI
Ajinomoto Co. Inc.
Fujitsu Limited
Kanegafuchi Chemical Industry Co., Ltd
Kirin Brewery Co., Ltd.
Kyowa Hakko Co., Ltd.*
Mitsubishi Kasei Corporation*
Nihon Digital Equipment Corporation
Nippon Roche K.K.
Showa Denko K.K.
Suntory Ltd.
Takeda Chemical Industries, Ltd.*
Tonen Corporation*
Toray Industries, Inc.*
Toyobo Co., Ltd

* One of the five original core participant companies

BERI
Asahi Chemical Industry Co. Ltd
Ajinomoto Co. Inc.
Fujitsu Limited
Hitachi, Ltd.
Hoechst Japan Limited
Japan Tobacco Inc.
Kaneka Corporation
Kyowa Hakko Co. Ltd.
Kirin Brewery Co. Ltd.
Mitsubishi Chemical Corporation
Sankyo Co. Ltd.
Suntory Limited
Shionogi & Co. Ltd.
Takeda Chemical Industries, Ltd.
Tanabe Seiyaku Co. Ltd.
Toyobo Co. Ltd.
Toray Industries, Inc.
Yamanouchi Pharmaceutical Co. Ltd.

REFERENCES

AETDC (Aerospace and Electronics Technology Deliberative Council) Kōkū, Denshi Nado Gijutsu Shingikai (1996) *"Kōzō Seibutsugaku ni kansuru Sōgōteki na Kenkyū Kaihatsu no Suishin Hōsaku ni tsuite" (Shimon dai 22 gō) ni taisuru Tōshin.*

Anderson, Alun (1992a) "Breaking barriers and expanding frontiers," *Science* 258: 568.

—— (1992b) "Japanese academics bemoan the cost of years of neglect," *Science* 258: 564–9.

Angier, Natalie (1988) *Natural Obsessions: Striving to Unlock the Deepest Secrets of the Cancer Cell,* New York: Warner Books.

Anonymous (1983) "Igakubu kyōju wa 'kane wa inochi yori tōtoshi,'" *Pureibōi* 9, 12: 90–5.

Aoyama, Gōshō (1996a) "Fubuki ga yonda sangeki," *Meitantei Konan* 10, Tokyo: Shōgakukan.

—— (1996b) "Tēburukurosu," *Meitantei Konan* 11, Tokyo: Shōgakukan.

Arai, Ken-ichi (1994) "Biotechnology and the new era of biomedical research: Gene technology and cell technology are critical in overcoming cancer, viral infections and genetic diseases," *Asia Pacific Journal of Molecular Biology and Biotechnology* 2, 1: 1–11.

—— (1996a) "Factors that influence the decision of young scientists to seek foreign training: How can we develop active biomedical research in Japan?" Workshop: Future Perspectives for Japan–US Cooperation and Exchange in Biomedical Science, Tokyo: R. Krause et al., Organizers (18–19 March).

—— (1996b) "21 seiki o mukaeru raifu saiensu to kenkyū shisutemu no danryokuteki na fukusenka: sangaku no renkei de, seimeikagaku to sentan chiryō kaihatsu o suishin suru, sentan kenkyū haiuei no kōchiku o," Tokyo: Unpublished position paper.

Asahi, Nobusuke (1993) "Hakasegō no nedan wa hyakuman-en," Takashi Ueda (henshūchō), *Oishasama, Bessatsu Takarajima* 184: 159–63, Tokyo: Takarajimasha.

Asahi Shimbun (1981) "Ronbun shōkoku kukkiri, inyō kaisū wa gyōseki no shōmei, beikoku no chōsa sekai besuto 1000 kagakusha-chū nihonjin wazuka ni 19 nin," 21 December.

—— (1996a) "Daigaku kyōin jikō shusshinsha wa 34%," 18 October.

—— (1996b) "Daigaku kyōin ni sentakuteki ninkisei, daigaku shingikai no tōshin," 20 October.

—— (1996c) "Daigaku kyōin ninkisei, kyōju no isu ni katsu," 29 October.

—— (1996d) "Daigaku kyōin no ninkisei, kumiai ga hantai shomei e," 31 October.

—— (1998) "Kenkyū kōhyōji no kyūsei shiyō OK, Kunigawa to daigaku kyōju, Tōkyō Kōsai," 27 March.

Barker, Brendan (1996) *Japan: A Science Profile,* Manchester, UK: The British Council.

Barker, Stephen (1995) "Japan opens new era in university funding," *Nature* 377: 378.

Bartholomew, James (1989) *The Formation of Science in Japan: Building a Research Tradition*, New Haven: Yale University Press.

Beck, John C. and Beck, Martha N. (1994) *The Change of a Lifetime: Employment Patterns among Japan's Managerial Elite*, Honolulu, Hawaii: University of Hawaii Press.

Bloom, Justin L. (1990) *Japan as a Scientific and Technological Superpower*, Springfield, Virginia: United States Department of Commerce, National Technical Information Service.

Brock, Malcolm V. (1989) *Biotechnology in Japan*, London: Routledge.

Chira, Susan (1989) "Japanese name-use law misses mark, women say," *New York Times News Service*, 14 January.

Choy, Jon (1992) "Japanese research consortia: Beating plowshares into tractors?" *JEI Report* 21A, Washington, DC: Japan Economic Institute.

—— (1998a) "Research and development in Japan: Squeezing more from every yen," *JEI Report* 29A, Washington, DC: Japan Economic Institute.

—— (1998b) "Diet considers freedom of information act," *JEI Report* 16B, Washington, DC: Japan Economic Institute.

Clark, Burton R. (1983) *The Higher Education System: Academic Organization in Cross-national Perspective*, Berkeley, California: University of California Press.

Coleman, Samuel (1990) "Riken from 1945 to 1948: The reorganization of Japan's Physical and Chemical Research Institute under the American Occupation," *Technology and Culture* 31, 2: 228–50.

—— (1996) "Obstacles and opportunities in access to professional work organizations for long-term fieldwork: the case of Japanese laboratories," *Human Organization* 55, 3: 334–43.

Collins, Steven W. (1992) "Genes and the state: The Japanese experience in biotechnology," Paper presented at the 44th Annual Meeting of the Association for Asian Studies, 4 April.

Deguchi, Masayuki (1994) "Comparison of Japanese and American philanthropy," *CGP Newsletter*, 5: 6–8.

Endo, Hideki, Yokoo, Yoshiko, Hirano, Yukihiro and Shimoda, Ryuji (1993) "Josei kenkyūsha no genjō ni kansuru kiso chōsa" (Female researchers in Japan), *NISTEP Report* No. 30, Dai 1 Kenkyū Gurūpu, Tokyo: Kagaku Gijutsuchō Kagaku Gijutsu Seisaku Kenkyūjo.

Endo, Masatake and Imai, Mikio (1991) "Zunō no kan'oke kokuritsu daigaku," *Aera* 4, 22: 9–14.

EPA (Economic Planning Agency) Keizai Kikakuchō (1995) *Kokumin Seikatsu Hakusho*, Heisei 7-nendo, Tokyo: Ōkurashō Insatsukyoku.

Evered, David (ed.) (1989) "Discussion," *The Evaluation of Scientific Research*, Ciba Foundation Conference. New York: John Wiley & Sons.

Fox, Jeffrey L. (1986) "Protein engineering: Biotechnology's hubris," *BioScience* 36: 516–19.

Frager, Robert (1970) "Conformity and anticonformity in Japan," *Journal of Personality and Social Psychology*, 15, 3: 203–10.

French Foundation, John Douglas (n.d.) *The John Douglas French Alzheimer's Foundation: A Non-profit Public Charity* [informational brochure], Los Angeles.

Fukui, Ken-ichi (1984) "Wakate kenkyūsha e no tegami: Kokusai butai de no hyōka o toō" (Seeking evaluation on a global scale), *Gakujutsu Geppō* 37, 1: 32.

Furukawa, Tetsushi (1963) "The growth of anti-religious rationalism and the development of the scientific method in Japan," *Journal of World History* 8, 3: 739–55.

Garfield, Eugene (1987) "Is Japanese science a juggernaut?" *Current Comments* 46, 16: 342–8.

Hackett, Edward (1995) "A longitudinal study of research groups in science and engineering: Report of progress during phase I," unpublished progress report, National Science Foundation (April).

Hall, Ivan P. (1998) *Cartels of the Mind: Japan's Intellectual Closed Shop*, New York: W.W. Norton & Company.

Hall, John Whitney (1970) *Japan: From Prehistory to Modern Times*, New York: Delacorte Press.

Hane, Mikiso (1986) *Modern Japan: A Historical Survey*, Boulder, Colorado: Westview Press.

Hashizume, Daisaburo (1996) "Nihon no kagaku gijutsu no hatten," *Asahi Shimbun* April 28.

Hashizume, Daisaburo and Kamiya, Yuji (hensha) (1997) *Kenkyū Kaikoku: Nihon no Kenkyū Soshiki no Ōpunka to Kadai* (Opening of Japanese Research Positions to the International Scientific Community), Tokyo: Fujitsū Keiei Kenshūjo KK.

Hicks, Diana M. and Latz, J. Sylvan (1996) "Where is science going?" *Science, Technology and Human Values* 21, 4: 379–406.

Hidaka, Satoshi (1991) "Nayameru sararīman kenkyūsha," Shinji Ishii (henshūnin) *Kenkyū Suru Jinsei: 'Rikei' no Karera wa Nani o Shite Iru no ka? Bessatsu Takarajima* 137: 114–21, Tokyo: Takarajimasha.

Honde, Christina (1996) "Beyond ambiguity: The characteristics of Japanese scientific and technical prose," unpublished manuscript, University of Chicago Committee on Human Development.

Honjo, Tasuku (1992) "Daigaku to daigakujin no hyōka," *Kyōto Shimbun* 25 February.

IFT (Institute for Future Technology) Mirai Kōgaku Kenkyūjo (1990) *Kisoteki Sendōteki Kagaku Gijutsu no Suishin no Tame no Kenkyū Jinzai ni kansuru Chōsa*, Part I, Tokyo.

—— (1993) *Ri Kō Nōgakukei Gakubu Sotsugyōsha no Shogū ni kansuru Chōsa*, Tokyo.

—— (1996) *Raifu Saiensu no Genjō to Kongo no Hōkō ni kansuru Chōsa*, Tokyo.

IHEP (Institute for Health Economics and Policy) Zaidan Hōjin Iryō Keizai Kenkyū Kikō (1996) *Amerika ni okeru Igaku Seimei Kagaku Kenkyū Kaihatsu Seisaku to Nihon no Kadai*, Hōkokusho, Tokyo.

Iinuma, Kazumasa and Iinuma, Teruo (1990) *Kisoteki Sendōteki Kagaku Gijutsu no Suishin no Tame no Kenkyū Jinzai ni kansuru Chōsa II: Kenkyū Katsudō no tame no Yokogata Shakai Shisutemu no Teigen*, Kagaku Gijutsuchō Itaku Chōsa Kenkyū Hōkokusho, Tokyo.

Iinuma, Kazumasa (n.d.) "Seven outstanding scientists since Meiji," *Japan*, Tokyo: Kyoritsu.

Ikehara, Morio (1991) "Sangakukan no chikara o atsumeta kiso kenkyū no suishin: tanpaku kōgaku kenkyūjo," *Kiso Kenkyū Suishin no tame no Kadai*, Tokyo: Kōbunshi Gakkai.

—— (1995) "Orijinaritī no genten," *CIBA-GEIGY Kenkyū Zaidan Kikanshi*, 7: 2–3.

Imada, Tadashi and Yamaoka, Yoshinori (1990) "Yūzā kara mita kenkyū josei–kenkyūsha e no ankēto chōsa kara–," *Josei Nīzu o ika ni Haakushi, dō Taiō suru ka*, Tokyo: Zaidan Hōjin Josei Zaidan Shiryō Sentaa.

Imamura, Kyoko (1993) "A critical look at health research in Japan," *The Lancet* 342: 279–82.

Isono, Katsumi (1991) "Japan has its own grant review process and postdoctoral system," *Chemical and Engineering News* 69, 48: 34–5.

Ito, Takao, Shimoda, Ryuji and Hirano, Yukihiro (1993) "Wagakuni no daigaku ni okeru kiso kenkyū: Daigaku kenkyūsha ni yoru kōen ni motozuku kōsatsu" (Basic research in Japanese universities: A study on the basis of the lectures on basic research by university researchers), *NISTEP Report* No. 28, Dai 1 Kenkyū Gurūpu, Tokyo: Kagaku Gijutsuchō Kagaku Gijutsu Seisaku Kenkyūjo.

Jankowski, Katherine E. (1993) *Inside Japanese Support 1993*, Rockville, Maryland: The Taft Group.

Japan Institute of Labour (Nihon Rōdō Kenkyū Kikō) (1996) *Japanese Working Life Profile 1995–96*, Tokyo.

Japan Techno-Economics Society/Kagaku Gijutsu to Keizai no Kai (1994) *Zainichi Gaikokujin Kenkyūsha no Kenkyū Kankyō oyobi Kenkyū Seika ni kansuru Chōsa Kenkyū*, Tokyo.

JBS (Japanese Biochemical Society) Nihon Seikagakkai (1997) Kakenhi Mondai Kentō Mondai Iinkai (1997) "Gakkai no uchi soto: Kagaku kenkyūhi ni kansuru ankēto shūkei kekka," *Seikagaku* 69, 11: 1304–14.

Johnson, Chalmers (1995) *Japan: Who Governs? The Rise of the Developmental State*, New York: W.W. Norton.

JPC (Japan Productivity Center) Zaidan Hōjin Nihon Seisansei Honbu (1990a) *Beikoku no Gijutsusha, Nihon no Gijutsusha: Gijutsusha no Kyaria to Nōryuko Kaihatsu*, Seisansei Jōkyū Gijutsusha Mondai Kenkyū Iinkai, Tokyo.

—— (1990b) *Doitsu no Gijutsusha, Nihon no Gijutsusha: Gijutsusha no Kyaria to Nōryoku Kaihatsu*, Seisansei Jōkyū Gijutsusha Mondai Kenkyū Iinkai, Tokyo.

—— (1990c) *Eikoku no Gijutsusha, Nihon no Gijutsusha: Gijutsusha no Kyaria to Nōryoku Kaihatsu*, Seisansei Jōkyū Gijutsusha Mondai Kenkyū Iinkai, Tokyo.

—— (1998) *Nihonteki Jinji Seido no Genjō to Kadai*, Tokyo.

JSC (Japan Science Council) Nihon Gakujutsu Kaigi (1988) *Nihon no Gakujutsu Kenkyū Dōkō*, Nichigaku Shiryō 1, Tokyo: Zaidan Hōjin Nihon Gakujutsu Kyōryoku Zaidan.

—— (1991) *Nihon no Gakujutsu Kenkyū Kankyō*, Nichigaku Shiryō 3, Tokyo: Zaidan Hōjin Nihon Gakujutsu Kyōryoku Zaidan.

JPRI (Japan Policy Research Institute) Staff (1996) "Foreign teachers in Japanese universities: An update," *JPRI Working Paper* 24, Cardiff, California: Japan Policy Research Institute.

Kagawa, Yasuo (n.d.) "Nihon no gakkai, gakkaishi no kaiseian," unpublished position paper.

—— (1993a) "Evaluation of Japanese universities by their contribution to life science," *Biochemical Education* 21, 3: 135–7.

—— (1993b) "Seimeikagaku no gyōseki ni yoru daigaku hyōron," *Seikagaku* 65, 2: 126–9.

Kamiya, Yuji (1996) "Zainichi Nihonjin," *Riken Nyūsu* 181: 8.

Katayanagi, K., Miyagawa, M., Matsushima, M., Ishikawa, M., Kanaya, S., Ikehara, M., Matsuzaki, T., and Morikawa, K. (1990) "Three-dimensional structure of ribonuclease H from E. coli," *Nature* 347: 306–10.

Kato, Takeshi (1991) "Nihon no minkan kenkyū josei no genjō to mondaiten – monbushō kakenhi to no kankei o chūshin to shite," *Kenkyū Gijutsu Keikaku* (Journal of Science Policy and Research Management) 6, 4: 281–95.

—— (1992) "Minkan zaidan no kenkyū joseikin wa dono yō ni haibun sarete iru ka," *Josei Zaidan* 24: 6–9.

—— (1995) "Joshu no idō patān kara mita kenkyūsha yōsei shisutemu," Shinichi Yamamoto (kenkyū daihyō) *Daigaku ni okeru Kenkyū Kinō no Hatten to Hen'yō ni kansuru Kenkyū*, Heisei 6-nendo Kagaku Kenkyūhi Hojokin Kenkyū Seika Hōkokusho, 147–64.

Kenney, Martin (1986) *Biotechnology: The Industry–University Complex*, New Haven, Connecticut: Yale University Press.

Kikuchi, Seishi (1950) "Scientific research," in Hugh Borton (ed.) *Japan* 207–18, Ithaca, New York: Cornell University Press.

Kinoshita, June (1994) "Biologist on the fas(t) track," *Science* 266: 1185.

—— (1996a) "System's rigidity reduces lure of science as a career," *Science* 274: 49–52.

—— (1996b) "Schools scramble for niche to keep up with competition," *Science* 274: 47–8.

Kobayashi, Shin'ichi (1991) "Kenkyūsha to iu yūbokumin, daigaku to iu sabaku o ika ni tabi suru ka?" Shinji Ishii (henshūnin) *Kenkyū Suru Jinsei: 'Rikei' no Karera wa Nani o Shite Iru no ka? Bessatsu Takarajima* 137: 162–71, Tokyo: Takarajimasha.

—— (1992) "Science funding system in Japan: Tackling with future," *Proceedings of the International Symposium on the Improvement and Development of Science Funding Systems* (Beijing, 26–31 October), National Natural Science Foundation of China, 205–9, Beijing: China Aviation Industry Press.

—— (1993) "Daigaku kenkyūhi no kōhi futan no suikei hōhō to sono mondaiten," *Kenkyū Gijutsu Keikaku* (Journal of Science Policy and Research Management) 8, 3/4: 223–37.

Kodama, Fumio (1989) "Some analysis of recent changes in Japanese supply and employment patterns of engineers," in D.R. Corson and S. Okamura (eds) *Science and Technology to Advance National Goals: Science Policies in the United States and Japan* 41–58, Fifth US–Japan Science Policy Seminar. Tokyo: Japan Society for the Promotion of Science.

Kornberg, Arthur (1989) *For the Love of Enzymes: The Odyssey of a Biochemist*, Cambridge, Massachusetts: Harvard University Press.

Kozaki, Jōtarō (1992) "Rebyū seido o saiyō shi kiso kenkyū bun'ya ni shinpū," *Nikkei Medeikaru* 278: 37–42.

Latour, Bruno (1987) *Science in Action: How to Follow Scientists and Engineers through Society*, Cambridge, Massachusetts: Harvard University Press.

Latour, Bruno and Woolgar, Steve (1986 [1979]) *Laboratory Life: The Construction of Scientific Facts*, Princeton, New Jersey: Princeton University Press.

Leflar, Robert B. (1996) "Informed consent and patients' rights in Japan," *Houston Law Review* 33, 1: 1–112.

Leibowitz, Brian M, (1990) *The Journal of the Institute for Hacks, Tomfoolery & Pranks*, Cambridge, Massachusetts: MIT/MIT Museum.

Lewis, Catherine C. (1995) *Educating Hearts and Minds: Reflections on Japanese Preschool and Elementary Education*, Cambridge, UK: Cambridge University Press.

Linhart, Sepp (1988) "From industrial to postindustrial society: Changes in Japanese leisure-related values and behavior," *Journal of Japanese Studies* 14, 2: 271–307.

Linton, Ralph (1936) *The Study of Man: An Introduction*, New York: Appleton Century Crofts.

London, Nancy R. (1991) *Japanese Corporate Philanthropy*, Oxford, UK: Oxford University Press.

Long, Susan O. (1998) "Becoming a master physician," in John Singleton (ed.) *Learning in Likely Places: Varieties of Apprenticeship in Japan* 172–89, Cambridge, UK: Cambridge University Press.

Maddox, John (1994) "How to pursue academic excellence," *Nature* 372: 721–3.

Maddox, John and Swinbanks, David (1992) "Reforming Japan's science for the next century," *Nature* 359: 573–82.

MAF (Ministry of Agriculture, Forestry and Fisheries) Nōrin Suisanshō (1995) Nōrin Suisanshō Nōrin Suisan Gijutsu Kaigi Jimukyoku, "Nōrin suisan kenkyū kihon mokuhyō" (Heisei 2-nen 1-gatsu), 2, *Nōrin Suisanshō Gijutsu Kaigi to Kenkyū Kikan*, Tokyo.

Makino, Noboru (1992) "Nihonteki aidenteitū o korosuna," *Kenkyū Gijutsu Keikaku* (Journal of Science Policy and Research Management) 7, 1: 3–5.

Matsuo, Yoshiyuki (1995) "Saiensu byū: Monbushō kagaku kenkyūhi no yukue," *Nikkei Saiensu* (*Scientific American Nihonpan*) 5: 18–30.

May, Robert M. (1997) "The scientific wealth of nations," *Science* 275: 793–6.

MCA (Management and Coordination Agency, Statistics Bureau) Sōmuchō Tōkeikyoku (1996, 1998) *Heisei 7/9 nen, Kagaku Gijutsu Kenkyū Chōsa Hōkoku*, Tokyo: Nihon Tōkei Kyōkai.

MHW (Ministry of Health and Welfare) Minister's Secretariat, Statistics and Information Department (1992) *Health and Welfare Statistics in Japan 1992*, Tokyo: Health and Welfare Statistics Association.

MOE (Ministry of Education, Science, Sports and Culture) Monbushō (1987) *1986, Shōwa 61-nendo Gakkō Kyōin Chōsa Hōkokusho*, Tokyo: Ōkurashō Insatsukyoku.

—— (1991) *Heisei 3-nendo Kagaku Kenkyūhi Hojokin Shiken Kenkyū (A/B): Kenkyū Keikaku Chōsho Sakusei Kinyū Yōryō* (Shinki), Tokyo.

—— (1993, 1996a) *1992, Heisei 4-nendo/ 1995, Heisei 8-nendo Gakkō Kyōin Chōsa Hōkokusho*, Tokyo: Ōkurashō Insatsukyoku.

—— (1996b) *Heisei 8-nendo Kagaku Kenkyūhi Hojokin Kōbo Yōryō*, Tokyo.

MOL (Ministry of Labor) Rōdōshō Fujinkyoku (1995, 1998) *Heisei 7/9 Nenban Hataraku Josei no Jitsujō*, Tokyo: 21 Seiki Shokugyō Zaidan.

Monmaney, Terence (1997) "Nobel Prize is vindication for pioneering UC scientist," *Los Angeles Times*, 7 October.

Motokawa, Tatsuo (1989) "Sushi science and hamburger science," *Perspectives in Biology and Medicine* 32, 4: 489–504.

Mouer, Ross and Sugimoto, Yoshio (1986) *Images of Japanese Society: A Study in the Social Construction of Reality*, London: KPI International.

Muramatsu, Yasuko (1996) "Daigaku ni okeru Senkō Bunya no Jendāronteki Kenkyū," *Heisei 7-nendo Monbushō Kagaku Kenkyūhi Joseikin Seika Hōkokusho,* Kadai Bangō 07301032.

Murata, Keiko (1996) "Nenkō chingin wa 70 nendai kara teika, chōki koyō no meritto mo genshō," *Shūkan Daiyamondo* 84, 26: 50–2.

Muto, Eiichi and Hirano, Yukihiro (1991) "Kokuritsu shiken kenkyū kikan to kiso kenkyū – kokken ni okeru kiso kenkyū no shinkō o mezashite" (Government laboratories and basic research – Toward the promotion of basic research in government laboratories), *NISTEP Report* No, 20, Dai 1 Kenkyū Gurūpu, Tokyo: Kagaku Gijutsuchō Kagaku Gijutsu Seisaku Kenkyūjo.

Nagakura, Saburo and Kikumoto, Hitoshi (1994) "New developments in the science policy of Japan," *Science* 266: 1189–90.

Nakamura, Masashi (1992) "Soshite daigaku ni kasu ga nokotta," *Shūkan Asahi* 97, 39: 30–3.

Nakanishi, Koji (1983) "Dokusōsei o sodateru ni wa wakai sainō ni katsuyaku no ba o," *Sankei Shinbun* (September 5).

—— (1990) "Naze Nihon de wa jinji no kōryū ga sukunai ka?" *Kagaku* (Chemistry) 45, 6: 363–4.

—— (1991) "Scientific research and education in Japan," *Chemical and Engineering News* 69, 48: 30–44.

Nakaoka, Tetsuro (1980) *Science and Technology in the History of Modern Japan: Imitation or Endogenous Creativity?* Tokyo: United Nations University.

Nakayama, Shigeru (1991) *Science, Technology and Society in Postwar Japan*, London: KPI International.

—— (1996) "Amerika no daigaku ni okeru ninkisei no jittai to nihon," *Nihon no Kagakusha* (Mini Tokushū: Daigaku kyōin no ninkisei o kangaeru) 31, 6: 316–18.

Narin, Francis and Frame, J. Davidson (1989) "The growth of Japanese science and technology," *Science* 245: 600–5.

Narin, Francis, Hamilton, Kimberly S. and Olivastro, Dominic (1997) "The increasing linkage between U.S. technology and public science," *Research Policy* 26: 317–30.

Nature (1992) "Semiprivate research: best of both worlds," 359: 577.

Negishi, Masamitsu and Yamada, Hisao (1992) "Ronbun no kyōdō shippitsu ni tsuite no ichi-kōsatsu" (Co-authoring of scholarly papers – A comparative study on Japanese and Western papers), *Gakujutsu Jōhō Sentā Kiyō* 5.

Nihon Keizai Shinbun (1998) "Nihon kigyō no kenkyū kaihatsu: Sofuto, baio de okure, honsha chōsa, Ōbei ga yūi," July 20.

Nihon Kokka Kōmuin Rōdō Kumiai Rengōkai (1998) *Kokkō Rōren Dai 43 Kai Teiki Taikai Taikai Shiryōshū*, Tokyo.

Nikkan Kōgyō Shinbun (1994a) "Josei kenkyūsha: Jidai ga motomeru jinzai 2," December 8.

—— (1994b) "Josei kenkyūsha: Jidai ga motomeru jinzai 1," December 7.

Ninomiya, Seiji (1993) "Shiroi kyotō no kenryoku no gensen wa ikyoku kōzasei to iu zettai shuken ni aru!" Takashi Ueda (Henshūchō), *Oishasama, Bessatsu Takarajima* 184: 82–90, Tokyo: Takarajimasha.

Nishigata, Chiaki and Hirano, Yukihiro (1989) "Shizen kagakukei hakasegō shutoku no ryōteki Nichibei hikaku" (Quantitative comparison of science and engineering doctorates in Japan and the United States: Training of researchers in Japanese doctorate courses), *NISTEP Report* No. 7, Dai 1 Chōsa Kenkyū Gurūpu, Tokyo: Kagaku Gijutsuchō Kagaku Gijutsu Seisaku Kenkyūjo.

Nishizawa, Jun-ichi (1986) "Guchoku ittetsu ga shinri e no tobira o hiraku," *Purejidento* (President) 24, 7: 42–51.

—— (1991) "University research faces difficult problems," *Chemical and Engineering News* 69, 48: 32–3.

Nozaki, Hitoshi (1990) "Nōberu Kagakushō wa naze sukunaika?" *Kagaku* (Chemistry) 45, 6: 364.

NRC (National Research Council) (1989) *The Working Environment for Research in U.S. and Japanese Universities*, Washington, DC: National Academy Press.

NRS/SCAP Natural Resources Section, Supreme Commander for Allied Powers General Headquarters (1948) Memo on Check Sheet, Scientific and Technical Administrative Committee of the Japan Science Council, 20 May, Record Group 33, Box 7399, File 6, Suitland, Maryland: National Archives and Records Administration.

NSB (National Science Board) (1996) *Science and Engineering Indicators 1996*, Washington, DC: US Government Printing Office.

—— (1998) *Science and Engineering Indicators 1998*, Arlington, Virginia: National Science Foundation.

Oberländer, Christian (1998) "R&D in Japan's pharmaceutical industry: The biological revolution, gene therapy and public policy," in Martin Hemmert and Christian Oberländer (eds) *Technology and Innovation in Japan: Policy and Management for the Twenty-first Century*, London: Routledge.

REFERENCES

Ohta, Tomoko (1990) "Kōun na tenkai," Akira Yuzawa, Katsuko Saruhashi et al., *Josei Kagakusha ni A karui Mirai o*, 14–8, Tokyo: Domesu Shuppan.

Okamura, Sogo (1986) "Kenkyū soshiki to inobēshon saikuru," *Gakujutsu Geppō* 39, 1: 9–13.

Okubo, Yoshiko and Miquel, Jean-François (1991) "International scientific collaboration of Japan: Co-authorship analysis," *Journal of Science Policy and Research Management* (Kenkyū gijutsu keikaku) 6, 4: 261–80.

OPM (Office of the Prime Minister) Sōrifu Kōhōshitsu (1991) "Josei," *Yoron Chōsa* 23, 3: 2–33, Tokyo: Ōkurashō Insatsukyoku.

—— (1992) "Josei no kurashi to shigoto," *Yoron Chōsa* 24, 7: 2–52, Tokyo: Ōkurashō Insatsukyoku.

—— (1993a) "Danjo byōdō," *Yoron Chōsa* 25, 5: 2–67, Tokyo: Ōkurashō Insatsukyoku.

OPM (Office of the Prime Minister) Naikaku Sōri Daijin Kanbō Hōkoku Shitsu (1993b) *Zenkoku Yoron Chōsa no Genkyō*, Tokyo.

OPM (Office of the Prime Minister) Naikaku Sōri Daijin Kanbō Naisei Shingishitsu (1994) *Josei no Genjō to Shisaku: Kawaru Kazoku to Josei no Seikatsu*, Tokyo: Ōkurashō Insatsukyoku.

OPM (Office of the Prime Minister) Sōrifu Kōhōshitsu (1996) "Kongo no atarashī hatarakikata," *Yoron Chōsa* 28, 4: 2–61, Tokyo: Ōkurashō Insatsukyoku.

—— (1998) "Danjo kyōdō sankaku shakai," *Yoron Chōsa* 30, 4: 2–71, Tokyo: Ōkurashō Insatsukyoku.

Orr, Robert M. (1996) "Japan's bureaucrats weave a choking web," *Nikkei Weekly*, 19 August.

Ōsaka Baiosaiensu Kenkyūjo [no Arikata o Kangaeru] Konwakai (1997) *Ōsaka Baiosaiensu Kenkyūjo no Arikata o Kangaeru Konwakai Hōkokusho*, Osaka: Zaidan Hōjin Ōsaka Baiosaiensu Kenkyūjo.

Ostrom, Douglas (1998) "Joblessness in Japan climbs into uncharted territory," *JEI Report* 22B: 1–2. Washington, DC: Japan Economic Institute.

Pollack, Andrew (1994) "The creative force behind Japan's Computer U," *New York Times*, 26 June.

Reed, Steven R. (1993) *Making Common Sense of Japan*, Pittsburgh, Pennsylvania: University of Pittsburgh Press.

Rohlen, Thomas (1974) *For Harmony and Strength*, Berkeley, California: University of California Press.

—— (1983) *Japan's High Schools*, Berkeley, California: University of California Press.

Sakakibara, Kiyonori (1991) "Increasing basic research in Japan: Corporate activity alone is not enough," *Current Politics and Economics of Japan* 1, 1: 83–8.

Samuels, Richard J. (1987) *The Business of the Japanese State: Energy Markets in Comparative Perspective*, Ithaca, New York: Cornell University Press.

Sankei Shinbun Shakaibu (1992) *Daigaku o Tou: Kōhai suru Genba kara no Hōkoku*, Tokyo: Shinchōsha.

Sasaki, Noriko (1990) *Dōbutsu no Oishasan* 4, 40: 123–38.

Satō, Makoto (1998) "Kiso igakusha o ikusei suru daigakuin no setchi o," *Igaku Shinkō* 46: 6, Tokyo: Zaidan Hōjin Nihon Shiritsu Ika Daigaku Kyōkai.

Schrage, Michael (1997) "To all PhDs: A 50-cent dollar for your thoughts," *Los Angeles Times*, 26 October.

Science (1992a) "Big spender, but little basic clout," 258: 564.

—— (1992b) "Wellcome Trust: Britain's big biomedical spender," 256: 1132.

—— (1993) "Task force: Level the playing field," 260: 868.

Science Watch (1990) "Japan captures bigger share of papers in top journals," 1, 5: 7.

Sehara [no first name] (1979) "Kyubetto: Fujin kenkyūsha no shūshoku mondai," *Tanpakushitsu, Kakusan, Kōso* (Proteins, Nucleic Acid, and Enzymes) 24, 13: 77–9.

Sekai Dai Hyakka Jiten (1981) "Daigaku," 24–5, Tokyo: Heibonsha.

Sekimizu, Kazuhisa (1991) "Wakate 30 saidai o taishō to shita kakenhi mondai ni kansuru ankēto," *Seikagaku* 63, 1: 44–51.

Shimao, Eikoh (1989) "Some aspects of Japanese science, 1868–1945," *Annals of Science* 46, 1: 69–91.

Sindermann, Carl (1985) *The Joy of Science: Excellence and Its Rewards*, New York: Plenum.

Smith, Charles (1989) "Tax, foreign pressure and the power of women," *Far Eastern Economic Review* 146, 52: 26–7.

Smith, Thomas C. (1988a) "Okura Nagatsune and the technologists," in *Native Sources of Japanese Industrialization, 1750–1920* 173–98, Berkeley, California: University of California Press.

—— (1988b) "'Merit' as an ideology in the Tokugawa Period," in *Native Sources of Japanese Industrialization, 1750–1920* 156–72, Berkeley, California: University of California Press.

STA (Science and Technology Agency) Kagaku Gijutsuchō (1994) *Kagaku Gijutsu Hakusho*, Tokyo: Ōkurashō Insatsukyoku.

—— (1996) *Kagaku Gijutsu Hakusko*, Tokyo: Ōkurashō Insatsukyoku.

—— (1997a) *Wagakuni no Kenkyū Katsudō no Jittai ni kansuru Chōsa Hōkoku*, Tokyo: Kagaku Gijutsuchō Kagaku Gijutsu Seisakukyoku Chōsaka.

—— (1997b) *Kagaku Gijutsu Hakusho*, Tokyo: Ōkurashō Insatsukyoku.

—— (1998) *Kagaku Gijutsu Hakusho*, Tokyo: Ōkurashō Insatsukyoku.

Stephan, Paula E. and Levin, Sharon G. (1992) *Striking the Mother Lode in Science: The Importance of Age, Place, and Time*, Oxford, UK: Oxford University Press.

Stewart, Thomas A. (1996) "The invisible key to success," *Fortune* 134, 3: 141–3.

Sun, Marjorie (1989) "Japan lays out welcome mat for US scientists," *Science* 243: 1546–7.

Swinbanks, David (1989) "Objections to Japan's system," *Nature* 340: 494.

—— (1991) "Japanese biologists produce 'hot' papers," *Nature* 351: 597.

—— (1993) "RIKEN wins reviewers' praise," *Nature* 365: 97.

—— (1996) "Japan's academics fight erosion of tenure . . ." *Nature* 383: 654.

Takagi, Haruo (1984) *The Flaw in Japanese Management*, Ann Arbor, Michigan: UMI Research Press.

Takahashi, Hideo (1990) "The long workweek in Japan: Difficult to reduce," *JEI Report* 11A. Washington, DC: Japan Economic Institute.

Takahashi, Junko (1991) "'Kekkon shite moraenai shōkōgun' o wazurau otokotachi," Shinji Ishii (henshūnin) *Kenkyū Suru Jinsei: 'Rikei' no Karera wa Nani o Shite Iru no ka? Bessatsu Takarajima* 137: 101–7, Tokyo: Takarajimasha.

Takahashi, Hiroyuki (1998) "Working women in Japan: A look at historical trends and legal reform," *JEI Report* 42A. Washington, DC: Japan Economic Institute.

Takaya, Hideo (1996) "Monbu kanryō no kyōju shūnin ni 'nō,'" *Asahi Shimbun Weekly AERA* 54 : 69.

Takeuchi, Hiroshi (1990) "Kenkyū no genba kara mita kadai" (Problems from the viewpoint of laboratories), *Kenkyū Gijutsu Keikaku* (Journal of Science Policy and Research Management) Tokushū: Daigaku mondai o kangaeru, 5, 3/4: 246–61.

Tanabe, Tsutomu (1996) "Rinshō shiken ni hōshū no rūru o," *Asahi Shimbun*, 19 December.

REFERENCES

Tanaka, Fukuko (1993) "Kekkon, shussan, otto no shi ... soshite watashi wa kyōju ni natta," Takashi Ueda (henshūchō), *Oishasama, Bessatsu Takarajima* 184: 60–6, Tokyo: Takarajimasha.

Tonegawa, Susumu (1994) "Shin wa bi nari" (Maegaki), Fuminori Yoshida *Baio no Kaitakusha Monogatari: Amujen Seikō no Kiseki*, Tokyo: Kodansha.

Tōyō Keizai Shinbunsha (1995) *Nihon Kaisha Shi Sōran* (Jōkan), Tokyo: Tōyō Keizai Shinbunsha.

Tsukahara, Shūichi (1996) "Daigakuin no Kagaku Gijutsusha Ikusei Kinō," *Kagaku Gijutsusha Seiiku no Arikata to Daigakuin Mondai – Yutakasa no Naka de no Inbaransu*, Yamada, Keiichi (Kenkyū Daihyōsha), Tokyo: Zaidan Hōjin Seisaku Kagaku Kenkyūjo (Institute for Policy Sciences).

Tsūsan Jānaru (1996) "Tanpaku Kōgaku Kenkyūjo no Seika to Kongo no Kadai: Zadankai," 29, 8: 20–5.

Ueda, Takashi (1993) (henshūchō) *Oishasama, Bessatsu Takarajima* 184, Tokyo: Takarajimasha.

Ui, Jun and Ogose, Tadashi (1976) *Daigaku Kaitairon*, Dai 1-kan, Tokyo: Aki Shōbō.

Umeda, Keiji (1991) "Shokuhin sōgō kenkyūjo no kenkyū suishin hōkō to shintaisei" (Research and development of National Food Research Institute), *Nōgyō Gijutsu* 46, 6: 279–84.

Wade, Nicholas (1981) *The Nobel Duel: Two Scientists' 21-Year Race to Win the World's Most Coveted Research Prize*, New York: Anchor Press/Doubleday.

Wanner, Barbara (1997) "Japanese corporate citizenship: Beyond the growing pains," *JEI Report* 1A. Washington, DC: Japan Economic Institute.

Watson, James D. (1968) *The Double Helix: A Personal Account of the Discovery of the Structure of DNA*, New York: New American Library.

Weber, Larry H. (1992) "Overview of ten bioscience-related research institutes in Japan," *United States National Science Foundation Tokyo Office Report Memorandum* 231 (13 May).

Yahara, Tetsuichi (1997) "Fōramu: Daigaku kyōin no ninkisei wa kenkyūkatsuryoku o kōjō saseru ka" *Kagaku* 67, 6: 426–9.

Yamamoto, Akio (1991) "Nihon no kenkyū taisei e no teigen," *Kiso Kenkyū Suishin no tame no Kadai – Kokusaika no Naka de no Nihon no Kenkyū Taisei wa ika ni aru Beki ka,* Kōbunshi Gakkai Kōenkai (26 February) 11–15, Tokyo: Kōbunshi Gakkai Kōenkai.

Yamamoto, Shinichi (1992) "Daigaku no kenkyū shien mekanizumu no kōsatsu – Beikoku ni okeru indirect costs gainen o chūshin ni," *Daigaku Ronshū* 21: 301–16, Hiroshima Daigaku Kyōiku Kenkyū Sentā.

Yamazaki, Shigeaki (1991) "Ronbun happyō kara mita Nihon no seimei kagaku," *Kagaku* 6, 8: 544–7.

—— (1994) "Ranking Japan's life science research," *Nature* 372: 125–6.

—— (1996a) *Seimei Kagaku Ronbun Tōkō Gaido*, Tokyo: Chūgai Igakusha.

—— (1996b) "Gakujutsu ronbunsū no kokusai hikaku chōsa – igaku ryōiki no bunseki," *Jōhō Kanri* 39, 6: 391–407.

Yamazaki, Toyoko (1965) *Shiroi Kyotō* (The White Tower), Tokyo: Shinchōsha.

Yanagida, Mitsuhiro (1990) "The grant-getting game in Japan," *Nature* 343: 111–12.

—— (1996a) "Koramu: jinshu, kokuseki o towazu," *Kōtōken* 11 , Zaidan Hōjin Kokusai Kōtō Kenkyūjo no Gekkan no Kōhōshi.

—— (1996b) "Editorial: About Japanese science," *TIBS* [Trends in Biochemical Sciences] 21: 1–3.

REFERENCES

Yang, Wei, Hendrickson, Wayne A., Crouch, Robert J., and Satow, Yoshinori (1990) "Structure of ribonuclease H phased at 2 Å resolution by MAD analysis of the selenomethionyl protein," *Science* 249: 1398–405.

Yoder, Stephen K. (1987) "Native son's Nobel award is Japan's loss," *Wall Street Journal*, 14 October.

INDEX